Know My Light

a Woman's journey through past life experiences

by
Susan Latner

First published by Dog Ear Publishing
4011 Vincennes Rd
Indianapolis, IN 46268
www.dogearpublishing.net

ISBN: 978-1-4575-4712-6

This book is printed on acid-free paper.

Printed in the United States of America

In loving memory
Eileen Connolly
Teacher, Counselor, Friend
You have blessed me all the world and back again

CONTENT

Encore

Francesca's Story

PROLOGUE

*N*ot aware of what her part was in the scam, Francesca spoke the word "Mama!" Her Mama spanked her for speaking. Francesca the toddler had seen her Mama take money from a stranger's pocket and was juggled uncomfortably in the process.

"He will never miss it," Mama whispered to Francesca who was in her arms. "Mama!" Francesca repeated loud enough for the man to hear her and see her mother with his wallet in her hands.

"Madam," he yelled as he grabbed her wrist and his wallet letting the child fall to the ground.

"See what you have done?" The mother scolded her child as she was being detained by the well dressed stranger.

"Officer! Officer!" the man yelled trying to find the local police. "This woman is a thief. Someone get an officer and have her arrested!"

The child Francesca started screaming as her Mama violently tried to free her wrist from the man's tight grip.

"Run Francesca. Go get Papa!" The child wailed and held tight to her mother's skirt. "Get Papa Francesca!" The mother screamed as she struggled with the man to free herself.

"Let go of my wife!" Her father yelled as he came charging toward the man.

The stranger took his cane in hand and started beating the irate husband over the head and shoulders with the golden handle. Papa was cursing and pulling at the man's arm, Mama was struggling to free herself and Francesca was screaming as the victim hit the Papa one last time on the head causing blood to gush out of his head alongside his right ear.

Francesca's Papa fell to the ground holding his head. Her Mama freed herself of the man's grip and dropped to the ground to aid her husband and Francesca continued to wail as she plopped down next to her Mama in a pool of her father's blood.

Mama grabbed a portion of her own skirt and held it to Papa's head to try and stop the bleeding, but, it was too late. Papa laid in his own blood eyes wide open and fixed in a blank stare.

"You killed him!" she wailed. "You killed my husband! Murderer! You are a murderer!"

The man stood in horror at the scene before him. How did this go from bad to worse in such a short period of time? He stood there clutching his cane in his hand.

The police arrived to survey the scene. "What happened here?" The officer asked looking from adult to adult not even seeing the young child.

The man spoke first. "This woman robbed me of my wallet." He pointed to the wallet which had fallen to the ground in the struggle. "When I tried to get it back her accomplice attacked me. I had no choice but to defend myself."

"Officer he is lying!" The Mama jumped into the accusations. "I was tending to my baby when he grabbed me. My husband came to my rescue and he beat him. He beat him to death for nothing! What am I to do? What will I do without a husband?" she wailed. This caused the baby to start screaming again even louder than her Mama was screaming.

The officer looked at the man dressed in his fine evening attire. A grey suit, formal shoes and a matching grey top hat. In his hand he held a black onyx cane with a gold handle. He looked at the woman dressed in poor gypsy clothing. The man she called husband wore the white shirt of a poor working man now drenched in his own blood. The officer jumped to the only conclusion possible. The man was telling the truth. This woman tried to rob him and she must pay for her mistake.

"Come Madam." The officer grabbed her arm. "Come with me." Being a very large man he pulled the woman up to her feet and dragged her along with him.

"My husband, my baby!" she shrieked. "You can't leave them here!"

"Your husband isn't going anywhere and the baby will be brought to the court house later."

He pointed to a man and a woman in the crowd. "You there. Bring the infant to the courthouse," he ordered.

They looked at each other and scooped up the frightened and screaming child and followed his carriage to the local courthouse.

Francesca's Mama was thrown into a jail cell and left there screaming and wailing until morning when the judge would see her.

The couple who obligingly brought the baby to the courthouse, volunteered to keep her until court resumed in the morning.

The jailing officer could not be bothered with the child and permitted it without recourse.

In the morning three young boys arrived at the courthouse demanding to see their mother. They too were dressed in poorly kept clothing. The eldest boy spoke for the three of them. "We have come for our Mama. She was brought here last night. We have money to pay so you can let her go." The boy, of approximately 12 years of age, opened up his sweaty hand to show a few coins.

"Let the boys through to see the judge," the officer on duty announced. The boys were escorted to a courtroom where a judge was seated behind a large desk.

"Stay here," they were told and were shown to a bench by the door. Their mother stood off to the side with an officer standing next to her.

"Madam. You are charged with theft. How do you plead?" the judge addressed her.

"I am not guilty of any of this. That man beat my husband to death in front of my baby and me. He is a murderer. Charge him with murder!" she cried.

"Mama!" The boys gasped loudly as their mother turned to see their three faces staring at her in horror.

"Let them through," the judge commanded. "Are these your children Madam?"

"They are," she said.

"And the baby too?" he asked.

"Yes sir," she responded.

"You have done them wrong Madam. You will repay this man the money you stole from him and will leave this area immediately. Should you ever be seen in this town again, even if you are just passing through, you will be arrested and will serve time in prison. Take your children and go NOW. Pay the officer on the way out. Do you understand me?" he commanded.

"Yes," she said and he banged his gavel dismissing the broken women and her children.

"Come Mama," the eldest son said as he and his brothers ushered her out of the door.

They gave the jailer all of their money and collected the baby on their way out of the building. They were not even permitted to gather their deceased father's remains. Instead they were escorted to the outskirts of town by the arresting officer who spat on them as he sent them on their way.

CHAPTER 1

*S*he stood on her spot ready to begin. Her arms poised. Her head
down. She was good to go. "Francesca are you ready?" Zeke asked
her as he always did before a performance. She glared at him coyly out
of the corner of her eye. Zeke always asked and he always knew that she
was ready. Just a little joke to get her riled. Zeke her oldest brother and
Gabe her second brother played fiddles while Aaron, the youngest
brother, played tambourine. They stood in a line several feet behind her.
Francesca stood in the center of the area allocated for her dancing. Not
too close to the tables of diners, not so far back that she lost their attention.

The boys began to play their soulful country music. It called to her,
spoke to her heart. Beckoned her to move, to join in, to express herself
with her entire body and she did. Each step rehearsed over and over
until she only needed the first few notes to cue her in to her next move.

Francesca was a little bit of a girl. With a swarthy complexion, long
dark straight hair matched her big dark eyes. The rich people came to
their shows wherever they went. They sat at the tables and chairs, ate
their food and watched the child move and twirl to the unusual beat of
the gypsy music. Gypsies they were called in the big city. It was true they
came from the north. Traveled in covered wagons to where ever the people gathered. Where ever someone would spend a coin for any form of
entertainment.

Mama was in her caravan wagon resting behind the show. Mama
was the fortune teller of their group and in charge of all of the money.
She used to read tea leaves for the ladies as they dined. But she had gotten too large to get out of her wagon without a lot of pain, so, she

remained inside and read cards or palms, or did anything for those who would venture inside her domain.

Francesca was too young to understand all that her Mama did for money. She only knew the wrath of Mama. Francesca was always in trouble for something. Always being scolded for something whether she did them or not. Zeke tried to protect her from their mother's scorn but to no avail. Mama always came up with something to pick at Francesca about. Truth be told Mama blamed Francesca for her lot in life. It was Francesca's fault she was fat, Francesca's fault that she had no man in her life, Francesca's fault she could not move her body any longer, Francesca's fault... well, pick a reason and that was Francesca's fault too. So, on this particular day the boys, all in their late teens, dressed in their puffy white shirts, colorful vests, and black pants played their instruments and Francesca was free. Free to shrug off the constant criticism of her much disgruntled mother by dancing to her heart's content. Dancing released the burden and permitted her to just be herself.

Before her sat a couple engrossed in conversation. The woman well dressed in a blue day gown and pearls wore a hat and shoes of the same color. The man, of equal status height and size, wore a grey morning suit with a pristine white shirt. He toyed with a walking stick while they conversed quietly amongst themselves as Francesca performed her routine. Concentrating on her steps, on the music, letting her arms fly freely she watched them as curiously as they watched her. Entranced by their intensity. Most people barely glanced at her while she danced. Usually it did not matter to Francesca what they did. She had her music and her dance. What could be more important than that? But this couple was different. They watched with critical eyes. Conversed only at breaks. The man nodded his head to the beat of the music. They were counting her steps as she did. Who were they? What did they want? Francesca was encouraged. She gave it her all to show them. Show them what? Show them all that she could do. All that she could be. Gain their approval the way mama never did. At the end of the performance she was winded. More winded than usual.

The couple motioned her over to their table. "Tell me child, what is your name?" The beautiful woman spoke with a funny accent.. Her brothers Zeke and Gabe each placed a hand on her shoulders as they crowded around her for protection and more out of curiosity. "Francesca," she said meekly.

Zeke spoke more assuredly. "She is known as the great Francesca." Trying to sound more grown than he was. This caused the couple to laugh.

"Well, great Francesca, we are very impressed with your style and your dance. Do you dance here often?" Francesca looked at Zeke for assistance. She did not know how often they came there. All the places they traveled to looked similar to her. As long as she could dance, everywhere was home.

"Sometimes," Zeke replied.

"We would like to see more dancing," the gentleman said casually.

"Our next show will be soon. Perhaps you would like some refreshments while you wait?" Zeke replied. Ready to sell whatever he could to increase their money. It was about the sale he always told his siblings. A good student at his mama's knee.

"Perhaps we will," the gentleman said. "What would you like my dear?"

"Only coffee for me," she replied reluctantly.

"Two coffees with cream," he replied.

"Gabe, get our friends their coffee and some pastries at my expense," Zeke instructed. "I hope you enjoy your refreshments while we prepare our show." He made an abbreviated bow and walked away. Followed by Aaron who was holding Francesca by the hand.

"What's happening here Zeke? Aaron whispered.

"They want to see Cesca dance some more. I don't know what they really want, but, I am sure it will come out once they see our next show. Prepare for Inter Metzo , let Gabe know what we will be doing next. The chumps must finish their coffee before we begin."

Francesca was confused but she did not care. Inter Metzo was her favorite dance. Always their final performance when they had an attentive crowd.

"You gonna tell Mama?" Aaron asked.

"Not until I know what they really want." Zeke could only guess what that was about. He felt something coming. Hoping it wasn't harmful to his baby sister. She was still so young. Naive to the ways of men, and some women. A child of only nine years should not know the wickedness that was a part of those fancy French elite. He protected her always. Securing her away from the lecherous men and boys. If it had been up to Mama, she would not have been so pure at her age. Her little body would bring good money for any man to do as he pleased. It was only due to Zeke's protectiveness that kept her in front of the music and not stuck in her cart on her back.

"Go get ready for Inter Metzo," he commanded to Francesca while yanking on a handful of her hair.

"Ow," she yelped to the sharp pain encompassing her head. Feeling the joy his assured protectiveness inspired. Off she ran to her wagon throwing her few clothes aside in order to find her favorite dress. Mama made it for her when she was in a good mood. It mimicked the outfits her brothers wore. A big puffy white shirt with a fancy embroidered vest all attached to a full length skirt. The skirt had hidden panels running down from her waist that flared out when she spun. Each piece was a different panel of vibrant color. She loved the spinning portion of the dance. It always caused the crowd to gasp and clap with joy. She loved the clapping and happiness of the reaction. Taking it all in as a personal reward for her expertly executed moves.

They took their places for the next show. Zeke asked, "Ready?" Francesca gave him her glare and they began. The performance began as it always did. So enraptured with the physical feeling she lost herself and flowed with the tune. At the moment the spinning began she waited for the reaction it always inspired and was shocked when there was no response. She glanced quickly to her brothers and Zeke just shrugged and nodded for her to continue. Surprised but still in step she continued until they finished. She bowed her head and stood very still. The boys bowed their heads too, lowered their instruments and then stepped forward to join her.

The couple clapped politely which caused Francesca to look to Zeke. He once again stepped forward to their table.

"I hope you enjoyed our show today (gesturing to the container he set out for donations, already containing some coins.) Our next performance will be at this evening meal."

"We wish to speak to your father," the man said as he stood up.

"My Father?" Zeke asked confused.

"Yes. The person who makes decisions regarding Francesca's future."

"I make decisions regarding Francesca!" he said proudly puffing up his chest.

"No son. We need to speak to her parent, her guardian. Who is in charge here?" his enquiry becoming more stern.

"You want to speak to our Mama," Zeke paled.

"If she is the one who handles Francesca welfare?"

"Wait here. I will be back shortly." Zeke did not like the turn this conversation was taking.

CHAPTER 2

*M*ost unsuspecting customers climbed into the wagon with all their finery only to be confronted with the stench of a woman who did not cleanse herself or her living quarters. For all of the complaining about how awful her life was Marie was surrounded by the finest collectables money could buy, or, so she thought.

She did not know how vile she was to others, but, deluded herself into believing that they were surprised at how wealthy a woman she was.

Mama had put her hair up in a turban to make herself appear more regal and ethereal. It only added to the misconception of her psychic abilities, of which she had none. It was all an act to bilk the unsuspecting victim of their hard earned cash. "Easy come easy go," she told herself as she concocted a web of lies to suit herself and convince the unsuspecting ruse of her powers. In the end it did not matter as she was always gone within a few days.

Zeke was horrified that these grand people wanted to see his Mama regarding Francesca's welfare. Didn't he take good care of her on his own? Under his guidance the boys always worked together to make sure Cesca ate and bathed when needed. Despite Mama's neglect and constant complaints about Francesca, he made sure she always had what they had. He was more her parent than Mama ever was.

"Get Mama some water Gabe," he instructed his brother before entering her wagon.

"Mama there are customers here asking about Francesca and her future. They want to see you. Talk with you about her." Gabe entered her wagon behind Zeke holding a basin with the water in it for her to wash herself. She usually asked for water before she saw clients. Today she just looked at the pan of water and pointed to a spot on the table beside her. Ignoring the water she looked at Zeke and Gabe. "What do they want with her?"

"I don't know," said Zeke. Gabe just shrugged. "They saw her dance, asked to see her dance some more, and then asked to speak with you."

"How many men did you say there were?" Mama enquired with a knowing grin.

"No Mama, it's not like that. They are very refined. A man and a woman. Very well dressed." Zeke continued trying to emulate with his hands how these people were garbed.

Mama stuck to her own single thought that these people wanted the child for sexual purposes. She would listen to their trumped up request and charge them accordingly for the brats virginity, a mighty valuable commodity.

It was a sight to be seen. While Zeke and Gabe pantomimed how these fine folk walked, talked and spoke. Marie kept insisting that these fine people were misleading the boys and were truly only interested in having sex with Francesca. It was sickening to the boys and frustrating as well. This was their little sister she was talking about. Their mother was never going to understand the nature of this meeting. Actually she flat out refused to understand.

"Go now boys and bring these chumps to me. Enough with your explanations." She waved them off as she settled herself in for her command performance. She adjusted her turban as they entered her wagon. Mama acknowledged her guests with her most jovial smile.

"Greetings my friends. Welcome. Welcome to my humble home. Forgive me for not getting up to meet you but my knees are not what they used to be. Please come in and make yourselves at home." She directed them to the two chairs before her. Resting her large arms on the table before her. "My name is Marie, but, everyone calls me Mama. You may call me what you wish." Forcing a grin she continued. "My boys tell me you are interested in Francesca, but, perhaps you would like a card reading or your palms read before we discuss the child?"

Pulling out a handkerchief to cover her nose from the stench in the confined quarters the woman entered first followed by the gentleman helping her to a seat.

"Madam, we are not here for a reading. I am Monsieur Louis Dupre and this is Mademoiselle Juliette Benoit. We represent the Academie

Royale de Danse in Paris. It was brought to our attention that the child Francesca has shown great dancing talent and might be a good candidate for our school. She would be a student of dance, primarily ballet. This is a very prestigious school, Madam, and only the finest most diligent children are permitted to enter it's hallowed grounds."

The tuition for this honor is quite a hefty sum, however, accommodations can be made to ensure her necessities are met should funding be an issue for you." Monsieur Dupre ceased continuing his introduction as he saw the dumb struck look on Marie's face.

"What are you saying sir? You do not want to take the child for your own use?" Marie could not grasp what he wanted Francesca for. He certainly was not asking her to pay for schooling for that brat?

"No Madam, certainly Not!" Monsieur Dupre was infuriated. "We are offering to take her and train her at the finest school of Dance ever created. She will be instructed in poise, in etiquette, given clothing, given nourishment for her growing body, and, should she learn as we suspect, she would be offered a position as a ballerina in the finest production company France has to offer. Even you could understand what a fine opportunity this would be for the child?"

"Louis," Juliette whispered calmly putting a soothing hand on top of his tensed arm.

"Sir. Your offer is quite unexpected for such a humble servant as myself. I am flattered that you think my Francesca has the qualities needed for such a course of study. Certainly you must see for yourself that I do not possess enough funds for such an illustrious establishment. However, if you were to offer payment to purchase my most important bread winner, and take her away from her loving mother, then we could hold further discussion. What am I to do without the meager sum my little bird brings in? I am no longer able to entertain as she does so freely."

"Certainly Madam, you are not trying to sell us your child?" Monsieur Dupre asked angrily as rose to his feet.

"I am only suggesting, sir, that some compensation be made for the fact that you are wanting to take my only income and keep her for your own needs. I do not need her to be trained in dance she already dances her heart out." Marie smiled feeling proud that she had won that point. She was not giving up the little brat without something to show for it. As much as she wanted Francesca gone, it would cost them to have her and that was her bottom line.

Monsieur Dupre was exasperated. Mademoiselle Juliette rose to her feet. "Madame, the Monsieur and I will need to discuss this further before we finish this discussion. Perhaps we could return tomorrow to conclude our offer?"

"Well, don't wait too long. We may be gone by tomorrow." This was Marie's final statement.

The Mademoiselle and Monsieur exited the wagon and walked off mumbling to themselves.

All four children came out from behind Mama's wagon and waited for the couple to move away before entering their Mama's wagon. Zeke spoke first.

"Mama what are you doing? Don't let them take Cesca from us! She belongs with us. We are her family and she is ours!"

Gabe chimed in, "Who will watch out for her if she goes with them? Will we go too? I don't like Paris. There are too many people there!"

"I don't want to play in a music hall," Aaron added. "It won't be the same being indoors. We all like it outside especially Cesca!"

"Hush children. No one is going anywhere." She comforted her boys without even glancing toward Francesca. But in her mind Marie was trying to figure out the sum of money she wanted for Francesca's release. Like a dowry. Yes, just like selling her to a husband. Just as she had been bartered for those many years ago. When she was young. Her father had taken chickens and goats for her hand. Let them give her coins for that little trouble maker. And, when they wanted to give her back, Marie and her sons would be nowhere to be found. Marie smiled to herself.

"No Mama No! Don't let her go!" the three boy voiced loudly one strong voice over another emphatically.

"Boys. Boys I give you my word!"

Her word! Her word! Francesca knew IT WAS DONE ! Mama would give her away. Her word meant nothing. It was a sham she used to distract the objector. Francesca had heard it time and time again. So while the boys stayed to emphasize their dismay Francesca ran. She ran out of Mama's wagon. She ran straight to the woods behind their camp sight. She ran as hard and as fast as her legs would carry her. Until she could not run any longer and then she would cry.

Cry for this final rejection was sharp and painful. She felt the words cut her like a knife. " I give you my word." The beginning of the end!

Monsieur Dupre and Mademoiselle Benoit watched from their carriage. They heard the loud cries of the boys refusals and saw Francesca bolt across the clearing.

"Look Louis. Look at her flee the oppression. We must do whatever it takes to get her away from this horrible life, that disgusting woman."

"I will discuss it with the benefactors my dear, but, I cannot promise it will be easy." He watched Francesca as he spoke. "She certainly has the talent but will we be able to save her from her heritage? I just don't know. Why are you so interested in this one? She will be quite the challenge to tame and to train." He glanced at Juliette and out of the carriage to Francesca. Have those maternal powers of yours finally kicked in?"

"I don't know why, but, the feeling is so strong. She will do great work I keep hearing over and over in my head. How can I refuse the will of God?" She resumed watching Francesca until they were so far away she was no longer a speck in the tree line.

"A business decision, yes. The will of God will remain to be seen," he mumbled.

*F*rancesca began her day with a run to the forest. She was joined by all three of her brothers. "We could help you escape," Aaron offered.

"Will you come too?" she asked hopefully. Aaron just froze. He had not thought about leaving. Could he exist without Mama and Zeke controlling his every move? Aaron did not want to think about it just yet. Maybe when he was older. Yes, when he was a grown man he would leave and perform on his own. Find his own way. But, for today he just shook his head no. Francesca sighed with exasperation.

"How about you Gabe, will you come too?" Gabe shook his head no as well. " Zeke, will you come with me?" She held her breath as she waited hopefully for his affirmative nod. Freeing her from Mama's domineering decision.

"Not at this time Cesca. We have work to do with Mama." He grabbed her by both arms stopping her from running and looked her square in the eyes. " But you should go with these people Cesca. It is an opportunity you should not pass up. To get away from Mama and have a better life. Who knows what would happen to you if you stayed here? Mama's anger with you grows as you get older. As much as I do not want for you to leave, I fear Mama will cause you more harm if you stay."

Francesca had not thought about it like that before. She trusted Zeke to take care of her. His decision weighed heavily in her heart. She took a deep breath and considered what he had said. Was this the chance to be free of Mama? A chance to dance all of the time? To be with other girls and do everything other girls did? Francesca took in a deep breath, held her head high and said, "Yes," out loud. "I will like this very much." Surprising even herself. She let go of the fears and tears that haunted her all through the night. It was a new day filled with sunshine. She took another deep breath and as she walked back to her wagon to prepare for her new beginning she felt lighter. So good she even began twirling as she walked. The boys let out a collective sigh of relief. They had saved her from Mama, but, what was in store for her now? They trudged back to their wagon without speaking. Glancing at each other with knowing looks. Francesca had her new beginning, but, what would they do without their star dancer?

Mama stood in her doorway watching the children as they returned from their run. "You boys are pathetic," she scolded. Mimicking them with an exaggerated tone. "We love you Francesca. Can we help you Francesca?" In a disgusted tone she went on," you act like dogs at her feet." Turning into her own space she said out loud to no one "Let's get this over with."

Monsieur Dupre and Mademoiselle Benoit arrived mid morning. Leaving their carriage outside of camp they walked the distance to Mama's wagon. Monsieur Dupre carried a case filled with papers. Mademoiselle Benoit slid a small package into her coat pocket while she walked.

"May we come in Madam?" He asked politely yet firmly. Strain in his disposition evident in his tone.

Marie beckoned them in. Without hesitation she began, "Well, what is your offer?" She glanced coldly to both of her visitors. Juliette bristled and Louis gave Juliette a sharp silencing stare.

"We have discussed with the benefactors of the school and have come up with a plan that should benefit us all especially Francesca."

Marie stared at them impatiently. Not caring how it benefitted Francesca apparent in her demeanor.

Monsieur Dupre opened his case and took out a sizable stack of documents.

"We wish to warn you that this is a onetime offer. Take it or leave it. There will be no further negotiations." Monsieur Dupre began. "Francesca is to leave with us today, immediately after the signing of the documents. She is to take nothing with her to remind her of you, her home, or her brothers. IS THIS CLEAR ?"

Marie nodded.

"She will reside at the school with many other students, teachers, faculty and guards and will NOT be permitted visitation by any of you at any time. IS THIS CLEAR?"

Marie nodded again.

"Should any of you come for her and take her so much as one step off of the school property you will be detained for kidnapping and prosecuted to the full extent of the law. IS THIS CLEAR?"

Marie nodded once more.

"If any of you go to the authorities claiming we have stolen her from you, we will show them these documents, which you WILL be signing today. Proving that we have full ownership of her. IS THIS CLEAR?"

Marie's eyes widened as she nodded.

"In return, we the owners of, the Acadamie Royale de Paris, do hereby issue to you funds in the amount of 50 livre to be paid in full and as payment in full for one Francesca. Francesca what? What is her given family name?" Monsieur Dupre inquired.

Marie's throat went dry. She was receiving more than she had expected. Not as much as she wanted, but a sizable amount none the less.

"Madame Marie, what is Francesca's family name?"

"There is no family name Monsieur. She is known only as Francesca."

"All right. It shall remain written as only Francesca. IS THIS CLEAR?"

Marie licked her lips and again nodded.

"Do you wish to read these documents over before you sign them?"

Marie shook her head NO.

Knowing that she probably could not read Monsieur Dupre instructed, "So, we will read them together and then we both will sign. One copy remains here with you and one copy for the school's records."

Monsieur Dupre went slowly through each line making sure Marie understood what she was signing.

In the end he took out a pouch from his inside jacket pocket containing the 50 livre coins.

He counted it out slowly with her overseeing so there would be no miscalculation. Marie followed the counting closely. Perspiration gathered on her brow and upper lip at the deliberately slow process. There was a note enclosed in the pouch signed from the funding officer. As Marie reached for the money Monsieur Dupre stopped her abruptly. He scooped up all of the coins and replaced them into the pouch.

"Please call her to us Madam, it is time for us to proceed on our journey."

Marie banged on her side table with an open palm with three loud strikes. So loudly that it startled Mademoiselle Benoit. As rapidly as the pounding ceased Francesca appeared up the stairs with her brothers standing like sentinels behind her.

"Francesca," the pair acknowledged her in unison as they stood. Marie watched the coin sack in Monsieur Dupre's hand very closely. Making sure there was no entrance into it by his fingers.

Mademoiselle Benoit addressed her first. "Do you know why we are here today Francesca?"

"Yes Madam," she said meekly.

"And why is that child?" Her soothing voice caressing the frightened child.

"You are taking me to my new dance school," she responded.

"This is correct. It is time to go now Francesca. You must say your goodbyes to your family so we may begin our journey."

Francesca froze in place. She had never said goodbye to anyone before. Let alone her family. She did not know what to do. She looked to Monsieur Dupre and then to Mademoiselle Benoit before looking at her mother.

Mama opened her arms wide to Francesca for the first time in many years. Francesca stepped forward into her mother's embrace awkwardly and stiff.

"You will miss me when you are gone," Mama whispered into her ear. Francesca said nothing and looked into her mother's big face for the last time.

As Francesca moved outside, Monsieur Dupre handed over the money sack to Marie sealing their deal for all time.

Her brothers waited for her at the foot of the stairs. Aaron came up to her first. Ruffling her hair with his hand he said, "Don't forget me."

"I won't," she exclaimed as she gave him a big hug.

Gabe came forward and embraced her awkwardly. "Remember our dances," he commanded.

"I will," she insisted.

Then it was Zeke's turn. This was the hardest release of all. He was her protector. Tears began to flow down her face. "Ready Cesca?" his voice cracking as he spoke their favorite game. She flung herself into his arms and sobbed not wanting to ever let go. Unable to contain his own emotions, Zeke took a handful of her hair and gave a strong tug.

"Ow!" she gasped grabbing her head.

Gently but firmly Monsieur Dupre took hold of her arm and ushered her away. "We must go now," he informed her. Francesca bent down to pick up the bundle of clothes and keep sakes she had gathered when Monsieur Dupre interrupted her. "You will leave those here." She looked at him quizzically but did as he said looking to her brothers for answers. Aaron and Gabe shrugged, Zeke just turned away.

Mademoiselle Benoit still inside Marie's wagon faced her and pulled out the small bundle wrapped in paper and ribbon from her pocket. "This is the gift we give to all of the mothers of our dance students. I want you to have it." Marie just looked at the package. She was still clutching the pouch of coins and did not respond. Juliette placed the pouch on the table and left the wagon to follow Monsieur Dupre and Francesca to the carriage.

Truth be told it was a very quiet exit. Monsieur Dupre helped Francesca into the carriage and waited for Juliette to assist her as well.

"You gave her the gift anyway didn't you?" He enquired.

"I did. Despite her despicable behavior she has lost her only daughter today. Perhaps someday she will understand what she has given up." Juliette climbed into the carriage and settled herself next to Francesca. Relieved, she took a deep breath and glanced at the tiny child this great big fuss was about. How could one small girl create such hatred in her mother and express such joy with her physical movements?

Francesca looked out of the window as they rode away. Craning her neck to see the boys she loved so much disappear from her sight.

" Francesca," Juliette said to her. "I have a surprise for you too." Forcing a joyful tone after experiencing such an exhausting event. Francesca turned to her with eyes wide. Taking another little packet out of her coat pocket she unfolded the paper for Francesca to see.

"Have you ever had candy?"

Francesca looked into the wrapping and shook her head no.

"Well then you must try this and tell me if you like it. It is my favorite," she exclaimed.

Francesca took a piece reluctantly. Juliette offered some to Louis, who shook his head no and held up his hands in refusal of the treat.

While Juliette sighed as she put one in her mouth. Francesca followed her lead. It was very sweet and different than anything Francesca had ever eaten before.

"I think I am going to like it," Francesca said with her mouth full.

Juliette laughed and glanced at Louis. Yes, she nodded to his unspoken words. This child has much to learn.

Marie waited for the carriage to leave before unwrapping her gift. "This is the gift we give to all the mothers of our dance students," she relived the words spoken to her only moments before.

Untying the ribbon she unfolded the paper to find a woman's broach. The design was the figure of a dancing ballerina.

Marie shrugged. What would she do with such a frivolous thing? She scowled as she tossed it aside. Having second thoughts, she refolded the pin into the paper and along with the signed documents put them together in the back corner of her room tucked into a safe place.

CHAPTER 4

*W*hen they arrived at the Academie Francesca was overwhelmed by the size and grandeur. Never had she seen anything so illustrious. Mind, body and soul were expanded in a brief second as to what she could become, what she could accomplish, but, being only a child, she did not retain that image of herself, but rather, filed it away as a fantasy. It was only her imagination. An adult would call it a revelation, the child just called it hope. She climbed the stairs holding the hand of Mademoiselle Benoit for support and guidance.

She was taken through mazes of corridors passing the chapel, dance halls, classrooms, necessities and finally her dormitory room where she would live the remainder of her formative years.

She had never seen so many beds, so many night tables, so many armoires. The mademoiselle directed her toward the only unadorned bed. "This one is for you child."

Francesca sat on it, laid across it, stretched her hands over her head and touched the wall. "It's mine? It's beautiful!" Francesca whispered.

"Come," Mademoiselle beckoned. "Let's go get the rest of your accoutrements." Her mind flashed on her bundle of clothes Monsieur Dupre would not let her take. Mademoiselle led her down a hallway to a store room.

"Simone, this is Francesca. She is joining us, starting today, and needs the supplies for her quarters."

Simone smiled. "So nice to meet you Francesca. Here is your bedding," she said as she made a pile of linens and a blanket and handed them to Francesca. "Once every month you will bring these back to me for washing and I will give you another set to put on your bed. Do you understand?"

Francesca nodded yes, not truly understanding but eager to please her new acquaintance. "Merci," Mademoiselle Benoit said as she left the room. Francesca picked up the sizable bundle. "Merci," she added and followed Mademoiselle down another hall to the clothing closet.

"Georgette this is Francesca our newest student. She will need her uniforms, dance clothes, and sleep gown, s'il vous plait."

"Oui Mademoiselle," looking Francesca over with a critical eye. She pulled out many garments.

Francesca had never worn that many clothes. It was overwhelming but she tried to appease the Mademoiselle. Stumbling behind the Mademoiselle who had scooped up the pile of clothing and was headed back down the hall to Francesca dormitory room.

The Mademoiselle hung her clothes on hooks inside the armoire, laid the rest on the shelf and turned to Francesca. "Let us make up your bed." Francesca froze with the pile of bedding still in her arms. The Mademoiselle smiled. "Ah child, you do not know how to make up a bed, do you?" Francesca shrugged.

"Let us begin your schooling right now. From this day forth you will prepare your bed like this." The instructions were brief, the demonstration specific while Francesca followed through the process. "Voila, it is done," Mademoiselle exclaimed with a smile.

"It is almost time for our noon meal. Let us refresh before we dine." Juliette took her to the necessities and poured some water into a basin. She showed Francesca how to cleanse her hands. Francesca was eager to learn everything from this wonderful loving teacher.

As they strolled into the dining room Francesca gasped at the sight. So many girls. Girl seated and chatting amongst themselves. Girls lined up along one wall waiting to get their plates of food. Kitchen workers lined up behind tables assisting the girls with their selections.

Mademoiselle handed Francesca some silverware and a napkin. She preceded the child in collecting a plate filled with food and helped the kitchen staff in a selection for Francesca.

"Francesca let us take our meal back to my office for today. I have so much work to do and we can chat while we eat."

Francesca let out a relieved sigh. Her family did not use so many utensils for food and she was not sure how to manage it with so many girls watching her.

Juliette placed her plate on her desk and made room for Francesca next to her. She opened her napkin, placed it in her lap and put out her silverware for Francesca to follow.

"We hold our fork like this and our knife like this." She demonstrated until Francesca did as instructed. It was like teaching a babe she thought to herself. For that is what Francesca was. A clean slate. What did that mother teach her? she thought. Not much was her only answer.

Francesca tried eating the peas on her plate only to have them fly everywhere. "I don't like them much," she exclaimed in embarrassment.

"I don't care for them much either," Juliette laughed. "But we must eat them so the kitchen staff will not be disappointed with us."

Monsieur Dupre appeared at the office door. "And how is our newest student finding her first day?" he enquired.

"We are having our first instruction on dining etiquette," Juliette explained.

"I see. Well, carry on. I look forward to hearing good things about you Francesca," he said as he turned and left the room.

Francesca began her first day of classes trying to figure out how to wear all the clothes she had to put on. Coming to her assist was her student advocate, Monique. She was also a new student. Ahead of Francesca by only a few weeks, Monique was slightly larger than Francesca with big blue eyes and a mass of very curly blonde hair.

"You must hurry so we won't be late," she exclaimed. "Madam does not like it when we are late." The girls scurried to their first class of conversational French. "Wait here," Monique instructed her as they stood by the teacher's desk. "Madam will be here shortly and will tell you what you need to do." In a whispered voice Monique said, "She is very mean."

Francesca smiled until she saw Madam, a very tall, thin, stern faced woman. Her brown hair with silver strands was pulled tight in a bun behind her head. "Yes, what can I do for you?" Madam enquired sharply.

"I am Francesca the new student," She replied softly.

"Ah yes. We have been expecting you. Take the seat next to Monique. She is your advocate, Oui?"

"Oui Madam."

French class was a long slow blur for Francesca. She could not read and could not follow the instructions. At the end of class Madam called

Francesca over to her desk. "We will speak to Mademoiselle Benoit about your performance today," she said harshly.

Francesca swallowed hard. She had done something wrong and would be punished but she wasn't quite sure what she had done.

Monique scurried her off to their next class Etiquette. "This is my favorite class. We pretend to eat grand meals and meet royalty. You will love it too!"

Francesca was hopeful. She liked Monique and wanted to be friends with her new companion. After French class anything would be better.

Etiquette class was instructed by an elderly woman the girls called Mademoiselle Grainier. She was barely taller than her students plump and squishy with wavy white hair.

"Mademoiselle this is Francesca our new student, she needs lots of etiquette," Monique volunteered.

Mademoiselle Grainier gave Francesca a sweeping once over with critical eyes. Francesca blushed at the expected criticism she would receive in front of all the other classmates, but, she was surprised. Mademoiselle Grainier smiled at her instead. "Well, I do like a good challenge. Take a seat behind Monique."

Francesca sighed with relief. She was sitting in the back row and not visible to all the nosy girls. Monique was right she did like Mademoiselle Grainier and was surprised at how much training there was for eating and walking and sitting.

The next class was Dance. The girls had to change into their dance clothes of which she had forgotten in her room. While everyone else was changing, Monique ran with Francesca back to the dormitory, grabbed the clothes and ran back to the dressing room to change. Francesca was feeling a bit proud that she was already starting to learn her way around the school only to be reprimanded for not being dressed and ready for class.

"It won't happen again Monsieur Ettinger," Monique defended. "She will leave her clothes here like the rest of us starting today."

Monsieur Ettinger nodded. "Let us begin." As with everything else Francesca found it hard to keep up. The directions were confusing. Every position had a name she did not know and after a while it all ran together in her mind. Throughout the class Monsieur Ettinger called out to her "Francesca, Head up! Francesca, Stand straight! Francesca, Relax your hand, hold it like this!" and he would position her body as she had never held it before. "Back to the bar Francesca!"

It was painfully demeaning. She was known as a good dancer and here she was the dummy of the class. All of the girls whispered behind her back. She was constantly embarrassed and there was nowhere to go to get away from it.

"I will do a good job. I am the great Francesca," she told herself. Her first job she thought was to go through a whole dance class without being yelled at.

Monsieur Ettinger called, "Class dismissed." Francesca sighed with relief. She was winded and sore in places she did not know could hurt.

"Francesca may I see you please?" he commanded.

What now? she thought to herself. "Oui Monsieur," she replied.

"You have worked hard today but I will work you harder. Are you up for the challenge?"

"Oui Monsieur."

"Good. Go get ready for your meal. You have earned it." His voice softened.

"Oui Monsieur." She looked at him. He wasn't so bad. She could live with that. Off she scurried to change back into her uniform and find Monique.

"He is a Bastard," Monique whispered. Her cheeks flushed from all the exercise. "Bas-tard," she emphasized. Francesca only nodded as she glanced back at the teacher as he retreated to the back of the dance studio. She watched as he practiced his own ballet moves.

The girls ran to the dining room and joined the many students standing in line to get their meal. It was a very noisy place. Lots of clatter from plates and silverware, girls talking and laughing. Monique talked to many of the girls never once including Francesca in the conversations. Monique jumped in line before Francesca and grabbed a roll of silverware. The cooks behind the counter asked her if she wanted this course or that item. Saying oui or no to each cook as they moved down the line, Francesca just mimicked whatever Monique ordered. They took their plates and beverages and proceeded to a table already filled with girls. Monique squeezed in between two girls and told Francesca, "Sit over there," and pointed to the far end of the table. She was being banished from her new friend. She felt hurt and alone but did as she was told without saying anything.

Francesca sat next to a girl she did not know, set her plate and glass down and just stared at the food.

"You better eat," the girl beside her said. "We don't have a lot of time and dinner is a long time away."

Francesca began unrolling her silverware. Thank goodness Mademoiselle Benoit taught her how to use these utensils or she probably would be in more trouble now.

"I am Giselle." The girl introduced herself. "But, everyone calls me Giza."

"I am Francesca," she said softly.

"I know. You are the one they like to pick on today. Wait, the next new girl will be scolded like you when she comes. They pick on me a lot too. It is to make us better dancers so they say," Giza sighed.

Francesca laughed. She decided she liked Giza already.

The remainder of the day went on as the morning had. Lots of confusion, ridicule, and whispers behind her back. She hated school. Why couldn't she just dance? She missed her brothers and how they took care of her.

After evening meal Monique pulled her aside. "We are free now to do as we please before we must go to bed. So go find something to do." Monique walked away. Again she was being banished. Where would she go? What would she do?

Francesca sought out Mademoiselle Benoit and found her in her office.

"Francesca how did your first day of classes go?"

Francesca had decided to tell her she wanted to go back to her brothers, but, all she could do was cry. She sobbed so hard she could not get a word out.

"There there child." Mademoiselle Benoit came to her and encircled her with her arms. "Was it really so bad?"

Francesca nodded her head yes as she continued to sob. Trying to stop herself the sobs became hiccups.

"Tell Mademoiselle everything and we will try to remedy it."

"I don't know anything," she wailed. "They want me to read, I don't know how to read. I love to dance and he yelled," she hiccupped.

"He yells all the time. It is not my kind of dance. I want to go with my brothers and dance my dances."

"I see." Juliette paused. "Francesca we cannot go back we can only go forward. I will think of a way for you to adjust. For now, after evening meal you will come to me and we will work on your studies. We will help you to read. Some nights you may go into the studio and practice your new dances. The room remains open until it is lights out. Is this agreeable to you?"

Francesca shook her head yes.

"OK then. For tonight you rest. Do not worry. Tomorrow after evening meal we will start.

Francesca left the room feeling better. Beaten but not beat. There was a glimmer of hope and she was going to hold onto it, or, she would leave and find her brothers, wherever they were.

Mademoiselle Benoit closed her office and went to the teacher's lounge looking for any of the beginning studies teachers. She found only Madame Harvey preparing to leave.

"Madam I understand Francesca is in your morning class?"

Madam stopped and contemplated the question. "Francesca, I don't know. Ah yes, the new girl. The idiot, no training, no knowledge, very backwards," she stated as she recalled her class time.

Horrified the Mademoiselle stood straighter. "Well she may be backwards, but she has a wonderful gift for dance. When you see her dance you will be amazed. For now she needs tutoring to get her caught up to your high standard of learning."

"Yes she needs tutoring but I am not able to spare the time to sit with her," Madam said as she continued preparing to leave the school.

"But of course. I am preparing to help her myself until we can find her someone to give her extra instruction," Mademoiselle interjected. Madam nodded her head as she moved to leave the room. "Since it has been quite some time since I was in a classroom perhaps you can give me some ideas as where I can start with her?"

Only too eager to voice her opinion Madam Harvey answered. "She must begin at the beginning. Use a beginning primer. If she is as sharp as you wish to believe, then she will catch up quickly. Now I must go," she said as she hurried out of the room.

"Merci Madam," Juliette uttered as she watched the Madam leave the room.

CHAPTER 5

*F*rancesca walked back to her dormitory feeling beat up from head to toe. She flopped herself down on her bed and started to relax. Her feet throbbed like nothing she had ever felt before. She was just too tired to deal the them. Zeke always took care of her pains. Where was Zeke now when she needed him? So, so tired she drifted off into sleep.

"NO!" Monique screamed startling Francesca awake. "You cannot sleep in your uniform. Mademoiselle Greinier will kill you if you come to class wrinkled."

Francesca got up, stripped her clothes off. Letting them fall to the floor she walked over to the armoire, got out the only dress that looked different from the uniform, pulled it on, and crawled back into bed.

"Are you an animal?" Monique shrieked. "Hang these up before they look any worse!"

Francesca could not believe anyone would be so interested in clothing. Her clothing no less. She dragged herself out of bed, picked up the pile, shoved it into the armoire, and went back to bed.

"Mon Dieu!" Monique sighed shaking her head. She went to Francesca's closet, shook out each garment, and hung them up carefully on the hooks inside. "You have to learn everything," she exclaimed and walked back to her own bed.

In the morning Francesca woke early to get herself ready for classes. she wanted extra time to prepare as she was still unsure about buttoning her clothes properly. "No discipline from teachers today!" she commanded to herself. However, when she and Monique walked into French class and went to take their seats Madame Harvey stopped her. "Oh no. You are to see Mademoiselle Benoit at once!"

Francesca was surprise. She thought she was to go to see Mademoiselle in the evening. But Madam ushered her quickly down the hall to Mademoiselle's office.

"Here is your student ready for her first class," Madam said hastily and left Francesca with a startled Mademoiselle Benoit.

"I have not yet located a primer for you. Let us see what we can do." Mademoiselle located some paper, an ink well and a quill pen.

"This is the alphabet." She wrote out. " You will copy it for me. Do you know how to spell your name Francesca?"

Francesca shook her head no. Mademoiselle wrote it out slowly for her to see. "You will copy if for me as well. Do both several times." And so they began the basics. The hour passed by quickly.

"Francesca, it is time for you to go to your next class. Come back here after evening meal as we discussed yesterday and we will continue your studies."

"Oui Mademoiselle," she said as she ran off to Etiquette class.

"We will prove Madam wrong about you," Mademoiselle Benoit said to her empty office after the child had left.

Francesca entered the Etiquette classroom just as Mademoiselle Greinier started her lecture.

Monique gave her a harsh look and turned her back to Francesca to focus on the Mademoiselle's instructions.

Francesca was just starting to relax into the flow of Etiquette class when the class ended for the day. "Off to dance class you go. We do not want to render the anger of Monsieur Ettinger do we?" She asked as Francesca scurried away.

She hurried putting on her dance clothes and joined the other girls at the bar attached to the wall. She found Giza and stood behind her. Watching and mimicking the girls as they stretched and practiced the routine of positions. Her body throbbing with pain became less noticeable as she let herself begin to acclimate to the movements.

Monsieur Ettinger moved to the center of the room and began his instructions. Walking up and down the row of girls he assisted each one with a command or a touch.

"Head up Monique."

"Point that toe Paulette."

"Straighten those legs Giselle."

To Francesca he just nodded and repositioned her hand and arm as she tried to hold it as he had placed it. "This is better already," she told herself. Only to be reprimanded later for all the same things she had been told the day before.

At noon meal she got her plate and sat next to Giza, excited to talk to her new friend.

"Francesca," Paulette called to her from across the table.

Francesca looked up surprised.

"I think you are teacher's pet," she chided.

"What is pet?" she whispered to Giza.

"A pet is an animal that lives with people. You know! Like a dog or a cat or a bird," she explained.

"She thinks I am an animal?" Francesca was confused.

"No, no. Like a favorite animal. She means you are the teacher's favorite student," she explained.

Francesca blushed. Like she was Zeke's favorite, she told herself. How could this be so?

"I don't think so. He yells at me all of the time." She smiled. Was Paulette trying to be nice to her?

"No. He watches you all of the time," Paulette countered.

"Oh, I don't think so. I am just the new one he has to train," she replied honestly. "Is she crazy?" She whispered to Giza. "He doesn't watch me any more than he watches you. Does he?"

"Oh, he watches you. But I don't think it's what Paulette thinks. She is just jealous. She wants to be the best. She would like to be teacher's pet. Watch her acting all grown up around him. Like she knows how to be a great dancer. We were told before you came that you were a good dancer and we should be grateful to have you join us. Paulette did not want to hear that someone else could be the best," Giza stated as she slid a forkful of food into her mouth.

Francesca just stared at Paulette and then back to Giza. "So she does not like me?" Francesca was very puzzled.

"No. Paulette likes Paulette and anyone else who likes Paulette. Watch out for her she is very mean," Giza replied quietly.

After evening meal Francesca went to Mademoiselle's office ready to continue her basics. Mademoiselle had a primer for her and she went through the introductory chapter. It was slow and hard to grasp but she practiced writing her letters and her name and anything else Mademoiselle asked of her. Too bad Mademoiselle could not teach all of her classes.

She wondered if Zeke, Gabe and Aaron knew all of this stuff. Did they know how to read? She never saw them read books, but, they were so smart they probably knew how and had not gotten around to teaching her.

Mademoiselle stopped her after the first chapter. "This is a good spot to stop. You have learned a lot for one day little one. Tomorrow morning we will continue. You may go and do anything you like. There is still time before you must go to bed."

CHAPTER 6

$\mathcal{F}$rancesca woke with a new sense of security. There were people, many people taking care of her. Her school needs and personal needs were met. She had food every day, she had dance class, and she had a new friend Giza. She still missed her freedom, missed her brothers with a passion, and missed her dance most of all.

Today after all of her classes she would dance her dance. Something fun to look forward to after a very structured day.

So she waited and waited. It was easier to get through the morning lessons with Mademoiselle Benoit, the silly manors in Etiquette class, and all the rules in dance class. Francesca did her best to follow all of the rules in dance class. It wasn't easy to keep her head up, point her toes, hold her arms and hands in those crazy positions and do it all at the same time, but, she would do it. She would show them that she was the great Francesca. She would!

"You have some place to go Francesca?" Mademoiselle Benoit asked as she watched Francesca hurry through her evening lessons.

Francesca blushed. "I just want to go dance," she explained.

"Of course you do." Mademoiselle realized that this little girl they were trying to mold into a functioning, normal, professional dancer was still the wild child who performed outside in unabashed joie de vivre.

"When you are done with your chapter you may go to the studio."

Francesca grinned and excitedly hurried to finish her work. She bolted from Mademoiselle's office running all of the way to the studio. Other girls called to her as she ran but she did not stop to hear their taunts. She was focused on one thing and one thing only.

She reached the studio and turned the handle, peering inside and sighed with relief to see it empty. She looked around and saw no one.

Not even Monsieur Ettinger. The joy in her heart rose and exploded out of every pore radiating from the center of her being. Rolling her head and shoulders Francesca relaxed her body.

She walked to the center of the room and closed her eyes. Wiggling her toes she imagined the grass beneath her feet. Felt her brothers standing behind her. She envisioned a crowd of people seated at tables before her, and heard Zeke call to her, "Ready Cesca?" She turned her head to him as if he were really there. And then she heard the music, her music, the music of her soul. She began with their opening tune. Freely moving as she liked to move. Focusing on all that she remembered. She was so focused on her dance that she forgot she was in the school's dance studio. One song finished and she began the next. She would not stop until she had done them all. Maybe she would do them all again. The more she danced the freer she felt and more expressive her movements became.

Monsieur Ettinger finished his evening meal with the other teachers and walked the hall back to his classroom. He would extinguish the flames to all of the lights and close up the room before leaving. Tomorrow was the weekend and he was free. He had plans to be with his friends. Other dancers his own age. Not the little girls who surrounded him day in and day out. What had he become? He was a dancer. A star among dancers. He was in his prime and ready to go back to performing when the right opportunity arose. Tonight he was getting rip roaring drunk with his friends and maybe even get lucky with a ballerina or two. Dimitri Ettinger was a handsome man. He was tall and lean with well defined muscles. He had a round face with chiseled features, blue eyes and thick golden blonde hair most women coveted for their own. Dimitri always had plenty of women to choose from since the majority of his dancing buddies preferred the company of other men. "More women for me," he grinned to himself. Even the little girls appreciated his good looks. Falling over themselves to catch his eye. Wanting him to give them special instruction or to just flirt. Mostly they flirted. Some used their lack of dancing ability to get close to him. But little girls were not his interest. Give him a fully grown woman ready to spread her wings for him.

Thomas had promised there would be women at this gathering tonight and he was ready to go get the party started.

He heard noises as he approached his studio. A soft swishing noise which made him curious. There better not be a little girl wanting his attention tonight, he just wasn't in the mood. Dimitri opened the door ready to scoot away the intruder when he saw Francesca in the middle of her performance. Trying to figure out who it was and what she was doing. Dimitri closed the door softly being careful not to disturb her. Ah, it was the new girl. Francesca was it? He was ready to approach her and stop the wildness of her movements but he paused. He became enraptured with her dance. Not ballet yet not quite anything he had seen before.

"She is something special," The school founders had told him and they were right. He was riveted by her movements. He wanted to go to her and correct her positions but he stopped himself and took in all she had to offer.

Francesca began her favorite, "Inter Metzo," and he knew she had the potential to be something great. He now understood why the elders spent so much time working with this backwards girl. He knew the children picked on her for being so different, but, he decided to join the adults and work with her to make sure she would achieve her potential.

When Francesca finished and bowed her head Monsieur Ettinger stepped forward and clapped for her. "Brava. That was excellent Francesca."

She was shocked to see him there. She stared at him as if he had two heads. When did he come in? She was so surprised that he liked her dance. For all of the complaints and corrections he assaulted her with during class time, this was the first time he approved of her. This touched her heart.

"I see now why Monsieur Dupre and Mademoiselle Benoit raved about your dancing."

"Merci Monsieur," she said fanning herself. She had danced in her school uniform which was too many layers of clothing to dance in.

"You must do it again, this time I will help you correct some of your mistakes," he volunteered taking off his jacket and throwing it aside.

"No Monsieur," she exclaimed backing away from him.

He stopped.

"This is my dance not yours. I made the steps and turns not you!"

"Whoever taught you this routine did not show you correctly. I only want to improve your performance," he offered.

"Monsieur Ettinger," she swallowed. "No one taught me this dance. It is mine. I feel the music and I dance. It is not from a book like your dance."

"Francesca we have a performance coming up before the holidays. All of the girls who wish to perform sign up. They will practice and then perform in front of the whole school. It would be a great opportunity for you to show the other students what a talented performer you are. With your talent and my instruction we could show off who you really are. What do you say?"

"No. No. This is mine. For no one to change. I am sorry Monsieur Ettinger, my answer is No," she said emphatically and ran off to her dorm room and the safety of her own space.

"We shall see." He sighed as he went around the room extinguishing the flames before closing the door for the night.

Francesca slipped into her bed clothes and prepared herself for sleep. She crawled into bed but sleep eluded her. Tossing and turning she repeated in her mind over and over again the conversation with Monsieur Ettinger. "With your talent and my instruction we could show these girls what a talented performer you really are."

No! She did not want them to change who she was. She wanted them to accept her for herself. Stop making fun of her. Stop taunting her for the things she said or the things she did that were different.

She WAS the great Francesca. Why didn't they see that? Why did she have to change to prove that to them. As hard as she tried to hold them back the tears flowed. She turned her back to Monique hoping the other girl did not hear her sobs. Why couldn't they just accept her for who she was?

Dawn came much too early. Francesca had not slept and she still was tormented with the struggle. To hold fast to who she was or give in and be just like the rest of them. The choice was disgusting. I am not like them. I will never be just like them!

Francesca dressed quietly and slipped out of her room. Wandering the halls of the school she looked into every classroom as they sat empty. "Why am I here?" she heard a voice in her head. "To be a great dancer," she answered back as she continued to wander the halls. "Then why do

I fight it?" the voice asked again. "I don't know why I fight," she answered herself. "Am I afraid?" the voice asked. "Yes," she said meekly. "Afraid of what?"

"What am I afraid of?" she asked herself. "Afraid of not being good enough?" the voice suggested. "NO. I am good enough." "Then what am I afraid of?" Again the question of challenge. She stopped outside of the dance class. She always ended up at dance class. Going into the room she walked up to the wall with the bar attached. One long wall with one long bar. She touched the bar feeling the wood. Her greatest challenge. So much discipline required at this bar. First position, second position, third position, forth position, fifth position. She went through the structured movements. "Was this so hard?" Of course not. "Why am I afraid?" she thought long and hard.

The morning bells began to chime encouraging the girls to begin their day. So many changes had already happened to her she did not realize how many of them she had already undergone.

"Why am I afraid?" she asked herself again as she proceeded to the dining hall to begin another day.

CHAPTER 7

"**W**hat am I afraid of?" Francesca asked herself. It was Saturday the day off from school work that all the other girls craved. A chance to sit together and talk. For those who lived nearby they would go home for a visit or have family come get them. For Francesca it was a brief respite from the cruel words the other girls flung at her daily.

Francesca wandered the halls stepping inside the Etiquette classroom. She mumbled to herself, "What am I afraid of?" Looking around she felt all of the girls staring at giggling about her as she tried to walk with a book on her head or use the correct fork for whatever exotic food they were being served.

She walked into the Conversational French classroom and remembered being embarrassed as she was rapidly escorted out.

But it was in the Dance studio where she had her revelation. "What am I afraid of?" she asked herself as she sat on the floor against the wall. "Not being a good dancer?" "NO!"

"Not being a great dancer?" No, not it.

" Not being the BEST dancer?" That was it! She wanted to be the best The very best. The ONE AND ONLY best dancer!

"I will be the best!" She exclaimed in joy. Jumping up and spinning around with her arms outstretched. "I am going to be the best this school has ever had!"

But how was she going to be the best? Monsieur Ettinger criticized her all of the time. Through every dance class without exception. "Head up Francesca!" "Head up Francesca!" "Francesca, Head up!" If she held her head up any higher it would touch the ceiling and that would be something. She closed the door to the studio on her way to the chapel. Mademoiselle Benoit was the spiritual leader for the girls on Sunday.

Perhaps she was in the chapel now and would tell her what she should do.

Mademoiselle was indeed in chapel on her knees praying when Francesca entered the grand room. Rows and rows of wooden pews faced the alter with a huge cross hanging on the wall behind it.

Francesca waited in a pew a few rows back behind the Mademoiselle waiting for her favorite teacher to finish her prayers.

Mademoiselle Benoit crossed herself and rose from her kneeling position. As she turned to sit again she saw Francesca in a pew behind her looking forlorn. That poor child she thought. Did they do right by bringing her here? It was on more than one occasion that the other teachers came to her asking the same question. "Does she really belong here?" Juliette always listened and reassured them that Francesca belonged. But, even she wondered at times if her first reaction was the correct choice.

"What brings you to chapel today little one?"

"Mademoiselle may I ask you an important question?"

"Of course child."

"I want to be the best dancer ever, but I am afraid. What do I have to do to be the very best?" Her question was earnest her face pained with contemplation.

"Have you discussed this with Monsieur Ettinger?"

"No Mademoiselle. He yells at me all of the time." Mimicking the Monsieur she lowered her voice. "Stand up straight Francesca!" "Point your toes Francesca!" "Head up Francesca!" she sighed a deep exasperated sigh.

Mademoiselle tried hard to muffle a laugh. "I would guess he says these things to help you be a better dancer. Once you learn them, then you are on your way to being the best, but, you know Francesca, all the very best dancers must practice. They practice all of the time. When they are not in school they practice. They listen to what their teachers tell them and then they do it. Does this help?"

She was just going to have to do like he said. She sighed in exasperation. She was there at this school and she would have to do it his way. It did not matter if she liked it or not. She rose, crossed herself, and left to find a place to think.

She found herself back at the studio and went inside. Walking over to the bar she stood and placed her hand on it. First position. Second position. She practiced all of the positions until they started to become as routine as her own dance moves were. She held her head up high as she could as she went through the movements. She pointed her toes until her feet ached. She would do it all flawlessly if it killed her.

She finally gave in to physical exhaustion late in the afternoon. She had missed midday meal bud did not feel empty. She felt better about herself for doing these steps correctly.

She walked slowly back to her bed to relax before it was time for evening meal. She would talk to Giza when she returned from her visit with her mother. Giza's father was much older than her mother and had died recently. To relieve her grief, Giza's mother was getting ready to go on a world trip and had to get herself ready with a visit to the seamstress for a new wardrobe. Giza was being rescued from school to aid her mother with much needed assistance. "Not a fun visit for Giza," Francesca thought. Better than a visit from my own mother. Francesca shuddered at the thought. She had heard nothing from her mother since she entered school. (Not that she had expected her mother to contact her) but, she was deeply disappointed that she had not heard from any of her brothers, especially Zeke. Tomorrow after chapel Giza would return and she would discuss her new decision with her then. She couldn't wait!

Chapel was slow and boring. Francesca tried to wait patiently to see Giza but the day just dragged on and on. The other girls began returning one by one. Finally Giza entered the school. She had a new hair style which startled Francesca. "What happened to you?" Francesca asked her friend.

Giza was the only girl in her grade that was shorter than Francesca. She was considered plump, had a fair complexion, straight light brown hair and blue eyes. Her hair had been cut short as if a bowl had been placed on her head and cut around it. "Mamma says it is the latest style for hair," she sighed. "I Hate it! She always treats me like a doll or a maid depending on her mood." Giza flung herself onto her bed.

"It is something." Francesca did not know what else to say about her friends strange haircut.

The girls giggled and talked until it was meal time. As they walked to the dining hall they passed Monsieur Ettinger entering the building. "Bonsoir Monsieur," they said in unison.

He nodded to them, "Girls." Still a bit hung over from his weekend, Dimitri Ettinger planned to do some practicing to get his body ready for an audition in an upcoming show.

Francesca and Giza talked during their meal about Francesca's realization that she wanted to be the greatest ballerina ever. After dinner she would show Giza just how much she had improved.

The girls strolled into the dance studio and halted. There in his dance pants and bare chest Monsieur Ettinger was deep into his practice. The girls were mesmerized by the beauty and form of his body as he stretched and leapt through the air. As if he could fly, Dimitri Ettinger was the personification of perfection. The power of his kicks, the lines of his body, and his arms out stretched all moved gracefully and strong. He was spectacular! Up on his toes he twirled across the room in perfected movement.

The girls just stood with their eyes wide gasping at every move. When he finally finished with one arm thrust upward, his head back and the other arm thrust downward the girls could not contain themselves any longer. They began screaming. Which surprised the dancer. He was breathing heavily when the girls ran up to him screaming at the same time. "Oh Monsieur Ettinger!" They were so excited they both started jumping up and down. Holding each other's hands. While they were headed in his direction they were so wrapped up in each other's excitement that they jumped and spun in one spot. Dimitri bent over to pick up a rag to wipe his face and grabbed a glass of water for a cool drink.

"Oh Monsieur," they squealed talking over each other trying to express how excited they were by his dance.

"Girls! Girls please!" annoyed he tried to quiet them down.

"Monsieur," Francesca had contained herself enough to speak to him coherently. Still jumping up and down. "Monsieur, I want to dance like that! I want to dance just like that! When can I learn Monsieur? Will you teach me?"

She didn't wait for his response she just started twirling.

Dimitri Ettinger could not believe his ears. "Finally the student has emerged." He acknowledged to himself. Watching her he smiled to himself. "What have I gotten myself into?"

CHAPTER 8

Francesca's training began immediately. It were imperative to her development that she start as soon as possible.

The instructions were subtle at first. While Monsieur continued to lecture the other girls, to Francesca he just made hand gestures. Two fingers raised sharply meant hold your head up, and she did. Full hands pointed out meant adjust your feet. Left hand only meant adjust your left foot, right hand out meant adjust your right foot. She absorbed the training like the starving with food. the more he instructed the more she absorbed.

The true training came in the evenings after her studies with Mademoiselle Benoit.

He would begin each private class with an instruction and a demonstration as to how it was to be performed. Francesca would follow his lead and repeat it over and over until she had it down. Given to her in small increments by the end of the week she had a succession of moves and steps that flowed together.

On the weekends when Dimitri was off with his friends or his women, Francesca practiced and practiced. If she had questions or had forgotten a particular pattern of steps or hand movements they would review it on Sunday evening after meal time.

This pattern of study went on for several weeks. The girls in her class began to notice the difference in her performance. Teasing her about being teacher's pet to her face only to ridicule her behind her back. The head back stabber, Paulette, was being eaten alive by her own jealousy. Her viciousness grew as her own talent for dance failed to progress. Paulette tried flirting with Monsieur Ettinger only to be give the brush off. This response only infuriated her more and caused Paulette to create lies about the Monsieur's and Francesca's involvement.

As the holiday rapidly approached Monsieur Ettinger worked with Francesca on her presentation. They had decided to begin with a Gypsy Folk Dance and enlarge the dance to encompass Ballet moves. The dance began as pure folk dance and slowly developed until it ended in pure ballet.

Monsieur Ettinger contacted a few of his musician friends to create the ensemble of sounds. Transitioning from one genre of music to another was tricky. The right amount of alcohol as payment went a long way to encourage the musician's creative talents.

Francesca asked Mademoiselle Benoit for a person to sew her costume and she was put in contact with the seamstress for the professional ballet. Since the woman's first assistant was also one of Dimitri's "friends" the costume proved to be unique. An overlay utilizing Gypsy colors and style that was easily removed to show the more traditional ballet costume underneath. It was brilliant and Francesca loved it. Dimitri did his best, in private, to show his gratitude to the costume designer much to her delight.

The day rapidly approached for the school holiday performance and Francesca grew more nervous. She had never performed in front of such a large crowd. Monsieur Ettinger was a professional and quite aware of how stars reacted to stage fright.

"You have no need for fear," he told her. "It only gets in the way. Focus on the dance. You know what to do. We will practice many times before you go on stage. We will even rehearse on stage before the performance. You are going to surprise them all with your ability and progress." He said most assuredly. How could she deny his words. He was the professional. Any accolades she had achieved so far were a mere pittance compared to the star she had training her for this show.

Monsieur Ettinger was such a talented performer that he was able to help all of the other girls put together their performances if they asked.

Paulette had her performance all orchestrated on her own. Several girls had decided to do group presentations. Each had costumes made and musical scores arranged. Many used popular dance tunes so their presentations were easier to assemble.

In the end the lineup of routines started with Paulette and was followed by a group and continued alternating with single performers followed by group performances and Francesca's dance was the finale.

Monsieur Ettinger winked at her when the lineup had been announced and posted for all of the girls to see.

They were all excited talking amongst themselves. Paulette turned to Francesca in front of the whole group and said very loudly. "I am sorry you have to go last Francesca, I guess the better dancers get to start the show." She flashed her biggest smile. While some of the other girls gasped many just giggled.

Francesca did not know what to say to her rival. "I guess you are right Paulette, maybe next time I will get to go first."

Giza pulled Francesca aside. "Don't listen to her. She is very jealous of you. Let her think she is the better dancer. We will show her how good you are at the performance!" Giza glared at Paulette. Francesca gave Giza a big hug. She was Francesca's biggest fan.

Regular classes had ceased several days before the performance to give the girls time to focus on their presentations.

The day of the performance finally arrived and nerves were at their highest. Many girls spent the day in the necessities throwing up or having other body ailments.

Francesca had tried to sleep the night before but tossed and turned the whole night. Going over and over in her mind every step and every turn. Her costume was being held in a special location back stage for her. Giza had volunteered to help her with her hair.

The audience was to be filled with special people. Family members of the girls were invited. All of the teachers and staff had special seating as well as their spouses and family.

The establishing founders had dignitary seating and a special box was cleaned and adorned for his highness and the royal family.

The girls had been given special instruction on how to bow to the royal box before they were to take their general bow. Each girl had to demonstrate the depth of their "Royal Bow," until it was approved by Monsieur Ettinger. This only added to the girls already high strung nerves.

Since the evening of the performance was well into December, the weather was very cold. The girls were instructed to have their coats on over their costume while they waited for their performance time.

Giza helped Francesca into her costume and then the overlay. Gasping at its beauty.

"Shush," Francesca whispered not wanting to draw attention to herself. Her hair looked beautiful as it hung down her back in the big braid Giza had woven for her. Giza stood in protection of Francesca just in case nasty Paulette decided to make an appearance. But Paulette was too wrapped up in her own dress ensemble to cause trouble for Francesca. After all, she was going on stage first.

The music began and the audience took their seats and quieted down. A medley of songs were played as Monsieur Ettinger walked onto the stage center front. He was dressed in his finest suit. A most handsome figure of a man. He spoke very loudly.

"Messieurs et Mesdames. It is my great pleasure as instructor of the Premiere class of Ballet at L'Opera de Paris to introduce you to the finest performers of the class." The crowd clapped. "It is for your pleasure this evening that our students have prepared an ensemble of dance routines. So, without further ado may I introduce our first performer Miss Paulette Girard." The crowd clapped politely again.

Paulette took the stage from the left, took her place and nodded to her musicians. As her music began she appeared noticeably nervous but Paulette performed her routine, bowed to the royals and then to the audience. She received a modest round of applause and exited the stage to the right. She was all aflutter backstage commenting to whoever would listen about her performance, how nervous she was, and how the crowd loved her. She was quieted by one of the assistants and ushered to the dressing area to put on her coat.

From then on the performances were a blur to Francesca. Monsieur Ettinger announced each and every performer most elegantly. The groups did their routines, some making minor mistakes but most did just fine. Everyone remembered to bow correctly to the royals and then to the audience.

Finally it was Francesca's turn to perform. She was numb from the cold and her stomach was tied in knots. She handed Giza her coat. It was going to be the most memorable performance of her life. She took in the whole sight of the stage and the auditorium. Never had she seen such a huge room and never had she seen so many people. She had rehearsed on this stage but no one was permitted to see her rehearsal except Monsieur Ettinger. Monsieur Ettinger stepped on stage and began his announcement.

"Messieurs et Mesdames. It is my great honor to end our show this evening with a special performance from our very own Francesca Duvallier. Francesca if you please." He turned to her but Francesca froze in place. Who was this Francesca Duvallier? She was the only Francesca at school. She walked to center stage and gave Monsieur a funny look. He nodded to her and winked.

Francesca turned to the musicians to instruct them to begin and the Gypsy music of her heart began. The musicians that Monsieur had hired did a wonderful job creating a tune similar to the ones that her brothers had played. As she started her native dance the audience gasped and a hushed whispers were heard throughout the hall.

Backstage Paulette saw the beginning of Francesca's dance and smirked to herself. She knew Francesca would do something awful and she was right! She walked back to her seat to wait out the report of how horrible Francesca's dance had ended.

But the music progressed and Francesca's earthy tune eased gently into a natural flow with the more formal ballet. As the tune changed tempo Francesca spun taking off the overlaying gown to reveal the exact same gown in the more subdued formal ballet hues. The crowd clapped with surprise. As Francesca's turns slowed down, she took her long braided hair, pinned it up on top of her head and transformed herself into the consummate ballerina. Completing her transformation by performing a routine only the most professional grown ballerina could maneuver.

She did it. No mistakes! She felt elated!

The crowd cheered and rose to applaud her performance.

She took a very deep bow to the Royal box and again to the audience. She had not heard such a loud cheer for the other girls so she did not know what to do. Monsieur Ettinger joined her on stage, held out his hand to her, and said, "Follow my lead."

He ushered her to stage right and had her bow again. The crowd cheered more loudly. He ushered her to stage left and had her bow again. And the crowd continued to cheer. He walked her back to center stage and left her there to go and gather all of the other student performers. Francesca stood there, put both of her hands to her mouth, flung her arms out and took one last bow.

The crowd continued to cheer as Paulette reached the stage to collect her final accolade. She was stunned to hear them cheering so loudly.

Was this for her? She beamed her finest smile as she bowed with the whole group. "We are stars!" she exclaimed to the girl standing next to her. "Don't be daft you moron. This crowd is enamored with Francesca's performance. Didn't you see it? She surprised us all. She started with that horrible folk dance but it then became a dance like a professional Prima Ballerina. She was amazing!"

Paulette was horrified but stood frozen on stage while the cheers and clapping continued. Only when the clapping died down were the girls ushered offstage.

"Congratulations girls! Congratulations to you all!" The Senior Monsieur Dupre had come backstage to address them. "You have all done us proud this evening. His Highness was most thrilled with your show. Go enjoy your holidays with your families knowing you did a wonderful job. We look forward to seeing you perform again next year." He finished his speech and sought out Francesca.

"Francesca you did us proud child. What a marvelous achievement you have earned. I hope you enjoy your gift from us. Monsieur Ettinger requested you be given a formal name since you have improved so dramatically. What could be better than a legitimate name to honor this fine achievement. A new status for a future Prima Ballerina." Monsieur Dupre gave an abbreviated bow and left her standing with Mademoiselle Benoit and Monsieur Ettinger.

Francesca was shocked. What just happened here? she asked herself. There were so many people rushing over to talk to Monsieur Ettinger and Mademoiselle Benoit that they were swept away from her. Giza slipped through the crowd to her side. Her trusted friend was always there for her. What would she do without Giza?

"Did you hear all of that?" she asked Giza.

"No I missed it. There are so many people and it is so noisy." She held her hands to her ears.

"Wait until you hear what he said!"

"Who?" Giza asked.

"Monsieur Dupre!" she screamed trying to be heard over the crowd. "They gave me a new last name to honor my work. He said I am the stuff of Prima Ballerina. Can you believe it? Me, a Prima Ballerina!"

Giza started jumping up and down. Grabbing Francesca's hands and grinning from ear to ear enjoying her friends accomplishment as though it were her own.

Back at the school, while the other girls were collecting their belongings and departing for their holiday break, Francesca slipped into her night clothes and fell into bed. Trying to go to sleep was near impossible. As exhausted as she was Francesca could not get over what Monsieur Dupre had said to her. "Our future Prima Ballerina." And the gift. She was a whole person now just like the other girls. No longer just Francesca. She was now Francesca Duvallier!

CHAPTER 9

*F*rancesca woke with a big smile on her face. Reliving the applause and cheers from her performance. She felt alive. Her feeling about herself were correct. She would be a great dancer and all those people including Monsieur Dupre agreed.

She was still tired but ravenous. Today she would eat. Yesterday she was too anxious, too nervous and excited to eat. Today she would eat everything they had in the kitchen. Maybe she would have cake for breakfast if they had it!

Dressing in her uniform she strolled down to the dining hall. The school felt strange without all of the girls. A limited number of staff members were there to tend to their needs.

Entering the dining hall she was greeted with a shout from the cook behind the serving counter. "There she is!" the Madam behind the counter announced loudly. "There's our star!" Francesca beamed a big smile at her. She was still the star this morning. "We have a limited menu today," the cook said. "But the star may have anything she wants!"

Francesca was not used to the adulation or special treatment. "Merci Madam," she said as she looked over the meager selection of food. "Everything looks wonderful. I want some of everything today."

The cook grinned and gave Francesca a larger portion that usual filling her plate to capacity. "So this is what it is like to be a Prima Ballerina. I like it already!" she said to herself.

"Come sit with us Francesca." The few girls who were in the dining hall called to her. She joined them graciously and began to eat. They joked and talked throughout the meal. Francesca felt like she had woken up into someone else's life. A life where she was loved and appreciated. Certainly not at her usual school. Thankfully Paulette had gone home the night before. She could relax from the constant worry of being a victim to a verbal attack. Even Monique was gone for the holiday. She still could not figure her out. Sometime she was nice and friendly and other times she was mean like Paulette.

"Have you seen Giza?" she asked the others. Just then Giza walked into the dining hall. She saw Francesca and gave a big grinned smile only to stop when she saw who Francesca was sitting with. Francesca made room for Giza next to her and motioned for her to come over. Giza walked slowly to her friend.

"Get something to eat and join us," Francesca insisted.

"With all of the stars?" Giza inquired snidely. Francesca rolled her eyes. "No, with your friends." Giza smirked and went to get her plate.

"Why do you like her? She's so odd," one of the girls asked.

"Because she is the only one who would talk to me when I first came here and because she is my friend." Francesca defended her.

Giza joined them and as they talked. Francesca observed her new friends. Did they really like her or were they just being nice because she did so well last night? Francesca was very puzzled by all of this attention. She felt the same, yet everything had changed.

Francesca and Giza left the dining room together. "I guess I am not such a horrible person after all," Francesca said.

"Yes. Now they can see who your really are and what you can do. They will want to know you more now that you are important," Giza affirmed.

"How did you get so smart?" Francesca asked but got no reply.

The days passed. Francesca and Giza remained inseparable. They went to practice dance by themselves and Francesca helped Giza with her positions and movements. "You are a good teacher Francesca, but, I think your student is stupid."

"That is nonsense!" Francesca exclaimed. "You remember how awful I was when I started. Monsieur Ettinger would not let me quit and I will not let you quit." Giza did improve slightly. Francesca was certain it was because she was not the masterful teacher like Monsieur Ettinger. "Just wait until he returns. Monsieur will see how well you are doing and will want to give you extra lessons too."

All of the girls returned after the holidays and school resumed. Although Francesca had learned enough to rejoin French class she still went to study with Mademoiselle Benoit every evening.

She was most excited to get to dance class and raced to change her clothes. She started her stretching and positions at the bar when a woman in dance clothes entered the studio.

"Mademoiselles s'il vous plait!" She clapped her hands to get their attention. "I am Mademoiselle Gifford. Monsieur Ettinger will not be here to teach you any longer. He is currently in rehearsals and will be spending all of his time preparing for his new production. We wish him well, oui? He has given me the format for your instructions and we will proceed from there. Do you have any questions?" She asked as she looked at all of the girls.

"Will he be coming back?" Francesca's upset voice rang clearly.

"Who are you Mademoiselle?"

"Francesca," she replied.

"Well Francesca, I do not know the answer to this. So we will proceed with our training and our dancing. Any other questions?" she asked looking at all of the stunned faces.

"No. Let us begin then. Stand up straight please. First position..."

Francesca followed routinely but she was in shock. He did not even say goodbye. She felt the ripping of her heart again. Another man she cared for and depended on take away from her. How was she to survive? This new teacher did not know who she was. Did not care for her. She was rough and unfriendly. She was going to have to prove herself all over again. She loved dance, but, she did not love this new teacher Mademoiselle Gifford!

Francesca sat at the dining table with her lunch untouched before her. Giza was by her side and all of her classmates around the table. They were all shocked by the turn of events they had just experienced. The only one eating happily was Paulette.

"Not the teacher's pet now Francesca?" she smirked.

"Be quiet Paulette," Francesca blurted out angrily.

"Be quiet Paulette," Giza and a few others chimed in. Giza looked at Francesca amazed at her friends bold response.

"Maybe Mademoiselle Gifford will see who the real stars of the class are," Paulette went on.

"Maybe she will." Giza voiced, "but it probably won't be you!"

Paulette got up in an angry huff and stormed out of the dining hall. The girls at the table sighed collectively.

"Now we have to prove ourselves all over again," Francesca exclaimed.

"That's easy for you," Monique chimed in. "You dance so well. The rest of us will have to work even harder," Monique sighed. She too got up and left the dining hall.

"She thinks it is so easy for me," Francesca said turning to Giza. "She did not see me practicing every night before bed time or every weekend when she was out having fun. Mademoiselle Gifford does not know me at all!" She threw her napkin over her untouched meal and left the dining hall before the tears came flowing down her face. Francesca looked into the dance studio and found it empty. She did not see Mademoiselle Gifford sitting on the floor in the back corner.

Staying in her uniform Francesca went to the bar and started to practice. Without thinking she stepped away and started the routine from her grand performance. Feeling Monsieur Ettinger's energy around her Francesca went through her steps. Throwing her raw emotions into every gesture and every step she executed her dance with precision. At the end she stood looking at the empty space before her. There was no Monsieur Ettinger to reward her with words of praise there was only silence.

"So you are the one they speak of." A voice came to her from the back corner.

"Who Mademoiselle?" Francesca turned toward the voice.

"Everyone. Mademoiselle Benoit, the other instructors, even Dimitri spoke of you," she answered as she rose and walked over to Francesca.

"Monsieur Ettinger spoke of me?" she asked hungrily.

"Oui child. He said you are his best student and I should take good care with your studies. He said that you are stubborn but have great talent. Is that correct?" She studied Francesca's face intently.

"Oui Mademoiselle. I suppose that describes me." Tears started rolling down her face and she hastily brushed them aside.

"You know Francesca, these performances do not last forever. Perhaps Monsieur Ettinger will be back to teach you once the show has completed its run," she said.

Francesca nodded her head, "I have to go to class now," she announced and left the studio in haste.

Mademoiselle Gifford watched Francesca as she left the room. "Another of Dimitri's love sick ballerinas. He does have quite an effect on us all," she sighed.

The following day in dance class Francesca began to prove herself to Mademoiselle Gifford. She held her body in perfect form throughout the class. "Impressive." Mademoiselle noted to herself. Her practice positions were excellent. It was only during instruction of new steps that the Mademoiselle saw the awkwardness of Francesca's true nature. But, just as Dimitri had said, Francesca became tenacious and practiced over and over again until she had a better grasp of the new routine. The other girls continued to fumbled over themselves trying to grasp the steps.

"S'il vous plait Mademoiselle, show us again." Francesca studied the new movement most intently until she inched her was to perfecting it.

After class Mademoiselle Gifford stopped Francesca before she left the studio. "You are very good Francesca. Perhaps I should have you help me teach the others."

Francesca was surprised. "You want me to help teach? But I do not know what you are going to teach us!"

"Yes, but you seem to grasp it far quicker that the others. You could help show them how you do it," She suggested.

"I will have to think about it," Francesca told her as she was getting ready to leave the studio.

"You will want to come practice in the evenings like you did with Dimitri."

"Why Mademoiselle?"

"Because you want to dance and you need to excel. You are a much better dancer than most of these girls and do well with private instruction. If you progress, as I suspect you will, you may be ready for productions on stage before the end of your schooling." The Mademoiselle studied her face for her response. It was difficult to compete on a professional level and she needed to see if Francesca had the determination to do it.

"Oui Mademoiselle. I do love to dance without the other girls around me, especially Paulette. She is very mean. She wants to be the best dancer and does not like it when I achieve."

"You leave Paulette to me," Mademoiselle informed her. Francesca sighed with relief.

Her private studies began again in the evening after her instructions with Mademoiselle Benoit. She told Mademoiselle Gifford how

Monsieur Ettinger taught her small portions at a time until she mastered the steps and could put them together in a flow of movements. Mademoiselle watched graciously and then did the instructions the way she wanted. She increased the amount of steps watching to see how well Francesca would absorb then. She continually pushed Francesca to do more than Dimitri had assumed she could do. Some days Francesca was able to learn more some days less, but, she was always the eager student. Francesca wanted to know everything and learn everything. Like a wild stallion, the Mademoiselle had to keep a tight rein on this wild talent and guide her in the right direction.

Spring was approaching and the girls were all eager to get outside and enjoy life. Mademoiselle Gifford knocked on Mademoiselle Benoit's office door and waited for a response.

"Come in," Mademoiselle Benoit called.

"Mademoiselle, I think it would be a good idea for all of the girls to see a professional ballet production. I believe it would inspire them to do better in their own work if they got to see how a true ballerina performs. Since the girls all studied with Dimitri Ettinger I thought they would enjoy seeing him perform in his latest production. What do you think?" Her mind already set to proceed she waited for Mademoiselle Benoit to agree.

"That would be a lovely treat for our girls. I know they miss their former teacher and seeing a staged performance would most definitely encourage our girls to try harder at their studies," she agreed. "Do you know when the performances are to begin?" she inquired.

"Oui Mademoiselle. I believe they will start the first week of March. I can contact the director to see when we can come. if you wish?"

"No no. I will make all of the arrangements. It will take some doing to get all of the girls to the theatre at the same time. I am certain they will enjoy some time off from their studies to see their teacher perform." Her eyes twinkled as she spoke.

"Merci Mademoiselle."

"Mademoiselle Gifford. Do not mention it to them yet. Let me see how it progresses before we include them. They would be very disappointed if it fell through. I will be in contact with you do not fear." Both women stood as they finished up their meeting.

"Merci Mademoiselle. It will be a glorious event for the girls," she said before she left.

"We all will enjoy a break from our regular schedule to see one of our own perform," Mademoiselle Benoit added as she waited for the younger woman to exit her office before she shut the door.

CHAPTER 10

$\mathcal{M}$ademoiselle Benoit made the announcement in chapel after
her service. It was a bleak February day. The girls were
delighted and became very animated to hear that they were going to see
Monsieur Ettinger perform on stage. Even the idea of a break from their
studies created an excitement that they were unable to contain.

"Are we going in our dance costumes?" one girl asked. "I want
them to know that we are ballerinas too!" she said emphatically. Many
other girls nodded their heads in agreement.

"No child we are going in our uniforms. We represent L'Opera de
Paris school of ballet. You will hold your heads up high and be gracious.
It is a great honor to represent the school in this manner," she instructed
them all. Although many girls had sighed in disappointment, others
acknowledged their level of acquired schooling and they sat a little taller
in their seats.

"If we are so fortunate, you may be able to go backstage after the
performance and speak to the ballerinas in person. This has not been
finalized yet. It will depend on your behavior at the show as to whether
or not you will receive this honor." She paused and looked around the
room. "If any of you are unruly, we will just return to the school. Make
no mistakes, behave as young ladies, sit dutifully during the performance
and you all may be rewarded with this gift. Have no misunderstandings
girls, this is a great gift we are giving to you."

Mademoiselle Benoit took a moment to let it sink into their heads
and the she proceeded to close her service.

"What do you think?" Giza asked Francesca excitedly. "A real ballet performance." She started jumping up and down. "And, Monsieur
Ettinger on stage. It has been a long time since we got to see him dance."

Francesca was not as excited as Giza thought she would be. "Yes I am looking forward to seeing a professional performance," she stated flatly.

"What is the matter with you?" Giza slowed her jumping. "Don't you want to see the show?" she could not believe Francesca's response.

"I just don't know how I feel. Monsieur Ettinger left us without saying goodbye. No words at all. Not "It's been great. You were good students. I will miss you." Nothing!"

"You wanted him to say goodbye?"

"Yes! I wanted him to say something to me. I saw him every day. Every day he instructed me, worked with me and then he was gone. Just GONE. No ending, just GONE." Francesca started to cry. Wiping her face "Like my Papa. Just gone."

"Oh, I see. Your Papa left you without saying goodbye and Monsieur Ettinger left you too. Too many men, not enough goodbyes." Giza nodded to herself.

Francesca gave Giza a little push and started laughing as she wiped the remaining tears from her face. "You will make a great priestess someday. Sister Giza the ballerina Priestess." She joked as they walked to their dorm room.

"How do I feel about seeing Monsieur Ettinger?" Francesca asked herself. The tears started flowing again. "Why would he leave without saying something? Anything at all was better than just disappearing."

Francesca did not have the answers to any of these questions. Being upset hurt her stomach and her head. She got up and strolled down to the dance studio. She peered inside and was relieved to see it empty. Not even Mademoiselle Gifford hiding in the back corner.

She went to the dressing room and changed her clothes. Standing at the bar she started the routine of warm up exercises followed with the routine of positions and finally the routine of basic moves that they did every day. It made her feel better to go through the basics. It made her feel more like herself.

She took a deep breath and started spinning. Moving herself across the great expanse of the room. From one corner to the far corner on her toes which made her move more quickly. She concentrated on what Mademoiselle Gifford had been teaching her and the pain of her loss melted to a tiny speck in her heart.

On the day of the performance all of the girls were aflutter with excitement. Francesca got caught up in the frenzy even though she still did not know what to say to Monsieur.

They were dressed in cleaned uniforms and Francesca let Giza braid her hair as she had worn it at her big performance.

The girls left the school in pairs following Mademoiselle Benoit. Francesca walked with Giza of course. "Remember your manors girls." Mademoiselle Grainier spoke up as she stood outside the school watching them exit. The procession of students in uniform was a very impressive sight to be seen.

The girls went to a matinee performance and were fortunate enough to sit close to the stage. Francesca looked around the enormous room once they were seated. It was overwhelming in size. I will dance here some day she told herself as she took it all in.

A large bell gonged alerting them that the performance was about to begin and the patrons all took their seats. Many theatre assistants went around the walls extinguishing some of the candle flames in order to dim the room.

The music began and the performers took the stage some walking some dancing. All of the girls looked and looked to find Monsieur Ettinger but settled into watching the show since the performers were so entertaining. The dancers were exquisitely gowned and the dance magnificent. No one made mistakes. They danced in unison, the precision spectacular. And then one of the school girls gasped. There he was. Monsieur Ettinger leapt onto the stage in amazing grandeur. His costume made him look royal. His command on stage over powered any activity by any of the other dancers. His long lines and strong movements were mesmerizing. When he danced with the Prima Ballerina every woman and every girl in the theatre wanted to be her. The whole show was glorious and ended way too quickly. Francesca's desire to be on that stage with all of those performers beat in her heart throughout the performance.

When the dancers took their bows at the end of the production all of the girls stood up clapping and roaring for their favorite dance teacher.

Monsieur Ettinger made a special acknowledgement of their approval by walking over to the portion of the stage closest to their seats and made an extra deep bow in front of them. The girls cheered even more loudly as he did this.

Monsieur graciously backed up and held out his arms for his cast of dancers to join him. Holding his hand was the Prima Ballerina who took her accolades with him and then by herself like the Monsieur had shown Francesca how to do after her grand performance. Giza nudged Francesca with her elbow to acknowledge the very same act.

The girls remained at their seats until the audience finished departing the auditorium before they were permitted to join the performers backstage.

Francesca waited for all of the other girls to step ahead of her. She held back because she had to say something to Monsieur but she still did not know what she should say.

She spotted him in a back corner deep in conversation with a man. Other people approached him, mostly women.

As the students flowed into the confined backstage area some went to speak to other ballerinas but most went to see Monsieur Ettinger. He excused himself from the other man, shook his hand and permitted the onslaught of attention to descend upon him. He talked to and answered many questions from his former students.

Monsieur Ettinger still talking to the girls looked around and finally found Francesca's sullen face. He cocked his head to the side and gave her a quizzical look. "How is my star student? Did you enjoy the performance today?" He gave her the once over not understanding her reaction.

"Oui Monsieur," she replied.

"Oui Monsieur?" he reiterated. "Is that all you have to say to me after all of this time?"

"You left without saying goodbye. You left me..." she started crying. "You left me alone without knowing where you went. I had no teacher. I had no one." She just kept crying and dropped her face to her chest.

Monsieur Ettinger wrapped his arms around the sobbing girl "Ah, the student becomes a wife," he chided. "I did not leave you just to leave you Francesca. I left to become myself. Just as you will leave to do what you have to do. We have this in common don't we Francesca? We have to dance it is in our souls. It is who we are. If we do not dance we are no one. Is this not true?" he asked talking into her hair. Still in his embrace she cried into his chest. She could not speak so she nodded her agreement. "You are still my best student. Never forget that. You will do me proud one day when you are famous and I am too old to dance. You will always be my favorite." He turned her face up to look into her eyes. "Always!" he said. He kissed her on the top of her head, let her go, and turned to talk to someone else behind him laughing as he spoke.

Francesca was left to contain herself. Bring herself back to balance, wipe her face and become the proud and gracious student of L'Opera de Paris school of ballet that she was.

Giza accompanied by Mademoiselle Benoit handed Francesca a handkerchief and gave her a moment to dry her eyes before they started their journey back to school.

CHAPTER 11

*F*rancesca woke with a troubled mind. She would never be as good a teacher as Monsieur Ettinger. What could she do to encourage the girls as he had done. Two fingers up meant hold your head up. Full palm moving left meant move your left foot. Full palm moving right meant move your right foot. Hands behind back meant arch your back. She tried this with Giza and it worked as long as Giza stayed focused. Giza easily slipped back into old patterns. She thought about how to get the girls to stand up straight. Then she remembered about Mademoiselle Grainier's trick about walking with a book on your head. This is why the Etiquette teacher did this silly game with them. To get them to remain standing straight. She continued developing signals for the different body parts and body movements.

In class she practiced with her friends. Paulette refused to cooperate. She caused such a ruckus with her refusal to participate that she was moved, by Mademoiselle Gifford, to the next class which was younger. Paulette and her family were so insulted by this move that she eventually dropped out of the academy.

Mademoiselle Gifford proved to be a excellent teacher for Francesca. She taught her hard and fast and made her stay sharp with her dance skills. She expected Francesca to perform professionally and pushed her to achieve at that level.

Having her assist as a teacher made Francesca focus on acquiring the skill before explaining it to the others. She had to demonstrate it and then assist others in achieving it. This process worked very well for Francesca's education and the education of all the dancers in her class.

Many girls came to her for extra assistance and she had to give up her special time with Mademoiselle Benoit in order to do so. By the time the second annual Holiday Show came around, not only did Francesca prepare her own theatrical presentation but she helped many of the other girls in creating their own.

Mademoiselle Gifford pushed Francesca to audition for a professional production. Out of her realm of comfort she prepared a piece for her audition only to have her work incorporated into the theatrical show.

With the guidance of Mademoiselle Gifford she only auditioned for specific shows utilizing her specific brand of showmanship. She was a trained classical ballerina and nothing short of that would do.

Auditioning at her tender age got her parts less than her capabilities proved worthy. Since the parts were so small she was able to continue at the school with her education and assisting the dance instructor with classes. Her life was unbelievable. Far beyond anything she had imagined as a child. Rarely did she think of her brothers, but, when she did it was with fondness of their antics together or their performances under Zeke's tutelage. How they would be amazed at her abilities now.

It was on a day at the theatre while she was in dress rehearsal for her small part that her life took another change.

Francesca was standing off stage waiting for her turn to enter when she heard a commotion at the back of the auditorium. Muffled voices followed by "You can't come in here!" echoed loudly. Francesca looked to see what was going on. Three grown men stood just inside the back door arguing with the attendant. "We must see her for a moment!" one man yelled. It was a voice she recognized. All three men wore billowy white shirts. Could it really be them? Francesca started running to the back of the auditorium. Was it really them?

"Francesca!" the stage director called. "Francesca come back here at once!" he commanded.

Francesca would not listen. Was it them? She ran faster and faster toward them. "Here she comes!" She recognized Gabe's voice, but, they all looked so different so old.

Francesca ran until she flung herself into the arms of her brother. It was Zeke! It was! They came back for her! They found her!

She was so happy and crying at the same time. She clung to Zeke while the two others patted her on the back. "Francesca. Francesca is that you?" They said over and over again. She hugged each one. She never wanted to let go of any of them. When she finished hugging each one Zeke commanded, "Let me see you." She stood back and did a small pirouette. Shaking their heads. "We would never have recognized you." "You are so grown up." "A real lady of the theatre." Each one spoke over the other. "Mama would be so surprised!" Zeke added.

Mama. She forgot about Mama."Where is Mama? Is she here too?" Francesca looked around but did not see anyone with them.

"No Francesca. That is why we are here," Aaron said.

""Mama has died. We came to tell you of her passing," Zeke claimed softening his voice.

"Oh no!" Francesca did not know what to say or how she felt. Actually she felt nothing. Nothing for the woman who hated her and gave her away. She just felt nothing. The boys looked grief stricken. She felt sorry for them. They looked old and worn out. Wearing the same clothes they were wearing when she left.

"Francesca!" the stage director called again.

"Boys. We are in the middle of rehearsal." She said as she wiped the tears from her face. "Please stay and watch. I want to visit with you some more. Let me finish my rehearsal and then we can talk. Have a meal together. I miss you all so much. I want to know everything that is going on in your lives. Are you married? Do you have children?"

"Francesca!" the impatient director called once again.

"Sit here and wait for me. I won't be long." She patted chairs and ran back to the stage.

The men sat reluctantly. "She looks good," Aaron said and they all agreed.

"She has really grown up. Not much taller but more...I don't know the word," Gabe sighed.

"Yes she is more lady like. More refined than she was before." Zeke finished Gabe's sentence.

They watched the performance very uncomfortably. They did not belong in Francesca's new world.

Francesca was very excited. Her brothers were here! Mama was gone. Wow, her Mama was really gone. She could not wait to spend time with her brothers and find out what happened to Mama.

Her time on stage seemed to go on forever. The director kept making demands He would then change his mind and give new directions. This forced all of the dancers to stay focused on their work.

Finally there was a break. She could talk to them and make plans to visit with them some more. But when she looked over to where they were seated they were gone.

Francesca ran to the back of the auditorium. Looking around frantically to find them. She found the attendant. "Where are they?" she demanded.

"They left a little while ago," was his response.

She ran out the front of the theatre and looked around the street. Nothing. No one was there. Heartbroken she walked back into the theatre. They had left her again. Left without a word. They told her Mama was gone and that was it. She had to get herself together to go back on stage. She did not belong with them any longer. She had the theatre and her dance and that was all. It would have to be enough. In her heart she felt a door slam between her past and her present. She took a deep breath and tried to clear her head. She began practicing to try to let go of the disappointment. Her fellow dancers looked at her and gave her space to deal with her grief. They whispered amongst themselves but said nothing to her directly. She knew they were talking about her but she did not care. Let them talk. She missed her brothers and there was nothing anyone could say to make up for it. She felt alienated. Caught between two worlds. Would she ever fit into the world of dance? She just did not know.

CHAPTER 12

"*F*rancesca" Mademoiselle Gifford came to her after a class they had conducted together. "I have heard of a new production I think you should audition for. They need a Prima Ballerina and you would be perfect for the part. Go to the audition. Do not take second best as you have in the past. This part is made for you."

Francesca listened with great awe. Mademoiselle thought she could be the lead dancer! It was worth checking out.

"Go in your finest costume. Be made up like the Prima Ballerina you are. Present the best of yourself. Expect nothing less than top billing. You can do it. This part is made for you!" she said again with emphasis.

Francesca did as she was told and went to the audition dressed for a successful performance.

"Mademoiselle, you have come from a production?" the assistant asked.

"Oui," she answered with assurance.

"Usually we have you join a group to audition but since you have taken the time to leave your current employ we can have you audition now on your own. Are you prepared?"

"Oui," she answered.

She was ushered into a dance studio set up with a row of people seated in chairs and a table before them. "Your name please?"

"Francesca Duvallier," she replied with authority in her voice. Rarely did she get to use her full name and it felt good, strong, and all grown up.

They continued to ask her questions and finalized with "Do you have a routine prepared?" Francesca agreed. She thought of Mademoiselle Gifford's advise "Prepare to show them the best of your talent."

She put forth her most challenging steps in a flow of movements she had planned to present for the next holiday production at school. She had been working on them with her advanced dance class and most of the students had not mastered them to her level of perfection quite yet.

"Merci Mademoiselle," she was courteously dismissed.

"Where may we contact you when we have made or decision?" one gentleman inquired. She gave them the school's name.

"You are at the school?" He asked with surprise.

"Oui. I teach at the school and you may leave your offer to me with Mademoiselle Benoit," she replied confidently.

God is going to strike me dead for stretching the truth on this one she thought as she left the building.

When she returned to the school she went directly to Mademoiselle Benoit's office. "Mademoiselle," she addressed her teacher.

"Oui Francesca." Mademoiselle Benoit looked up from her desk surprised to see Francesca all made up and in costume.

"I am expecting a post. I do not know when it will arrive. I just want you to know that I am expecting something."

"Of course child. I will most certainly inform you when it arrives."

Francesca went back to her room and changed her clothes. Removed the stage makeup and waited most impatiently for the post to arrive. She went to the studio in frustration and decided to practice until she heard or went mad with anticipation.

Mademoiselle Gifford was in the studio finishing a class for beginning students. Francesca had completely forgotten the school's scheduled classes.

"So tell me!" Mademoiselle Gifford inquired eagerly.

"It went well. I did as you instructed. Went in full makeup and costume. They permitted me a private audition and now I must wait for a post," she replied.

Mademoiselle Gifford smiled broadly. "This is very good. Now you must be patient. It can take some time for them to view all of the applicants. But we know you are the best. They must see the others to recognize your worth."

"How much time?" Francesca needed to know.

"It could be days maybe even weeks. Do something to take your mind off of it. I know. Do your job. Help me teach."

Francesca did her best to stay focused on helping the younger girls and practiced on her own in the evenings to relieve the stress of waiting. It was ten days later when she got the notice.

Mademoiselle Benoit entered the studio holding a sealed letter addressed to Francesca Duvallier. Mademoiselle Gifford dismissed her to go take the letter. She stood in the hallway outside of the studio and opened it in a hurry. It was written in very formal script She could barely focus she was so nervous. She handed the letter back to Mademoiselle Benoit. "What does it say? I am too nervous to read it," she exclaimed.

Mademoiselle read it and sighed. "You are being offered the premiere role of Lise in La Fille mal Gardee in the upcoming production. Should you agree to accept the part, rehearsals begin in February and performances to start in May. What is your response?" the Mademoiselle asked with a broad smile on her face.

"I accept, I accept!" Francesca clapped and started jumping up and down like a school girl. Mademoiselle Gifford joined them in the hallway grinning and clapping for her assistant while Francesca did pirouettes and continued to exclaim "I accept, I accept!"

When she calmed down she turned to Mademoiselle Gifford. "How do I accept their offer?"

Mademoiselle Gifford told her she would help her write an acceptance letter. It was done! She was now a Prima Ballerina!

She went to the theatre to begin production for the first time. A grand new beginning. She followed Mademoiselle Gifford's advise about how to act. She was escorted on a tour of the theatre. Shown her dressing room. Her own private dressing room! Then led to the stage where she would be performing.

"Ah here is our Lise, our star, Prima Ballerina Francesca Duvallier. Francesca meet your new cast. She said hello to a whole group of people she had never met before. "We will do a walk through tomorrow and begin class after that. But, today we get to know each other and learn each other's secrets." The group laughed. "If you do not know me my name is Pierre and I am your stage director. Over here is Jean-Luke the choreographer an Michel the conductor. We work well together and will get this show up and going very soon. Now tell us your names and a little about yourself so we can remember who you are after we have had a few drinks." He pointed to Francesca and she froze. What did she say about who she was.

"I am Francesca Duvallier. I was a student and then a teacher at L'Opera de Paris school of Ballet."

"Thank you Francesca. Very impressive credentials. Are you married? Have a boyfriend?"

"No and No Monsieur." She replied uncomfortable with the direction this was starting to take.

"Are you taking auditions for either role?" He enquired in a flirtatious tone. Everyone laughed.

"Monsieur," she laughed. "I think your wife would be most upset if you applied." Everyone laughed again and it set a jovial tone for the remainder of the afternoon. So many names and faces to remember.

"Monsieur I have a question?" she asked. "I need to find a room to stay. Is there someplace close by that I may let?"

"Well Francesca, there is always my home, although my wife may not be as pleased as I am to have you there. We have made arrangements for you for tonight. See my assistant later for recommendations of rooms available in our fair city for your long term needs. Have you any further questions? No. Let us resume tomorrow early morning after your meal. Bring your dance clothes for we will begin our preparation class for the production immediately after our first walk through. Get a good night sleep children, tomorrow will be a busy day!"

The group was escorted to two locations, one for the men and the other for the women. They were fed and left on their own to complete their evening. Francesca chose to go to her room and rest while the others stayed in the common areas for entertainment. Although she was tired she tossed and turned most of the night and woke to a loud knocking on her door.

"We are leaving for the theatre in half an hour Mademoiselle Duvallier. Come get something to eat before we go," someone yelled through the door.

Francesca raced to get dressed and pull her dance clothes together. She ran to the dining room and slowed herself to a stroll as she entered the dining room. The others were already eating and chatting. They stopped to look at her and then began their conversations again. She was motioned to by one of the women she had met the day before. "There is a spot here Francesca. I am Babette. I play your mother in this show. Since I gave birth to you I think we should get to know each other. Don't you?" Francesca smiled. She would have loved having a mother like Babette.

Once they arrived at the theatre the day flew by. Lots of talking amongst the creators about set construction, cue points, and walk on spots.

The dance instructor was a tough task master and got them all right into work. They were to have warm up class prior to execution where they would jump into rehearsing and memorizing their dance routines.

It was fast and hard and Francesca loved it. She worked closely with the choreographer and his assistant in preparing her dance numbers.

Every evening after meal time she practiced the steps she had learned that day. Everyone was a professional and this Prima Ballerina would not fall short of their expectations. She pushed herself until she collapsed in joyous exhaustion.

Finally it was the day they had all prepared for. Opening Night. She was so keyed up. She tried to calm herself by remembering what Monsieur Ettinger had told her before that first performance. "There is no need for fear, it only gets in the way." She found her dressing room and began to prepare her makeup. Someone knocked on the door.

"Oui," she called.

"Flowers for Mademoiselle Duvallier," a voice responded.

Francesca opened the door to see a huge bouquet of red roses. "Thank you," she said as she pointed to a spot for them to be placed. The young man handed her a card and left. It read, "May all your dreams come true," signed Dimitri. She could not believe it. Monsieur Ettinger remembered her on this special day. How did he now where she was performing?

She received another smaller bouquet from the school and every-one had signed the card. Her heart was full from all the love they shared.

Her performance went as perfectly as she had planned. The show had a few glitches that were worked out the next day and then forgotten. The audience went wild with approval. They had standing ovations from the first day. She took her bows as Monsieur Ettinger had shown her and received flowers from admirers in the front. It was truly a magical experience. Francesca was on top of the world.

Every day they had class to keep limber and every evening she danced her best and received the accolades to acknowledge her efforts. Life just couldn't get any better than this.

The show was blessed with a nice long run.

CHAPTER 13

1794

*F*rancesca was approached by the newest ballerina to join the ensemble, Jacqueline. "Mademoiselle Duvallier my friends are joining me for dinner after the performance this evening and we were wondering if you could join us? My friend Etienne asks me about you all of the time. He is a big fan of yours and would like to meet you. Are you available?"

Usually Francesca declined such an invitation. But tonight she felt like experiencing life. She agreed to meet them at the restaurant in the city.

Francesca had recently hired a seamstress to create a new wardrobe and she was very glad she had. She wore a gown designed for the show stopping Prima Ballerina that she was. The gown was gold and white brocade over white chiffon with a matching hat. She wore white pearl earrings and a pearl necklace to complete her ensemble.

She arrived at the restaurant and was escorted to a small private room where the others waited for her to arrive. She spotted Jacqueline who waved her over. "Mademoiselle Duvallier I am so glad you could join us. I want you to meet one of my dearest friends Etienne. He has been to see you in many performances and claims to be your biggest fan. Etienne meet Francesca Duvallier."

Etienne's face lit up as he bowed to take her hand and kissed it. "The pleasure is all mine Mademoiselle," He said smiling at her.

Francesca was mesmerized by him. Etienne was tall and blonde and well built. Not muscular like a dancer but sturdy.

Etienne escorted Francesca to a table where they sat and talked all during dinner. He was charming and a good talker and Francesca thought she could listen to him forever. He told stories of his work and his childhood. He entertained her for hours and long after the others excused themselves to go home. Etienne bought them after dinner drinks to sip by a fireside. They stayed until the restaurant closed and Etienne offered to escort Francesca home. She had never been so enraptured by a man before.

At her door Etienne asked if he could see her again and when she agreed he bent down and kissed her. It was soft and gentle and the most exciting experience Francesca had ever felt before.

Her head and her heart were alive. Francesca found it hard to concentrate on her dancing but her body remembered what to do without her mind cooperating.

On two occasions during class the instructor called to her. "Mademoiselle please, we need you here," he exclaimed in exasperation. She scolded herself. She would stay focused. This was her job. She regrouped, apologized and put her mind back into her dance.

The evening performance went as glorious as always. The audience cheered and stood clapping at their seats.

Etienne sat most nights in the first few rows on the far left side of the stage in an aisle seat. His long legs sticking out into the aisle.

He approached the stage each night after the performance with a bouquet of flowers. The exchange between them was as entertaining as the ballet.

Some nights he would bow to her before handing her the bouquet and she would bow back to him. The audience cheered and clapped.

Some nights he would grab at her and try to get a kiss. She would snatch the flowers, back up and shake her index finger NO and the audience roared and clapped harder.

The interaction between them made the critic's newspaper reviews. The audience would wait and see what would happen after the performance as much as they enjoyed the show itself.

Francesca and Etienne were accepted in social circles and were invited to glamorous soirees. Sometimes they went to these parties most often the snuck off to have a private dinner.

Etienne was an attentive date. He showed her the sights of the city at night and took her to all of the finest restaurants. If they were on the dance floor she had to be the public Francesca and talk graciously to the attentive admirers. She preferred their private time together.

She was deeply in love with this man and wanted to spend eternity with him. Her life was perfection. She could dance all day and have him all night.

She had become such a public figure that their private moments had to be protected and structured. Many evenings she would invite him to her home for a meal. Since she did not cook she would have something prepared and made sure the cook was dismissed for the evening after the meal was served.

They made love well into the night and Etienne did not appreciate having to leave her before dawn. She needed her rest more than she needed him he thought and he would leave her pouting.

They had been dating a year and the public started enquiring about and encouraging a marriage between them. Francesca was in total agreement but Etienne claimed he was not ready, so she waited.

At the theatre he continued to give her flowers after the show and she played with him as she always did in front of the crowd. Other men began to do the same, trying to grab her and get a kiss. She played back but would never let them catch her.

Etienne was furious with her in her dressing room after the show. "Why do you let them grab you?" he demanded angrily.

"I do not let them do anything! You started this. They just want to play too. You know they mean nothing to me. I love you! Their attention is the price I have to pay to dance."

"You don't have to be so nice to them," his anger went on.

She tried to brush it off. She had told him the truth. She loved him. He just had to accept it. The evening was theirs but his anger got in the way of their joy.

Performances continued to full houses. Etienne started coming to the theatre visibly drunk. He would struggle to the stage with his flowers in hand and grab her forcefully for a kiss. If he succeeded in grabbing her she would kiss him back and exaggerate fanning herself.

The crowd always responded with roars of laughter. She would never permit any other man to touch her. In her dressing room she yelled at him. "How dare you come to the theatre like a commoner. They watch us like hawks!"

"Well Francesca, that is me. I am just a common man." He left her to get herself home from the theatre.

Etienne stopped going to every performance and the critics made comment in their articles, "trouble in paradise."

Francesca was hurt and confused at her inability to change what was happening between them. On the nights that he did come to the theatre Etienne was distracted and less attentive to her.

Francesca did her best to put on a good show. While her personal life was shattering all around her she was too upset to eat as she should. I will take better care of my health when things settle down.

Days later Etienne showed up to a performance obviously sober and Francesca sighed with relief. They could finally get their lives back together. Perhaps he was ready to settle down with her. She looked forward to hearing what he had to say.

She performed the best she had in days throwing more joy into every movement. At the end of the show he got up as he usually did and brought her the flowers to the stage. She looked into his handsome face and the look there was flat. There was no excitement to see her. What now? she thought with disappointment. She had an overwhelming feeling of dread which she brushed off. She loved him, everything would be all right.

She put on a happy face, received the rest of her flowers graciously, and waved to the crowd as she left the stage.

Back in her dressing room Etienne paced the floor. She entered the room and put her flowers down on a side table went to pour herself a glass of water and turned to him.

"Sit down Francesca," he commanded.

"I can't. Not yet. Just tell me Etienne, what is it?" she looked into his face for a hint as to what he had to say.

"I am getting married," he blurted out.

She was shocked, blindsided.

"My family and her family have known each other for many years. She needs me Francesca, and you do not. You have your dance and your audience who loves you. How can I compete with all of this?" He held up his arms and let them fall heavily. He turned and left. Left her alone in her shock. He left her for another woman. She could not believe all that had just happened. She loved him deeply and he left her to marry someone else. She sat in her dressing room staring into nothingness.

Sometime later someone knocked on her door. "We are closing the theatre Mademoiselle Duvallier. Do you need someone to get you home?"

"No. Thank you. I am fine." She got up still in her performance costume and makeup and somehow got herself home. She was so cold she went to bed but could not sleep.

He was getting married to someone else. The horrible conversation went over and over again in her mind. She could not change anything. She was alone. She was all alone.

Late the next morning there was a pounding on her front door. She had slept briefly. Sometime during the night she had changed into sleepwear but she could not remember when.

She opened her front door to find a stage hand staring at her. "Monsieur wants to know when you will be at the theatre?" he asked hesitantly.

"Give Monsieur my apologies. I am not well today. I will be there tomorrow," she replied. Closing the door she went back to bed. She could not eat, food made her violently ill and subsequently dizzy.

The theatre sent someone to get her every morning for a week and every morning she sent her apologies and closed the door.

The next week Mademoiselle Benoit appeared at her door. She invited her in and took her to a sitting room. She had stopped eating and looked affright. "Child, what is going on with you?" she was deeply concerned. "The theatre contacted me, you have missed all of your performances for over a week. This cannot continue." She gave Francesca a once over. The child was very thin. Thinner than normal and very pale. "Tell Mademoiselle," she pleaded gently.

"Oh Mademoiselle. He left me!" she sobbed. "We were to be married and he left me to marry someone else. I am consumed with grief. I just can't get myself together. Not yet."

"Francesca, when did this happen?"

"I don't know," she tried to think. "I don't know."

"Well you must come back with me to the school for a brief time to recuperate. Regain your health," she implored.

"No I am fine here. Just a day or two and I will be better. Thank you for coming. It means so much to me." She stood and ushered her beloved Mademoiselle out.

The Mademoiselle contacted the theatre several days in a row and received the same response. Francesca had not returned. Her roll had been given to her understudy until she returned.

Mademoiselle Benoit then contacted Giza. Giza had left her schooling to do a few performances but had retired to get married and was now expecting her first child. It took some doing to get her friend to Francesca's door. She was eager to see her best friend after so much time.

Giza was greeted at the door by a maid who ushered her into the front room. "I will tell Mademoiselle your are here. What is your name?" she asked dutifully.

"Tell her Giza is here to see her." Giza was excited to be seeing her friend, have a reunion and giggle about all they had found so humorous. She was also most eager to hear about Francesca's magnificent new career.

Francesca made her way to the front room very slowly dressed in an expensive sleep gown.

Giza was horrified at the sight of her friend. Francesca's hair was a mess. She was noticeably way too thin, her lips were dry and her skin color was off. Giza tried to make pleasant conversation but something was very wrong with Francesca. She tried to enquire but Francesca brushed her question aside. "I am fine. Feeling stronger every day. I will be back at the theatre in no time," she assured her friend. "I am sorry Giza, I have an appointment and I must ask you to leave. We will have to do this again soon." Giza could not believe what she was hearing but accepted Francesca's dismissal and left to return to the school.

"Mademoiselle," she urged. "Something must be done. She needs someone to help her!" Giza was stricken.

Mademoiselle sent one more urgent notice. This one to Monsieur Ettinger. If anyone could get her to respond it was him. It read:

"Monsieur. Please help. Our Mademoiselle Francesca is in dire need. Come quickly!" Mademoiselle Benoir.

Dimitri took action immediately. His star pupil. What could she need from him that was so urgent? He went to the school to get her address and then to find her. No warning as to what the matter was he banged on her door. He was greeted by a maid. She permitted him in. He was impressed how she had made something of herself. Her modest home was lovely but felt empty. He was ushered into her bedroom and looked all around for her.

"Where is she? Mademoiselle Francesca?" he demanded.

The maid pointed to the bed where a very frail figure laid under the covers.

He took a deep breath. Why did they not warn him? She was barely breathing. "Francesca?" he called to her.

But she did not hear him. She heard Zeke call to her, "ready Cesca?" She let out her last breath and she was gone.

Dimitri cried out in anguish. He sat for the longest time unable to fathom what had happened to her.

He called to the maid sadly. "Get the undertaker." He knew she had no family. He had to take care of this himself.

His contact with the school was minimal, but, they finally agreed to accept her remains.

Dimitri contacted his friends at the theatre where she had been performing to deliver the sad news and then to the man at the newspaper,

"On this day our beloved star, Francesca Duvallier, met her maker.
She will be deeply missed by all those who enjoyed her dance."

Francesca Duvallier
1775 - 1795

EPILOGUE

*A*s you may imagine I was completely shocked at Francesca's inability to overcome the emotions of this break up. Another devastation in the continual feeling of being left by all of the men she loved. Poetically it would be called Dying of a Broken Heart, but truthfully, Francesca just gave up and literally starved herself to death.

Spiritual guidance wanted to help me save face by finding a medical reason for her demise, but, none was found. She had no one to pick her up and dust her off regarding relationships with men. Today we would gather our best friends, eat comfort food and talk badly about the man who did us wrong. Francesca's beloved Mademoiselle Benoit, with all of her loving motherly attributes, was a spinster and did not have such knowledge. Her best friend Giza married her first love and did not have this kind of knowledge either.

Francesca did not know or understand that God had a much better love match planned for her further down her path. She was supposed to have experienced expansion in her career with worldwide fame. Many of us give up prior to receiving our intended share. Faith was never a part of Francesca's upbringing. In fact the opposite was instilled in her by her mother's negligent and cruel ways. Too much negativity piled on too ferociously over a continually early time period is what did her in. Most people plan their lives by separating the difficult relationships with joyous ones. Francesca wanted to get it over with early so she could enjoy the rest of her life with her perfect love. Unfortunately, this proved to be too much for her. It sounded very easy to get it all over with first, but, in retrospect the burden was too heavy.

Burying the Lead

Mary Louise Elmers' story

PROLOGUE

*S*he read her literature like it was food for the hungry. Devouring every written word. Savoring the story like it were her own. "Only if it could be true," she sighed.

Mary Louise Elmers picked up her latest novel and swooned as if the tall handsome stranger was really pursuing her. She loved it, loved him, loved, loved, loved to read!

By day light she was the spinster Elmers. Everyone knew her as a hard working girl. By night she was the ravaged heroine in her current novel.

Mary Louise glowed as the hero took her in his arms and made mad passionate love to her. Declaring, in the end, his eternal lust for her and only her. "Ah," she sighed as she put the book down before turning out the lights.

Darian, her downstairs neighbor, knew her pattern well. She came home early in the evening, never made a sound, and turned out her lights before middle of the night.

"What could she be doing up there?" He asked himself as her lights went out on cue. He took a piece of paper and a pen and began to write. Imagining his heroin in the most unusual circumstances. Creating a fictional world of abstract thoughts and ideas all to be laced together at the end. It was his signature style. It made him moderately famous and kept the bills paid. That was for damned sure!

Darian wrote and wrote into the wee hours. When the dawn first began to break he put his pen down, stretched his tired hands and walked around his flat. Not seeing anything in particular he stretched his legs, rotated his head and shoulders, swung his arms in an exaggerated fashion and went to look out of his widow to see what the new day had brought. He did not see the piles of dirty dishes laying all over the tables, the mounds of dirty clothes scattered across the floor, or the quantity of crumpled papers over flowing the meager trash bin.

He looked out of his window and saw the spinster Elmers bundled up and walking briskly down the street to her job he supposed. "What does she do?" he asked himself. A librarian he imagined or maybe a caretaker of the elderly. "Boring as hell," he said out loud to himself as he blew out the candles and headed for bed.

O N E

*M*ary Louise went to work early. It was Tuesday and on Tuesdays she walked the Pomeranian dogs her employer owned (and did not take care of properly.) "Crying shame!" she said to herself as she put the leashes on Mitzi and Fritz.

She walked down Main Street and passed by her favorite book seller to see what new edition might decorate the window. She slowed the dogs down so she could stroll past the display. "Hmmm, a new book by Mikail Decature. Interesting!" She may just have to check it out when she got off of work.

She doubled back across the street, made sure the dogs did their business, and then walked them back home. She knocked lightly on the door before entering. "Mr. Jamison, It's me, Mary Louise bringing the dogs home," she yelled as she bent to unleash them.

Mr. Jamison was in his office behind a big desk scratching his chin.

"Mary Louise have you ever read any of Mekell Deecatur's books? he asked her.

"Why yes. Why do you ask?" She enquired as she took her coat off.

"I am thinking of taking him on at the paper. You know to write a column or a short piece. What do you think?"

"I think he would be well received. He writes a compelling fiction. Do you want him to write fiction for the paper? I thought you wanted more feature items?" she asked as she went to hang her coat by the door.

"I haven't decided yet. Just tossing around a few ideas before I broach the subject. He lives around here you know? Met him at a bar on Second Street a while back and had a rousing discussion about football with him. He does have a command of the English language I must say."

And a devil make care attitude toward the fairer sex she thought to herself. Not quite right that all of his female characters were blond, buxom and leggy. I guess it's every man's fantasy.

She sighed as she thought of her own mousy brown locks, short legs, and not quite there chest. Nobody's fantasy woman.

"What would you like me to do first sir, edit, layout, advertising?" She rolled up her sleeves and approached his desk.

"Take these to review the content. I thought they had merit but need a woman's opinion. These here need spelling checked and editing." He handed her two piles of paper. "The rest we'll get to after lunch. I have an appointment and will be back later. I f anyone comes by just take a message for me."

Mr. Jamison got up, put his suit jacket on and proceeded to leave his office. A portly man of middle age. His thinning brown hair brushed off his face with his fingers. He was a tyrant in the business world. Using unnecessary force to get what he wanted with everyone except Mary Louise.

Mary Louise got right to work focusing diligently on the tasks at hand. He sure expected a lot of her. Being an assistant was more demanding than she had imagined it to be. At least she got to be involved in the process of publishing the newspaper even if she never got to write anything of her own. Maybe someday she would get up the nerve to show Mr. Jamison her stories. Most men did not think women could write about anything but home making. Maybe she would use a male pen name. Well, food for thought.

Darian woke with a start when he heard the front door of the building open and shut. Miss Elmers must be home. Maybe I should make her a spy, he thought of his latest novel's leading lady. By day she worked at the Embassy and at night she wove her way down streets of ill repute following Ambassadors to back rooms where they make shady deals. Using her female wiles to gather intelligence and save the world. Nah, used that one before. Sold well.

Maybe Miss Lonely Heart upstairs is a nurse at the Veteran's Hospital baring her chest for the dying soldiers. He felt his body getting hard and ready for action. "Down pal," he scolded himself. "No action around here tonight."

He scoured the kitchen for something to eat. Only dirty dishes everywhere. "Damn," he said to his only audience, himself. Darian roamed the flat for a clean shirt to throw on. Most of them had stains on the front. He found one, the least offensive, put it on and grabbed up a pile of the rest and headed out the front door. On his way to the bar for some food he would drop off his dirty clothes to be washed. He could hold out with the shirt and slacks he had on for a day or two while the others got cleaned. All right now he had a plan.

He found Mrs. Simmons, the laundry mistress, getting ready to close up shop for the night. Using his power of persuasion and guileless charm, he talked the giggly older woman into taking his clothing off of his hands. Promising her they would behave themselves while she did her magic on them. The flirting was merciless and Mrs. Simmons was powerless under his spell. He toasted his good fortune with a Guinness and a shepherd's pie at the pub. He ordered himself a second meal to take home for later and a slice of pie to celebrate his victory over Mrs. Simmons.

Mary Louise hunkered down in her night clothes and crawled under her covers to start her new book. Maybe Mikail Decature would surprise her and lust after a not so blond, not so voluptuous heroine this time. The story took off at a fast pace. Lots of leaps and bounds. The hero always a good looking man in his thirty's vaguely resembled Mikail himself on a good day. He was always a man of the world who would do anything for country, his beloved Mum, saving the maiden in distress on his way to fighting crime or saving the world from unnatural disasters.

It was just starting to get good when there was a banging of the front doors downstairs. Darian Miles must be home from his evening sojourn into the bottle. She shook her head. What a waste, she thought, he was almost good looking. She didn't know what he did all day, but cleaning his flat was not one of them. On the rare occasion they passed in the hallway she had a chance to peak into his space only to gag at the sight and horrendous smell that emanated from the open door. How anyone could live in such filth escaped her understanding. It only takes a few minutes a day to keep everything tidy. Apparently he never learned that.

She tried to stay focused on her book but the noises just kept on coming. Mary sighed and put her book down. She got out of bed, put on her robe and tip toed to the front of her flat. She opened the door a crack to see out into the hall. No one was there. She closed and locked her door and went back to bed.

Before she could take off her robe a loud knocking sounded on her front door. "What now?" she said out loud as she went to her door.

Opening it a crack she saw a very inebriated Mr. Miles at her door.

"Yes?" she enquired mildly.

"Mum. Someone has broken into my home," he stated loudly.

"Really? How could you tell?"

"What? Oh, they have stolen all of my clothes. All of them! They were in a pile and now they are gone. Did you see anyone carrying them away?" he asked seriously.

"Someone stole your clothes?" Who would want HIS clothes? she thought to herself.

"Yes I had them before I went to dinner and now they are gone!" He was swaying while he spoke smelling like he had gone swimming in ale.

"Did you see em?" he asked.

"See who?"

"The THEIF Mum!" he belched in her face.

Mary Louise turned her head away to get away from the horrid smell. "No sir. I saw no one. Maybe you should go downstairs and look some more for your clothes. Perhaps they will show up on their own." She looked at him in the face for the first time. He was rather good looking. Or he could be if he wasn't such a mess.

He stared back at her for the first time as well. "God you are ugly," he said in a surprised tone.

"Thank you sir. Now why don't you go downstairs and look for those clothes of yours. I bet they will turn up." She smiled as she closed the door in his face. She would have been hurt and humiliated if he hadn't been so blind stinking drunk. "He'll think better of it when he sleeps off his alcohol stupor," she assured herself as she took off her robe and crawled back into bed. Thanks to Darian Miles she couldn't concentrate on her book any longer so Mary Louise went right to sleep.

Darian woke with a raging hangover. He had slept in his clothes last night. "What the hell happened?" He thought he had kissed the woman upstairs. What's her name? Something about her clothes being

missing. Well he certainly would remember if her clothes were missing!
He scratched himself through his clothes as he walked around his flat.
His pile of clothes were gone. "Ah I am a fool. It is my clothes that are
missing." He shook his head as he remembered that he had taken them
to Mrs. Simmons for washing.

TWO

*I*t took a few days before Mary Louise could get back to her new story. Work had been too demanding. It drained her of all of her energy. She had fallen into bed each night in an exhausted heap.

She had just settled into her book when she heard a loud crash coming from downstairs. "What the hell!" she thought. "What is that drunken fool up to now?" She got up and went to the front door to peak out into the hall. She saw nothing and the noises had stopped so she quietly shut her door. Again she heard another loud noise. Something large fell like maybe a bookshelf and this noise was followed by a human moan.

That was it! She ran to get her work clothes back on, slipped on her shoes, and ran down the stairs to see if she could help. Help do what? She did not know, but, she needed to find out what that idiot had done now. Maybe the bookshelf had landed on his stupid head and knocked some sense into him. Drunken fool! "Not likely," she mumbled as she approached his door.

Knock - knock- knock "Mr. Miles?" she said loudly.

Knock - knock - knock "Mr. Miles are you all right?" The door was closed loosely and swung open as she knocked on it.

She gasped at the sight of the tall man laid sprawled across his floor. He had obviously bumped into the large coat rack he had by the front door. A beautiful piece of workmanship.

The large carved wood back has brass hooks coming out of it and a wooden rail about knee high to hold canes and umbrellas. It would have been a beautiful piece had it not been split and now laid on top of the downed Mr. Miles.

"Oh My God!" She screamed as she ran over to him and bent to remove the wood from the struck man. "Mr. Miles are you all right?"

She asked as she rolled the furniture off of him as best as she could.

Darian Miles had a good sized egg forming on his forehead and a matching bruise on the cheek below it. He appeared all right otherwise.

"Mr. Miles." She called his name but he did not answer. Instead he snored or snorted. She did not know what came out of him but she was disgusted none the less. He smelled of beer as he just lay there. "You fool," she said to no one listening. She stood up and looked around at the horrible mess. "How do you live like this?"

Mary Louise went to his bedroom and found a blanket crumpled on top of his bed. She held it as far away from her body as possible and dragged it to the front room to cover him. "You are too big for me to drag anywhere so you will just have to sleep it off here," she said to him. No response came her way.

Mary Louise was overcome. "It's a wonder you don't have rodents or vermin in here!" She rolled up her sleeves and began cleaning. It was automatic, if she saw a mess she had to clean it away.

She started in the kitchen on the pile of dirty dishes. Finding a box for trash she scrapped the stale food into it best she could. She found a basin to put the dishes in and then moved to his desk. She threw all of the wadded up papers into the box, straightened up the remaining pile and place his chair neatly in front of it. She went around the room throwing garbage in the box. She then took the box outside and around behind the building. Perhaps some kind soul would burn these with their own in the morning she thought. She pumped some water into a bucket and took it back inside to her flat. She set some water to boil in her kettle and took the rest with some of her own cleaning rags back to his flat. She poured some water over the dishes to soak while she waited for the water in her flat to boil. She wiped down tables and checked on Mr. Miles who had not moved.

Once the water boiled she took her kettle downstairs and completely cleaned his dishes. Drying them with her own rags she set the dishes in a pile on his table.

Darian Miles had snorted a couple of times but remained unmoved on his floor. Exhausted, Mary Louise took her rags outside to clean and hang on the line before she went back to her own flat. She closed his door gently. She put on her night gown, fell into bed, and went right to sleep.

Darian woke with a start. His own moaning startled him awake. "What the hell?" His head hurt worse than it normally did. His forehead and cheek on the right side of his face were on fire and pounded like nobody's business. He blinked his eyes. Where am I? He looked around and his head throbbed even worse. Without moving his head he looked around and saw the wall with his favorite painting on it. Ah, he was home. On the floor? Turning his head he saw his grandparents coat rack in pieces on the floor next to him.

"Damn!" he mumbled. He loved that coat rack. Reminded him of his Granddad. He looked down and saw a blanket covering his body. He was puzzled. He lifted the blanked to see that he was fully dressed. How did this get here? He started to get up and the pounding in his head continued. Closing his eyes in hopes that it would deaden the pain, but, it had no effect. Slowly standing up he rubbed the back of his head which had a good sized egg on it. He looked around slowly hoping the room would not spin. Instead he found a room he had not seen in a long time. Neat and clean. "What the hell!" Someone had broke in and CLEANED the place. He could not believe what he was seeing. His stomach started rumbling so he lunged to the basin in the kitchen. Trying not to get sick he noticed the basin was clean as well He was really in a bad way. Someone must be pretty desperate to break in to clean his place. He looked around and saw nothing missing except his trash. Ah, the little bugger wanted his story! Now it made sense. Someone hit him over the head to get to his next manuscript. Brilliant but stupid! He would get to the bottom of this and have the thief hung! Stealing his trash was one thing, stealing his livelihood was punishable by death!

Darian took his time making his way to his bedroom. Content to find it as he left it. A complete mess. He looked around in all of his hiding places and nothing of value was missing. He then stuck his hand into his pants pocket and found his money was still there.

He sat on his bed and put his sore head in his hands. Who would break in to steel his manuscript? Darian's head hurt so badly he laid back on his bed and fell asleep again to avoid the pain.

THREE

*M*ary Louise scurried out the front door on her way to work. She had overslept due to all the cleaning she had done for his highness, the slob, and was running late. Making her way past his door she noticed it was still closed. Hope he is all right in there she thought as she ran all the way to work.

She thought about him off and on all day hoping he didn't need medical attention. Maybe she would bring him some soup when she got home. Or, maybe she would just stop in and see if he was all right. If she asked did he need anything and he said no that she would be off the hook to bring him something to eat. She liked the second idea better. Making her way home she walked more slowly than usual. Tired from the last evenings cleaning tirade. She made her way into the building to find Darian waiting for her at the foot of the stairs.

"Mr. Miles," she acknowledged.

"What is your name Mum?" he asked.

"Mary. Mary Louise Elmers," she said.

"Did you happen to see anything going on down here last night?" he asked her.

"What do you mean?"

"Did you see anyone come into my flat or run out?" he asked looking directly at her. The egg on his forehead more pronounced the bruise on his cheek more colorful than they had been last evening.

"No," she said as she started to climb the stairs.

He grabbed her arm and looked her in the eyes. "You heard nothing?" he asked more loudly.

She looked at her arm where he was holding it firmly. He let go immediately.

"Oh that," she said.

"Oh that. What do you mean?" he asked more intently.

Well, last night I heard a loud crash and heard you moan, so, I came downstairs to find you sprawled across the floor with your furniture on top of you. It's a shame. It was a nice piece of antiquity," she said as she started to climb the stairs again.

Again he grabbed her arm more firmly this time. "And you did what?" His anger coming to a slow boil.

"I moved the furniture off of you, retrieved a blanket from your room and left," she responded looking him square in the eyes. She tried to remove his hand from her arm. He tightened his grip.

"That's not all that you did is it Miss. Elmers?" He had his thief right in his hands.

"No I suppose not," she responded.

"Ah ha!, It was you! Do you always clean up at the scene of your crimes Miss. Elmers?"

"Crime? What crime? The only crime is the stench and filth you let accumulate in that hell hole you live in Mr. Miles!" She said as she force-fully removed his hand from her arm, turned and pointed her finger into his face. "Every day I walk pat your door and hold my breath because the fumes are so bad I could pass out. Didn't your mother teach you that cleanliness was next to Godliness? I did you a huge favor Mr. Miles and you stand here calling me a thief. For taking what? Your garbage? If you are so attached to that trash than why don't you go retrieve it. I left it in boxes out back by the incinerator bin! Good day to you sir!" she yelled as she ran up the stairs. What a fool I am. And to think I was going to offer him some soup. Thief indeed!

She ran into her flat and slammed the door behind herself.

Darian stood in disbelief. She had come in and cleaned his place, covered him with a blanket, and left his trash outside. What was wrong with her? He went outside and around back of the building to see three boxes of trash laying neatly by the incinerator. On top of one of the boxes were the crumpled pieces of paper he had discarded. He opened them one by one and found them all there. All of them! God, I am an idiot! She did a good deed for him and he called her a thief. Why would she do this. Why clean his flat? Oh, she must like him. Well isn't this a fine how do you do. He smiled to himself. She fancied him and he never noticed her. Well he noticed her, wondered about her, but, was never interested enough to venture into anything more.

Mary Louise was so angry all she could do was pace. She took off her shoes and threw them at the front door. "THIEF! What an idiot!" She pulled the pins out of her hair so hard that she pulled some hair with them. "Thief!" She dropped the pins in a pile onto her very clean side table.

"I helped my neighbor and this is the thanks I get!" She walked into the kitchen and walked back out. She was too angry to eat. All she wanted to do was walk. She opened cupboards and slammed them shut. She walked into her bedroom but did not feel like changing out of her work clothes. She didn't know what to do with herself. She finally landed in the chair in her front room and picked up her newest book. Mikail Decature would take her mind off of Darian Miles.

She sat and tried to read, but, she just couldn't concentrate on the words. They made no sense. She finally put the book down and went back into the kitchen. She would force herself to eat something and then go to bed. There was barely anything to eat in her kitchen. She had forgotten to stop at the butcher's shop on her way home. This neighbor of hers was making her crazy. Maybe she could move closer to work. No, she loved this flat. Maybe the demon downstairs would move away. Find someplace larger he could trash up. This thought made her smile. He could go find a nice pig stye to live in. He and all the pigs on the farm could snuggle together.. The picture in her mind was so ridiculous it made her giggle with the absurdity of it.

She decided to change out of her work clothes when she heard a knock on her door. What now? she asked herself as she got up to answer it.

There standing at her door was a man she had not seen before. A cleaned up Darian Miles. He had a bunch of flowers in his hand that looked like he had picked them out of the front yard. Wilting daisies and scraggly thistle all wilting in different directions.

Mary Louise looked at him in shock. She was not interested in going another round with him. Certainly his insults and miscalculations would hold him until his next absurd thought, unless this was it.

She looked at him with a questioning stare. He tried to look around her, but, she kept the door close to her. She was not letting him inside. "Mr. Miles," she stated.

"Uh, I came to apologize," he said still trying to look around her.

"So apologize," she responded sharply.

"Can't I come inside?" he said looking over her head.

"Say what you want out here."

"But it's too private for all of the neighbors to hear."

"What neighbors?"

"Oh, you know..."

"No. I don't know. What do you want Mr. Miles?" she demanded.

"Call me Darian," he said with a grin on his face.

"All right. What do you want Darian?"

"That's better," he said as he pushed his way into her flat. Looking around he whistled. "Wow you are a neat one aren't you?" He walked around her place looking at how clean and tidy everything was.

"And this is your business because?" she demanded. She followed him around as he inspected all of her little trinkets and collectibles.

"You helped yourself to my things. I guess I thought I could do the same to yours." He grinned as he sat down on a chair. "Look I came by to apologize for jumping to the wrong conclusion. And to thank you for helping me with my Granddad's furniture. I guess I was out of line calling you a thief."

"You guess?"

"All right I was out of line. But, you had no right coming in and cleaning my flat. Why did you do that anyway?"

"It helps me think. Calms me down until I can figure out what to do in unusual situations. It's just, Mr. Miles, I mean Darian, your place was so...unkempt that I just couldn't stand it. How do you live in such a mess? Doesn't the smell get to you?" she asked honestly.

He shrugged "I never think about it."

"Well you should. That much garbage is chaotic and it attracts vermin."

Now she was sounding like his Mum. He stood up. " I just wanted to thank you for your concern." He handed her the very wilted flowers and turned to leave.

She got up to escort him out when he turned back to her. "That was very kind of you." He bent over and kissed her on the cheek as he walked past her and out of the door. She held her face where he kissed her as she locked her door and got ready for bed. Thank God this day was over. It just couldn't get any stranger.

FOUR

She glared at the door while lying in bed. He was probably right. It was a strange thing to do. Cleaning someone else's flat without their request or permission. She would apologize to him when she saw him next.

Mary Louise got to work on time the next morning but was distracted all day. What would she say to apologize to him. She hated apologizing! She just wanted to make his flat smell tolerable. No one should live like that.

"Miss Elmers!"

She jumped. "Yes Mr. Jamison?"

"I said you should go home if you can't get any work done. Are you all right?"

"Yes sir. Just caught up in thought. If someone needed to apologize for their actions what would be the best way to do it?" she asked.

"Just be direct. I hate people who slither around what they are trying to say."

"I see," she acknowledged. Short but sweet it will be.

Darian was waiting for her on the front stoop when she got home. She was surprised to see him. He looked better than she had remembered. Sober and wearing clean clothes did wonders for his appearance.

She sat beside him and started her rehearsed apology. "I suppose I overstepped my rights as your neighbor by cleaning up your mess." There she had said it. Now they could be done.

He just nodded his head and looked at her waiting for the rest. Well there was no rest. She had to wing it if there was anything else she was going to say. Just say it Mr. Jamison had said. "So I am apologizing for my actions," she sighed. "But, you should have someone come clean for you Darian. It's not good to live in such filth!"

His eyes opened wide when she added that last little bit of advice. Uh oh, she must have overstated her apology. She got up to leave.

He grabbed her arm. "Have dinner with me." A statement not a request or a demand.

"Not in there." She pointed to his flat.

He laughed. "No not in there. I am hungry and there is a place I like to go to around the corner."

"Only on one condition," she responded.

"A condition for a meal? And what would that condition be?"

"No alcohol. You are a mess when you drink. You accuse me of all sorts of oddities when you drink."

"I do? What do I accuse you of doing?"

"Stealing mostly. You accused me of stealing your dirty clothes and then of course there is that trash business." She look at him only to see a smirk on his face. "Mr. Miles, Darian, you are not taking me seriously."

"Oh but I am girl, I am." He got up and offered her his hand to do the same.

She slipped her hand in his and was shocked to feel the warmth from his hand filled her from her finger tips all the way to her heart.

She was presented with a dilemma. Did she accept his offer and open herself up to who knows what emotional outburst he had in store for her next or just let it go and get back to her nice quiet life.

These situations never worked out well in the past. Usually the man making the offer wanted something from her. Not her company of course, but, something having to do with her position at the newspaper. It was the toss of a coin. She might as well. He was probably just trying to repay her for her kindness.

So she accepted and went with him to the pub for a meal. It just a meal and then she could back to her life.

It was a small but cheery place. Filled with locals who all knew each other. They all watched her intently as she followed Darian to a table in the back corner. He nodded to everyone as they made their way to a table. All of the patrons gave her the once over and whispered to themselves as she passed.

"Do I have something on me?" she asked as he helped her to her seat.

"Why do you ask?"

"Because everyone is staring and talking about me," she whispered back.

"Oh that. They're not used to seeing me bring anyone here," he said as he nodded to someone at the next table.

"Why do you come alone?" She inquired hoping it did not come off too personal.

He shrugged. "Don't have anyone to bring. I come here at unusual hours, not conducive to socializing."

The barmaid came over to the table and brushed herself up against Darian's shoulder. "What'll you have love?" she asked smiling intimately at Darian.

He looked to Mary for her choice.

"I'll have tea," she said.

"Make that two." Darian turned to the barmaid who was dumbfounded by Mary's request.

"Two teas coming up," she said as she walked away shaking her head.

Mary watched the other people staring at her. "You must come here often."

"I suppose I do."

"What do they expect me to do?"

"I don't know and I don't care," he was now annoyed.

"Then why did you bring me here? Everyone seems very busy talking about us."

"I eat here often, so, I suppose they feel attached to me. Just not used to me with a date."

"I see." He thinks I am his date.

The barmaid returned with their tea and they ordered two steak and kidney pies.

"What do you do in your flat all day?"

"Daytime I usually sleep."

"Then what do you do at night besides come here to drink yourself into oblivion?"

"I write a bit."

"Oh, you are a writer! How lovely, what do you write?" Now this was something she could get excited about.

"This and that," He offered very little.

"What does that mean?"

"A little fiction a little non-fiction depends on my mood."

"Have you ever submitted your work to the local newspaper?"

"No not yet. I was thinking about it though. Why, do you like to read?"

"Oh yes! I'm reading Mikail Decature's new book. Have you read it?"

"Yes as a matter of fact I have," he agreed.

"Good story, very fast moving, don't you think?"

"Yes. If you like the story you'll love the ending. Don't want to give it away but it has a nice twist," he said as he sipped his tea.

"Do you know him?"

"Know who?"

Their food arrived and they began eating.

"Mikail Decature. I hear he lives around here. I would love to know how he gets his ideas for his stories. Although, I must admit I am bored with his choice of female characters."

"How's that?'

"Well, they are all tall and blond and well, you know?"

"Know what?"

"Well endowed."

"Ah yes that," he smiled.

"So, do you know him?" she asked eagerly.

"I may have met him a time or two," he said shoving a large piece if steak in his mouth.

"Well, what did you think? Is he well spoken? Well educated? Is he handsome?" she blushed.

"I don't know about handsome, but, I guess you could say he was a man about town. Went to the top schools for his education." Darian motioned to the barmaid for more tea.

"And what is it you do Mary Louise Elmers that takes you out every day at the same ungodly hour?"

"I go to my job." She too left the rest out. Most men did not like to hear about women in the business world. They wanted women home sewing and raising children neither of which were in her realm of experience.

"And what do you do at this job?"

"Oh, a little of this and that," she replied.

"There seems to be a lot of that going around," he added sarcastically.

"Yes well, my employer needs assistance doing odd jobs. Some days I walk the dogs and others I read papers for him. You know, this and that." She was anxious to be done talking about herself and wanted to know more about Mikail Decature. "Do you see him here tonight?"

"Who?"

"Mikail Decature!"

Darian looked around the room. "No. I don't see him. But, if I do I will be sure to let you know." He smiled half heartily. Wish she would be more interested in me than old Mikail.

"You want to know a secret?" she whispered.

He nodded yes hoping to hear something erotic and totally out of the ordinary from this little frump.

"I've read all of his books and I think they're grand. I would love to write like that someday." There she said it. She voiced her highest hopes and dreams. To be a famous author and travel the world. To write about exotic places and escapades. Not correcting someone else's words and sending them to type.

"You want to be a writer then why don't you write? You just put your pen to paper and let it go."

"Oh you make it sound so easy. Some days I just don't know what to write about. I feel I need to see more of the world and I'm just stuck here," she sighed.

"You don't need to go anywhere special to write about it. Just use your imagination. Want me to look at some of your work and give you my opinion?" He saw for the first time her twinkling green eyes and shiny auburn hair. She really came to life when she talked about writing.

"Really? You would do that? If you have the time. I have several stories tucked away that I could show you!"

"Would you like anything else to eat. Some pie, more tea?" he asked politely ready to be done with the evening.

"Oh no, I couldn't take another bite."

He motioned to the barmaid and helped Mary Louise out of her chair. He spoke privately to the barmaid, handed her some money and waved to some other patrons as he escorted Mary Louise out of the bar.

They chatted lightly as they walked back to their flats. Mary Louise was very animated gesturing with her hands as they strolled back to their respective homes.

"Well this was lovely Darian. Thank you for inviting me. You're not half as bad a person as I thought you were. Much nicer without all that beer getting in the way."

He walked her to her door, said goodnight and went back downstairs. Instead of going inside he went back to the bar for the beer he had missed with dinner.

Mary Louise was on cloud nine. She had dinner with "The Cretin" who actually knew Mikail Decature personally. Maybe Darian would introduce her to Mikail Decature sometime! That would be a dream come true too. And, oh yes, he did show some interest in seeing some of her stories.

FIVE

*D*arian sat at the bar alone sipping his beer. Why do all the women want to meet Mikail Decature? Even the homely ones are enchanted by him. If they only knew the truth. He scratched his stubbly chin. That Mary Louise was all alive when she thought she might meet the great author.

"Ah, there you are. I thought I might meet you here." A large older man came up to the bar. "We talked about you writing a column for our local paper."

"Yes, Mr. Jamison is it?" Darian acknowledged.

The two men shook hands.

"Have you put any more thought to my offer son?" Jamison waved to the bartender and ordered himself a beer.

"I've been a bit busy with my next novel, to tell you the truth, I haven't given it much thought," Darian replied.

"I had a feeling when I didn't hear from you that that was the case. Mrs. Jamison and I are hosting a party for our local authors at our home a week this coming Saturday. Why don't you come and meet the others. My assistant will be there. I want you to meet her. You'll be working closely with her to get your pieces to publication. She's a real spitfire that girl. Knows what she's doing around a word or two."

"Sure I'll be there. What day is that?" Darian asked.

"Saturday December Eleventh, 5 p.m. We'll have cocktails and dinner following. Give you a chance to mingle before the serious business begins." Edward Jamison raised his eyebrows and his drink to Darian, told him the address and walked back to his group.

Mary Louise got to work early Tuesday morning. Got the dog's ready for their walk and was just about to head out the door when Mrs.

Jamison walked into the room. Edna Jamison was a strikingly beautiful woman. With crystal blue eyes and light brown hair. She was Edward Jamison's second wife after the first Mrs. Jamison passed away. She was much younger and very fashion conscious. She always dressed in the most beautiful and flattering clothes, unlike Mary Louise who wore a more dowdy style.

Edna was also a very sweet woman and would not hurt a soul on purpose which made her even more attractive.

"Mary Louise you are here so early!" she exclaimed.

"Yes Mrs. Jamison, I wanted to walk the dogs past the book store to see if there was anything else that had come in," she said as she finished getting the dogs ready.

"You know Mr. Jamison and I are hosting this work party next Saturday and it is very important that you attend."

"Yes I know."

"I don't mean to pry, but, do you own something festive to wear? Your work clothes just won't be appropriate."

"I had not thought about it yet," Mary Louise replied.

"Well dear, I hear we have some very illustrious guests coming and we all must put on our best appearance. I would consider it a great honor if you would allow me to assist you in selection of a gown. I may even have something you could borrow for the evening," she suggested.

"I don't know," Mary Louise hesitated.

"Why don't you take the dogs out and when you return we will look through my wardrobe for something for you to wear. If there is nothing that suits you we will have to get something made and that would take some time," Edna insisted as she opened the door for Mary and the dogs.

"All right," Mary said softly as she went out the door.

By the time she had returned Edna Jamison had turned the front room into a fashion house. Gowns laid across every piece of furniture.

"What's going on here?" Edward bellowed as he walked into the room.

"I am assisting Mary Louise in a proper gown for the party I hope you can do without her for some time while we decide on the best one for her to wear." She kissed her disgruntled husband on the cheek. He shook his head, grumbled something under his breath, and walked into his office and shut the door loudly.

Mary Louise was shocked as she looked at all the beautiful gowns Mrs. Jamison had brought to the front room. She unbuckled the dogs and took of her coat. "You went to so much trouble," Mary Louise said as she scanned the dresses.

"It's no trouble to look good. It is our duty. We represent Edward and the paper and must show our respect to the hard working staff that we value their efforts."

"Just by wearing fancy clothes?" Mary Louise was dumbfounded.

"Yes. Your clothes say a lot about you. They should convey a message that says I care about myself and honor you by dressing nicely for this occasion." Edna smiled sweetly.

"Oh I don't think mine say anything." Mary responded looking down at her plain dress.

"Yes they do," Edna insisted. "They say I care more about work than about my appearance."

"I guess you are right," Mary agreed.

"So, let us find you something that says I am confident in my job and care about this holiday celebration," Edna said smiling.

"All right if you put it that way. I would like to be taken more seriously in my work," Mary Louise agreed.

"And look beautiful for the holiday too," Edna added grinning.

Mary just sighed. No one ever cared how she looked and never found her beautiful. "That will be a big undertaking for a gown," Mary Louise added.

Edna laughed and put her arm around Mary Louise's shoulder, "You would be surprised what a well made gown can do."

The task took most of the morning. Mary Louise tried on gown after gown and Edna kept shaking her head no.

Mary Louise tried on a simple green satin gown. It hugged her chest and hung straight down to the floor. The green matched the color of her eyes.

"That's it!" Edna exclaimed. "It's perfect. Let down your hair Mary Louise so we can get the full effect."

Pin by pin Mary Louise let her dark auburn hair down. It was full and wavy and hung to her waist.

"Beautiful! You should wear it down more often. That bun you keep it in is way too tight for your lovely face."

Lovely face. Was she mad? No one had ever said she had a lovely face before.

"Edward come see!" Edna called to her husband. She went to his office and knocked on the door before opening it. "Come see your assistant's gown for the party!" She was more excited than Mary Louise.

Mary Louise felt very awkward as she stood waiting for her employer's opinion.

Edward came out of his office and looked at Mary Louise. Edna motioned for her to turn around so Mary Louise did as she was told.

Edward nodded. "Yes, my dear, you did it again. She looks lovely. Just right for a holiday party. Now can we get some work done?" Mr. Jamison went back into his office and closed the door.

"When you are done working today you come find me. There are a few other things to go with the dress that you must have. I don't want to make Edward angry. This is going to be fun!" Edna clapped her hands like a little girl. She started gathering up the discarded gowns and taking them away.

Mary Louise changed back into her regular work clothes, tired from all the unusual morning activity, and went into the office to work.

At the end of the day, when she was getting ready to leave, Edna appeared with a tray of food.

"I hope you don't mind, but, I put a few things together for you to try on. This snack should hold us over until you are fully adorned." Her smile was so contagious that Mary Louise did not have the heart to decline.

Mary Louise followed Edna upstairs to her dressing room. The dressing room alone was half the size of Mary Louise's flat.

Her armoires stood next to each other with a dressing table by itself in front of the window. A beautiful comb and brush set sat on top of the table. A wood box housing jewelry of all kinds was fully open next to the brush set.

Edna had Mary Louise put on the dress again and sit in the chair at the dressing table. She pulled out some earrings and studied them next to Mary Louise's face. Shaking her head yes or no depending on what she pulled out.

"What do you think of these?" She asked Mary Louise about some simple green drop earrings.

"Oh, they are lovely," Mary Louise sighed.

"Then you may have them. A holiday gift from me to you."

"I couldn't take these. They are much too valuable!" Mary Louise exclaimed.

"Nonsense. They are the first of many lovely things you should have. I have lots of earrings." Edna bent down to open a drawer. "Do you have scented water at home?" she asked.

Mary shook her head no.

"Which one do you like?"

Mary just looked at the jars.

"Open one and put a little on your wrist then smell it. See if you like it."

Mary tried each one and picked a scent she liked.

Edna brought the tray of food over to the dressing table for the two of them to share. "You are going to dazzle everyone with your beauty and charm," she assured Mary Louise. "The guests will arrive around dusk, so, why don't you come over at four and we will get you dressed. I want you looking extraordinary for this occasion!"

SIX

The week flew by in a whirlwind of chaos. Edward had Mary Louise prepare a presentation for the prospective authors. The house was in constant motion. Deliveries of food and decorations came at all hours. If Edna wasn't there to accept and direct their destination, Mary Louise stood in as hostess to sign and supervise their placement.

On the day of the party Mary Louise was a wreck. She paced the floor in her flat willing the hours to fly by. She left her flat and crept down the stairs hoping not to see Mr. Darian Miles. Since their dinner at the pub she had not seen or heard him. At least the building did not smell of decaying animals. Maybe her words sank into his thick skull.

She arrived at the Jamison home and was directed up to Edna's dressing room. Edna was seated at her table putting on the last pieces of jewelry. She was perfection in her gorgeous white gown embellished with red and green woven cords adorning her waist and shoulders. She looked like a Queen about to hold court. Mary gasped as she saw how lovely Edna looked. Oh to be that beautiful for just one day she thought.

"Oh good you are here." Edna turned to get up. "I have this chemise for you to wear. I wasn't sure if you have one to wear under your formal gowns."

Mary Louise felt like a princess getting ready for a ball. She slipped on the under gown and then the beautiful green satin dress. Edna helped Mary put on her new jewelry and started brushing Mary Louise's hair.

"Now you look like the business woman you are!" Edna said emphatically. "I hear we are to have a special guest tonight." Edna teased. "I hear Mikail Decature is coming."

Mary gulped "The famous author?" she squeaked.

Edna laughed and nodded. "The one and only."

There was a light knock on the dressing room door.

"Yes?" Edna called through the closed door.

"The guests are arriving Mum."

"Thank you," she answered back. "Well, duty calls. You come down when you are ready. I must do my wifely duty and greet my guests." Edna floated out of the room.

Mary stood in the dressing room for the longest time breathing deeply and telling herself over and over again "I look like the business woman I am." When she finally began believing it she took one last deep breath for strength and proceeded to go downstairs. She was going to meet Mikail Decature tonight! She would politely ask about his next novel and then she would enquire about how to get her own work published.

The room was noisy and full of handsomely dressed people. Most she knew as contributors to the paper. Some were advertisers. All of them had their spouses with them. She talked to everyone briefly welcoming them to the party and expressing how excited she was to finally meet the famous Mikail Decature.

There were maids roaming the room serving platters of finger food and a bar set up in the back corner with a bartender serving drinks.

As she made her way across the room she spotted Mr. Jamison handsomely dressed and Mrs. Jamison standing next to him smiling her most vibrant smile.

"Here she is." Mr. Jamison held out his hand to Mary Louise. "I want you to meet my assistant. She will be working very closely with you to get your articles to print. Mary Louise come meet our newest contributor Mykell Deecatur. Mykell this is my assistant Mary Louise Elmers."

As she stepped forward the tall man elegantly dressed standing before Mr. Jamison turned to meet her. He was beautiful and clean shaven and....her neighbor Darian Miles!

She blinked twice and gasped. "YOU!" was all she could get out.

He took her hand "Pleased to meet you," he said before he took a good look at her. "Well isn't this a fine how do you do," he said softly.

"YOU!" she said again loudly. Dumbfounded by the sight of him she tried to pull her hand out of his grasp.

He held on tighter and pulled her toward him and bent in to whisper in her ear. "I can explain."

"YOU! YOU! You lied to me!" was all she said as she yanked her hand free and backed away from him. She looked around the room and made her way quickly out the closest door to the balcony overlooking the garden.

Darian made his apology to the puzzled Mr. and Mrs. Jamison and went after her. Closing the door gently behind himself. "Mary!" he called to her back.

She was in shock. How could this be? How could that Neanderthal who lived downstairs be the Mikail Decature she admired. This is not happening. It was a cruel joke. Darian Miles had only seen Mikail Decature a couple of times. God, she was a fool. Spilling her guts about how much she admired Mikail's work right to his face. How could this be?

"Mary stop and listen to me!"

"You lied to me! You told me you barely knew Mikail Decature. Why? Why did you lie?"

He turned her around and grabbed both of her arms and bent down to look her in the eyes. "I tell everyone I barely know Mikail Decature to protect myself. I am a writer that's all. But, because I have a few published manuscripts everyone wants a piece of my fame. They try to steal my work. That's why I went so crazy the other night. I thought you were after my livelihood. Don't you understand?"

She had started crying she was so confused. "So, who are you?" she sniffled.

He took out his handkerchief and handed it to her. "Darian is my given name. I use Mikail as my pen name. I have other names I have written under but none of them have gone as public as Mikail."

Mary Louise had started shaking. Darian put his arm around her shoulder and walked her to the door. "Let's go inside. You've gotten a chill."

When they reentered the party Edna came to her rescue and whisked her away to a private room. "What just happened? That was the strangest introduction I have ever encountered."

"That man is my neighbor. I did not know he was Mikail Decature when we conversed before." She took a deep breath to gather herself.

"Do you think you can rejoin us or do you need a few minutes?" Edna asked.

"Give me a few minutes please," she said. Edna left her and Mary Louise sat down trying to gather herself and digest all that had been said. There was a tapping at the door. Mary Louise thought Edna had returned, but, when she offered "Come In," Darian, or was it Mikail, walked in with a glass of whiskey in hand.

"Drink this," he commanded.

"She took the glass and looked at it. "I don't drink alcohol," she admitted handing it back to him.

"Yes, well just this once you need a shot. It will warm you up."

She took the drink back and held it looking at the amber liquid. "My parents died drunk," she said still staring at the liquid. "They were too drunk to notice a moving carriage coming at them in the street. Trampled to death in their own stupor." She handed the glass back to him. Now he understood her aversion to beer.

"One shot won't get you drunk Mary. It will just warm your insides a bit." He took the glass and put it aside. Squatting down to be at her eye level he ran his hands up and down her arms to warm her. "You all right?" He looked into her face. "Do you think you can forgive me for not telling you the whole truth?" he asked softly.

Mary Louise nodded.

"Good," he paused and then said softly, "You look very nice tonight Mary girl."

"So do you," she responded.

"Let's go back to the party before the tongues start wagging," he said standing and offering her a hand to help her up.

She stood and took a deep breath and went to join the party.

SEVEN

They went their separate ways talking to the other writers in the room. Every so often she would remember that this man was Mikail Decature and she looked at him. If he saw her looking he would nod to her in response.

At dinner they were seated across from each other. In between bits of conversation with the people on either side of them they would glance at each other. He would smile or nod. She would just stare in disbelief that her neighbor Darian was Mikail Decature.

In between courses Edward took his knife and tapped it against his beverage glass. "Everyone. Edna and I are very happy to have you all join us on this occasion. Before we continue with this delightful meal I want you all to give Mary Louise your fullest attention."

Mary Louise stood up. "I want to take this opportunity to thank you all for coming. I have enjoyed working with each of you this past year. As Mr. Jamison has led you to believe we have a special guest with us tonight. He will be joining the family of contributors to our fine paper. Please accept warmly our newest staff writer, Mr. Darian Miles, also known to many as Mikail Decature."

Everyone started clapping. Darian stood up and bowed and then sat down again.

"A man of few words," Mary claimed and everyone laughed. "Darian would you like to tell us what kind of articles you will be submitting to the paper?" she asked.

"Certainly," he stood up again. "Since my specialty is fiction, I decided I would like to try my hand at gardening." Everyone laughed again.

"Seriously, I have not finalized my decision. I promise I won't step on any toes. Ed, uh, Mr. Jamison and I have not discussed exactly what he would like, but, I promise it will be an eye catching feature." He sat down. Everyone clapped softly and the meal continued.

He looked to Mary Louise who gave him a calm and reassuring smile. He relaxed and smiled back.

The evening ended on a nice note. Everyone went home happy. Mary stayed till the end making sure everyone got their hat and coat before she got herself ready to go. She checked with the wait staff to finalize any payment and made sure they were out of the house. She went from room to room checking to make sure they were empty before snuffing out the lights. She found Darian standing out on the balcony looking over the grounds.

"Everyone has gone. It is time to leave," she told him softly.

He turned to look at her. "I was waiting to escort you home. You are going home aren't you?"

"Yes I am going home."

She waited for him to enter the house before closing and locking the balcony door.

Edward was waiting for them in the entry. "You will see her home?"

"Yes sir it's on my way."

They shook hands. "Welcome aboard son. It's going to be a grand ride."

Darian helped Mary Louise put on her coat and escorted her out the front door. They walked quietly down the street. Mary Louise did not know what else to say. Tonight was quite a shocking event. Good thing tomorrow was Sunday. She had the whole day off to rest and recuperate.

Darian could not believe this was the same bombastic neighbor. Something had happened tonight. She looked different, womanly, softer, almost pretty. Not like the women he usually went for. Tonight she was comfortable to be with. He couldn't stop looking at her and she always seemed to be looking at him.

They walked up the stairs to their building. Darian opened the door for Mary Louise. As she crossed the threshold she turned to him. "If you are serious about writing for the newspaper we need your submission by Tuesday. Mr. Jamison will review it and return it to you by Wednesday for corrections or additions. If you can get it to me sooner that would be better. If I don't have it Tuesday you forfeit your spot in the paper for the week." She was exhausted, but, the directions were ones she had to give all of the authors. "Thank you for walking me home," she said and went into her flat and closed the door.

Darian stood there watching her act so businesslike. She was undeniably professional. Now all he had to do was find a topic to write about. That would be easy. He went back to his flat and found the newspaper lying on the floor where he had left it. He read it again cover to cover noticing what had been written and by whom. Remembering the people who had written the articles. He laid on his couch with his hands behind his head contemplating what kind of an article he should write. Nothing came to mind so he put the paper down and gave himself time to ponder his next step. Usually ideas flooded his brain. This one was proving to be a challenge.

Mary Louise spent Sunday cleaning her home and washing her clothes and bedding. She looked at her clothes with a new perspective. What did her clothes say about her? Not much. An old hag, a spinster, tired and worn out, all business and no fun. Perhaps Edna could give her some help on dressing more appropriately. Edna had said she should project how a successful business woman dresses. Most women did not want to be successful in business. Their husbands would not permit it even if they did. She had no choice so she did the best she could with what she had. Mr. Jamison had been very kind to let her work for him. She started out as an errand girl and slowly grew into performing an assistant's position.

EIGHT

$\mathcal{M}$onday came and went. A few authors had dropped off their articles and Mary Louise went to task editing before handing it to Mr. Jamison for his approval. No submission from Darian yet she noted to herself.

Tuesday she woke with joy in her heart. Filled with anticipation for the article he had promised. She spent the day wondering and imagining what he would write about.

By day's end Darian had not shown up and no delivery had been received of his work.

As she was preparing to leave Mr. Jamison called her into his office.

"Miles hasn't been in?" he questioned.

"No sir." she replied.

"You live near him, right?"

"Yes sir."

"Find out what happened. We expect his piece like everyone else."Mr. Jamisone was fuming.

"Yes sir."

"I want a response and his work as soon as you get it!" he demanded standing up. "He'll not make a fool of me," he said glaring at Mary Louise.

"I'll see what I can find out. Hopefully it was just a misunderstanding," she said as she went to get her coat and hat.

Mary was disappointed. How could he do this? This was his first time to prove what a great writer he was. She hurried home. No Darian waiting for her outside of the building nor waiting for her at the bottom of the stairs up to her flat.

She knocked on his door. No response. She knocked again on it much stronger and waited. A noticeably sleepy Darian answered the door.

"Yes," he said groggily.

"Your article is late. Do you have it ready?"

"No not yet."

"Mr. Jamison wants to see you first thing in the morning," she said as she backed up and went upstairs. She was disheartened. She knew what was in store for Darian once he met eye to eye with Mr. Jamison and it was not going to be pleasant.

Darian showed up late Wednesday morning. Mary was looking over the layout of the articles that had been approved with tentative space for those coming back from revision.

At least he looked presentable. She knocked on Mr. Jamison's office door and waited for his response before entering and closing the door behind herself.

"Mr. Miles is here," she announced.

Mr. Jamison looked at her. "Let him in," he glared at her.

"Mr. Jamison will see you now," she said backing into the office to let Darian inside. As he passed her she slipped out the door and closed it softly.

Darian looked back to see only a closed door. She sure moves quickly he thought.

"Have a seat." Jamison motioned to a chair before him.

Darian obliged.

"You've missed your first deadline." He got right to the point.

"Well, you see..." Darian started.

"NO" Jamison bellowed. "You see!" He was getting red in the face.

"We have a paper to run. Didn't Mary tell you your article had to be in by Tuesday at the latest?"

"Yes, but..."

"NO BUTS Mr. Miles. The paper doesn't operate on excuses. Do you have your article or not?"

"There's sort of a delay," he started mildly.

'NO DELAYS ARE ACCEPTIBLE! WE HAD AN AGREEMENT. DIDN'T WE?"

"Yes"

"And you are expected to fulfill your portion of the obligation. Were you not at my home at a party just this weekend when we announced your coming aboard?"

"Yes. But..."

"And did you not tell everyone you would be contributing your share?"

"I did. But..."

"WELL MAN WHERE'S YOUR PIECE?"

"It's not quite ready."

NOT QUITE READY! NOT QUITE READY! I CAN'T RUN A PAPER ON NOT QUITE READY. YOU'LL MAKE ME THE LAUGHING STOCK OF THIS TOWN AND THAT IS NOT GOING TO HAPPEN, DO YOU HEAR ME?"

Darian sat eyes wide open. No one had ever spoken to him this way. He could always squirm his way around his deadlines with a wink, a bottle of booze, some flowers for the editor's wife or gifts for the staff.

'YOU WILL HAVE SOMETHING READY TO BE IN PRINT BY THE END OF THE DAY TODAY OR I WILL RUIN YOU! DO YOU UNDERSTAND ME MR. MILES? NO ONE PLAYS THESE GAMES AT MY EXPENSE! NO ONE !!! Now Get Out! I want Mary to have that article before she leaves here today or you will NEVER be able to publish a book again. EVER!"

Darian walked out of Jamieson's office in a daze. White as a ghost he walked past Mary Louise without even seeing her.

They all looked like that when they left Mr. Jamison's office. Cruel and to the point. He took no excuses. They toed the line or they were gone. Mr. Jamison came out of his office. "If he's not back today we'll print a notice of his untimely departure from our staff. Find the last copy of our notice and have something ready in case he doesn't show."

He walked back into his office and slammed the door.

Darian went straight to the pub. He was shocked. What was he going to write? He still had no idea. He sat at the bar and ordered an ale.

"A little early even for you," the bartender acknowledged.

Darian just nodded. He was half way through his first pint when he noticed an old man sitting at the far end of the bar by himself.

"What's his story?" He motioned toward the old man with his glass.

"That's old Joe," the bartender said. "You should talk to him. He has quite a colorful past."

Darian grabbed his drink and moved to the stool next to Joe. "Mind if I sit here?"

Joe motioned his acknowledgment.

"I'm Darian." He stuck out his hand for Joe to shake. Joe waved if off.

"Joseph McGill. Joe to my friends," he said.

"Paddy says you have quite a story."

"Ay. I had quite a time." He nodded in agreement.

"Care to tell me a story or two over a full Irish?"

Old Joe nodded his head in agreement.

"Paddy. Two full Irish breakfast for me and my friend Joe here." Darian called out.

Paddy waved and Darian turned back to Joe.

Joe started, "You would probably want to know me life from the beginning." So Old Joe told a tale of running away from home at the age of fourteen to venture out to sea in order to find his fortune. The two men sat and ate their breakfasts as the tale of adventures in far off lands unfolded.

Darian was mesmerized. Not only was the story full of daring challenges and suspense he had no idea that this crumpled old man had such intrigue in his bones. When the story wound down Darian ventured to ask "So, Joe do you mind if I tell your tale to our local newspaper? These city folk are dying to know about lands far away. I myself make up stories of adventures, but, your story is more interesting because it's true."

Joe thought about it. "What's in it for me? If I let you tell my tale then everyone will know more about me than they should. I am left with the old salty recall and you get the glory of my travels."

"I could pay you a small amount. Kind of a finder's fee. I don't make much on the articles and they do have to be accepted by the paper first."

Joe nodded his agreement and stuck out his hand to shake.

Darian went home fully charged and filled with his purpose. He would tell the tales of local folk. Kind of a human interest feature. Did you know this about your neighbor?

He went to his flat and wrote for hours about Joe's exciting tale of adventure as a young boy. He was full of exuberance and could not wait to show Mary Louise his accomplishment. He finished shortly before it was time for her to get home. He paced the hall outside of his flat waiting for her to arrive.

Mary opened the door to the building and found an excited Darian waiting for her. She was exhausted from her day's work but the sight of him so animated and happy to see her set her heart all aflutter. No one was ever this happy to see her. It was enervating to feel so important.

"So you are here!" he said waving the papers in the air. "I have my story. I hope it's not too late?"

She took the papers in hand and sat down on the stairs and read what he wrote.

"This is quite appealing." She told him at last, "We don't have anything like this in our articles. It's not fiction, right?" she asked.

"Oh no. I met this old man today and this is his true life story. Fascinating isn't it? he asked proudly.

"Yes it is. I suggest you take this to Mr. Jamison right away. Tell him I saw it and gave it my approval," she said as she got up to go to her flat.

"Can't it wait until the morning?" He did not want to deal with Jamison again today.

"No. No. Don't wait. Mr. Jamison is very impatient. He'll want to put it to type right away. The sooner you give it to him the better."

Darian watched her climb the stairs then he turned to go back to Jamison's office.

Edward Jamison was dining with his wife when the butler came into the room. "There is a Mr. Miles here to see you sir."

"What the devil does he want?" Jamison demanded.

"He says he has his article ready to go. Claims Mary gave it her approval before he got here."

"All right. Show him in." He turned to Edna. "This better be good."

I'm sorry to disturb your meal Mum," he said giving a slight bow to Mrs. Jamison.

"Nonsense Mr. Miles. Would you care to join us?" Edna offered.

"He won't be staying," Edward announced before Darian could consider the offer. Not that he would want to spend any more time with Jamison than he had to.

Darian offered his article to Jamison. Edward pushed his plate away from himself and started reading. He nodded his head in agreement and smiled as he read. "This is good," he finally said. "I don't know if we have any room for it this week. Mary Louise will work on it in the morning. You may go Miles." He brushed him aside and went back to his meal.

Darian left in haste. He did not care that Jamison was a social pariah. His article was accepted and Mary Louise would work on it in the morning. He was happy. It was a good piece and his self esteem was restored.

He ran up the stairs to his building and continued up to Mary Louise's flat. He knocked on her door jubilantly. When she finally opened the door Darian could not contain himself. "He accepted it," he exclaimed as he moved into her flat. He grabbed her by the waist, hoisted her up and swung her around in a circle.

Mary laughed. His joy was contagious. "I told you it was good!" she said.

"The old man said you would work on it in the morning. Does that mean I'm in?"

"Apparently so," she agreed.

Darian and Mary Louise talked and talked into the wee hours of the morning the paper came out Friday morning with Darian's article inside. Because it was the last article to arrive it was printed on the last page.

Darian rushed to pick up a copy when he woke that afternoon. He went to the pub to show off his printed work. Thumbing through the paper he found an abbreviated version of his story. He was furious. How could she do this to him? He finished his ale and rushed home finding Mary Louise as she was approaching the building.

He opened the door for her, but, Mary Louise could tell he was not a happy man. Before she could speak he grabbed her by the arm and shook the paper at her.

"How could you do this to me? You butchered my article and buried it among advertisements!"

She yanked her arm free and turned to him.

"ME!" "I did nothing to you! You turned your article in late. You are lucky we had some space for it at all! Mr. Jamison wanted to drop you all together, but, I impressed upon him the need for a famous author's work in our newspaper. I also reminded him of the great show he put on welcoming you into the fold. You want a better place for your work? YOU get your article in on time! The earlier the better! We hold no place sacred for any author. It's the first to come with a publishable piece who gets the better spot in the paper!" She turned and ran upstairs to her flat opened and slammed the door shut.

Darian just stared at her. God she's a spitfire. The first to submit their work gets the best spot in the newspaper. He will remember that for the next time. He sat on the stairs and read the paper from cover to cover. Critiquing what the others had written. Rereading the butchered piece he had submitted. It actually was not too bad, he'd give that to her. He looked back up to her closed door. Now he got it. Jamison held the hammer but she wielded the axe!

NINE

*T*he following Tuesday an article was written and waiting for her outside her front door with it a bunch of flowers. The flowers had a note. "Forgive me for my stupidity," he signed it "D".

She took the article and left the flowers on the ground.

"Here we go," she thought. It was not the first time an author tried bribing her for a better spot in the paper.

She liked him, despite himself, and his feeble attempts to impress her were juvenile. Or, maybe she just liked what he wrote. She would have to explore the difference at a later time. Tuesday she always walked the dogs before starting on the stories. She couldn't wait to finish their walk and see what Darian had done this week.

Like the previous week it was an interview with a local character and his sojourns in the past. It was wordy and puffed up with saying like, "in this author's opinion." Mary Louise wrote notes for corrections "Too wordy," "Take out your impressions," "Return Wednesday," and left it at his front door. She walked upstairs, stepped over the dead bouquet of flowers and went inside her refuge.

Wednesday morning corrected papers were waiting for her and the flowers were gone.

There were three other corrected works that had been submitted before his and were printed in the next paper ahead of his piece.

Darian went to the book seller, picked up the paper expecting to see his article on the cover and was annoyed to find it on the third page. "Well, at least I'm moving up in the world," he said sarcastically.

The article was modified slightly but stayed true to his original intent.

The following weeks were replicas of his second work. He left his article on her doorstep, minus the flowers, and got his revision requests that evening. He made his changes and returned the article to her doorstep the next day. Darian found his article sometimes printed on page two, but, usually he found it on page three or four.

By week seven he had run the gamut of characters at the pub and was desperate to find something else to write about. Without an article to submit he tried writing a story about a character in one of his novels.

Mary Louise got the article Tuesday morning and read it. She could not believe what she was reading. She wrote in big letters on his front sheet "NO! Mr. Miles I have read ALL of your books. NO PLAGIARISM WILL BE TOLERATED! NOT EVEN IF YOU WROTE IT TO BEGIN WITH!" She signed it "Mary."

Hmmm. She had all of his books. He liked that about her. Liked that she was so sure of herself. Now he liked her for her choice in literature.

He turned in a different article of a young man's search for self expression. It was charming and had such heart. "He should have submitted this to begin with," she thought to herself. She felt like she was looking into his soul. She already liked him. Well, she like the serious Darian not the drunken, sloppy, self serving Darian.

Darian was waiting for her when she got home. Looking like he had just rolled out of bed. "Hand it over," he said motioning for her to give him his paper back. "No corrections," she said smiling at him. " Mr. Jamison took it as it was written."

Darian stood dumbfounded.

"You should have given it to me before. I think it's the best piece you've written," she said softly.

"I just threw it together," he admitted.

"Well, it came across as an honest account of his life. Or, is it your life?"

He nodded in agreement.

"Very touching Darian. It was a very moving piece," she said honestly.

"Have dinner with me," he said finally.

"Not tonight. Tuesdays are always grueling another time," she said.

"I'll hold you to that," he said.

"You do that," she answered and made her way up the stairs.

The next few days were intense as usual as the newspaper's deadline rapidly approached. She did not see or hear from Darian. She thought of him often and wondered what he was doing, but, always came to the same conclusion. He did not really care about her. It was just her connection to the publication that made him attentive to her.

The paper was completed Thursday and off to print late in the day for delivery early Friday morning.

Late Thursday as she was getting ready to leave the office Darian showed up. Surprised to see him. "You have an appointment with Mr. Jamison?" she asked.

"No, I came to walk you home," he responded. "I invited you to dinner and I was hoping tonight would be agreeable."

"Tonight would be lovely," she responded as they exited the office together.

"I have ordered a basket of goods from the bakery on 5th Street. I thought we might take it to the water side and watch the boats or birds or something."

"Oh how nice." The thoughtful plans really perked up her spirits.

They walked chatting lightly about the weather. He held the door open to the bakery for her. The smell was delightful and mouth watering. Breads and pies lined the counters. Darien spoke to the clerk and was handed a basket laden with edibles. They walked out of the bakery and strolled to the water side. Darian teased her with guessing what could be inside. It was a nice relief from the tense and focused day she had.

They found a spot to sit on the ground. Darian put the basked down, opened its covering, and pulled out a napkin wrapped around a small pie.

"Oh that looks good," Mary Louise said with eyes wide with anticipation.

"What do you suppose it is?"

"Let's try it and find out," Mary encouraged.

Darian held it out at mouth level for her to take a bite. When she got close and ready to taste it he snatched it away and took a big bite of it himself.

"Oh, you are right. It is good!" he said.

Mary Louise gasped and pulled on his arm until the pie was close to her mouth.

Darian grabbed it with his other hand. "Oh, did you want some?" He asked as he turned his head away and took another bite.

"Darian Miles!" She exclaimed as she struggled against his outstretched arm to get some of the rapidly disappearing meat pie.

She pulled on his arm trying to bring the pie closer to her own mouth but managed to pull Darian almost on top of her instead.

Darian smiled as he teasingly brought the pie closer to her. Knowing he was going to pop that last bite into his own mouth, Mary Louise reached for his other arm and pulled.

Somehow Darian had managed to hold his arm and the pie up just out of Mary Louise's reach and landed a kiss on Mary's seeking mouth instead. Mary gasped. She was in shock. Everything she had secretly wanted was happening.

Darian backed up to look at her and decided to go in for a second taste. With one hand on her shoulder and the other holding the pie close to her face he pulled her in for another kiss.

Mary was in heaven. The kiss was warm and soft and the scent of the meat pie filled her nose. It was glorious. In a quick move Mary Louise turned her head and sucked the remaining morsel right out of Darian's fingers.

"Mmm good," she said as she chomped on the pie.

Darian looked shocked and Mary started laughing. She laughed so hard she started crying. It was great fun.

Darian looked indignant and hurt that she tricked him with the promise of a kiss when she was really after the pie.

"Awww," she said looking at his hurt expression. She grabbed his coat collar and dragged him closer for the kiss he had sought only to have him turn his head away and pretend to be upset. All of which made Mary Louise roar with laughter. Trying to calm herself Mary Louise took deep breaths between laughs.

Darian, in the meantime, took another meat pie out of the basket and started eating it not even pretending to offer her a bite.

"Oh, so that's how it's going to be! If you're not going to share than I am leaving!" she said indignantly as she stood up. "Some date this turned out to be," she said in an exaggerated huff. As she bent to reposition her skirt Darian got up and lunged at her causing Mary Louise to topple over backwards with Darian on top of her. She gasped again and he kissed her more deeply than before. Mary Louise moaned and moved her hands to hold his face close to her own.

The kissing got deeper. Darian trying to devour her lips, her face, while his hands moved up and down the outside of her dress setting her whole body on fire.

"You know this is not going to guarantee you front page for your articles," she said humorously.

Darian stopped moving and pushed away from Mary Louise to look at her. "Is that what you think is happening here?" he asked.

"Well it did cross my mind," she said as she straightened her clothes and sat up.

"God Mary. I wanted to kiss you for the longest time. It has nothing, NOTHING to do with that stupid paper. Is that what you think of me? That I would stoop to seducing you to get the prime spot on the front page!" He was outraged. He stood up and started pacing.

"So what were the flowers for? My influence with Mr. Jamison is not for sale Darian. Do you think you are the only one who has tried to use me to get to Mr. Jamison?" She stood and dusted off her dress.

He grabbed her by the shoulders. "Who else has kissed you?" he demanded. Mary Louise laughed heartily at the thought of all the other authors. Most were old men and a few were women. The thought of any of them trying to kiss her was so absurd. Most of them barely acknowledged her existence. She was an annoyance they had to deal with to get their words published.

"No one has kissed me but you Darian. The others have brought gifts and flowers hoping to further their ascension to the front page."

"So that's why you left my flowers on your door step?" he questioned.

"Yes. I won't be bought."

"Well that's good to know." He picked up the basket and started walking her home.

"So that's it? I don't get fed?" She looked at him in shock This was turning out to be another bad date. She shook her head in disbelief.

"You still want to have dinner with me even though you think I'm only after a front page posting?"

"I was hoping you wanted to spend time with me and not have ulterior motives for the invitation. I was hoping we were becoming better friends and not just work associates." I was hoping you wanted to kiss me passionately over and over again.

"Friendship was not what I had in mind," he mumbled.

"What?"

"I want to get to know you better, but not as friends and not as work associates." There he said it. Now she knew.

"All right," she said.

"All right," he said. He put his arm around her shoulder, pulled her close, and kissed her on the forehead.

Mary Louise was content. A man interested in her. They walked up to their apartment building and Darian put the basket down. He sat on the stairs and made room for Mary Louise to join him. He opened the basket and handed her a bun and took one for himself. They sat and ate in silence. This was lovely. She never had anyone bring a basket of food to her before.

"Are you working on another book?"

"Not at the moment." He answered as he dusted some flour off of his hands and reaching into the basket for a fruit tart. "I'm still working on an idea for the next one. I have to submit more details to the publisher and I don't have it formed just yet." He took a big bite.

"I have a suggestion," she said leading into her pet peeve with his work.

"What's that?" he inquired.

"You need to have your leading lady look different. All of your heroines look the same. They are all well built leggy blonds and we are not all made that way."

"Really, I hadn't noticed," he smirked.

"Well I have. It would be really great if the female lead was short and with brown hair."

"Oh really? And would she work at a newspaper and live upstairs from our hero too?" he asked smiling.

"She doesn't have to. She just needs not to be so perfect. Many of your readers are women, you know this right? It's hard to relate to a perfectly built crime solver. Just give her some flaws and some ugly hair that's all," she stated as she reached into the basket to see what else was inside.

Darian laughed out loud. "All right. The next female character will have other characteristics. The male readers won't like it, but, as long as the women do that's all that matters."

"Don't be condescending Darian. I am sure that some of the men like other characteristics. Look at all of the married women. They are not only blonds and the rest of us poor brunettes and red heads are not all wandering around alone in the world."

"Point taken. Any other ideas I should consider for my next book?"

"No. The rest is up to you. Your writing is brilliant." She blushed. Oops, she had said too much.

He looked at her, finished chewing, wiped off his hands and mouth and moved closer to her. He gave her a quick peck on the cheek.

"Thanks for the suggestion," he said. He waited for her to finish her fruit tart before he stood, picked up the basket and opened the door for her to enter the building. He placed the basket next to his front door and motioned for her to climb the stairs to her apartment.

"Mary?" he asked as they reached the landing. "What is it you do at night before you go to sleep?" Curiosity got the better of him.

She turned to him surprised at the intimate question he was asking.

"I read your books," she said as she opened her door, went in and closed it behind her.

"Good answer!" he said to himself as he made his way downstairs.

TEN

*T*heir romance progressed with no one else the wiser. Due to Mary Louise's consistent work ethic she went to her job at the same time everyday and forced herself to stay focused. On a few occasions Mr. Jamison came out of his office wanting to know what the noise was about. Mary blushed. She had been humming or singing to herself.

Darian left the building at his usual time, but, rather than heading straight to the pub, he would walk around and reentered his flat after dark.

The nosy neighbors still talked about the poor spinster not finding a husband or about that wild author who stays out at the pub all night.

It was only Mary Louise and Darian who knew how their romance was blossoming. Spending hours together in her flat after she got home from work. Darian was shooed out the door at her normal bed time. It was then that he ventured to the Pub to visit with friends and gather stories for his newspaper articles. Everyone there was happy to tell their tales and adventures in hopes of seeing it in print the next week.

If he was asked why he got to the pub so late in the evening he would claim it was the book he was working on that kept him so busy. His time with Mary Louise had become precious to them both.

Mary Louise loved to play what if with him. If he wasn't so enamored with her lust for life and for himself he probably would have been annoyed.

"What if your hero meets a pirate ship on his trip around the world? And what if your heroine stashes the gems in her undergarments and swims ashore clutching them?" She asked with excitement.

He kissed her on the brow. "What if, my love, you write a story of your own and leave my characters alone?" he winked at her.

"Funny you should mentions that!" she said her eyes glistening as she pulled open her armoire drawer and showed him stacks of hand written papers.

"Well you have been a busy girl." He bent over to pick up a stack and pulled out quite a hand full.

Mary Louise moaned and grabbed her stomach doubling over in pain.

"What is it Mary?" Darian asked putting down the stack of papers.

"I've been feeling funny all day," she said. "I thought it would pass." She groaned again and clutched her stomach.

Darian picked her up and carried her to her bed.

"I've been meaning to ask you about your monthlies," he said. "I've never noticing you having them."

"I never really have them," she confided. "Only once in a while."

"You don't suppose you are with child do you Mary?"

"I don't know what that feels like. I just figured I would never have children so I don't really think about it." She groaned again and clutched her stomach.

"We need someone to help you who knows about stomach or womanly things. Do we know a midwife or anyone who has had a baby?"

"Oh Darian. I don't think I'm with child. It's just a stomach ailment." She tried to reassure him and herself as well.

"Mrs. O'Leary, who lives two houses down, has children. Maybe she knows someone who can help."

Darian darted out of the room and ran out the door leaving it wide open. If she had felt better Mary Louise would have gotten up to close it. She tried to use the chamber pot but was met with a gush of blood instead.

"Oh God!" she moaned. She stayed there for the longest time. Finally she made her way back to bed when she started feeling woozy.

Darian came storming into the flat. "Mary!" he called loudly.

"Mrs. O'Leary is getting a midwife to come help you. Are you all right?" He stopped as he saw the chamber pot full of blood and his Mary lying on the bed with a towel between her legs drenched with more blood. He went stark white. Mary Louise was perspiring and shaking. "Are you cold? Do you need a blanket?"

"Yes please," she whispered.

He looked around her room. Unable to find more blankets he took the one at the foot of her bed and wrapped it around her. Feeling totally useless, Darian went to the front room to look out of the window hoping to see someone coming to the building. "Can I get you something? Make you some tea?"

"No. Just sit with me. Hold me. I'm so cold."

He sat on the bed and rearranged the blanket to cover her feet. He gently rubbed her legs as she continued to moan.

Darian heard a tapping at the front door and bolted to the front room. "She's back there. I covered her but I don't know what else to do for her." He was terrified.

"I'm Gloria, a midwife. Let me look at her and see what needs to be done. You stay out here." She motioned to the front room and closed the bedroom door behind herself.

Darian tried to stay calm as he paced the small room. She had to be all right. What would he do without her? He couldn't imagine his life without her. She grounded him, made him stay focused and added joy to his meager existence.

Gloria came out of Mary's room hours later. Her clothes were covered in blood.

Darian turned three shades whiter.

"She's fine." Gloria assured him. "I am sorry she lost the baby, but, these things happen."

He nodded. So there was a baby. Why didn't they know?

"She needs her rest. It may be a while before she feels up to running the house. Give her a least a month before she resumes her wifely duties." She patted him on the shoulder and left the flat.

Darian sat there in shock. They lost a baby. His Mary had been with child, his child and they lost it. He could have lost her too. Thank God she would be all right. He got up and softly went to her room. He had to see that she was fine. He had to see his Mary's face. She looked so serene lying on her bed. The midwife had cleaned up. A pile of bloody sheets and towels lay next to the full chamber pot.

He pulled a chair over to her bedside and sat next to her. Picking up her hand, he kissed it and placed her cold hand in both of his for warmth.

He needed her, wanted her laughter and her liveliness. Her feisty, no nonsense ways. God, he loved her! Why hadn't he noticed that before. He was too busy loving her to notice how deeply their lives had intertwined.

Mary Louise woke to see him sitting by her side. "Darian," she said softly.

He opened his eyes and smiled a smile of relief. "Don't ever leave me," he said desperately.

"How could I leave you when you are holding my hand so tightly," she kidded.

"Do you know what happened?" he asked.

"Tell me," she said closing her eyes.

"We lost a baby. Our baby Mary." He searched her face for recognition.

"I'm sorry Darian. I did not know. I didn't know I was pregnant."

"Mary I can't do this again," he said choking on his words.

"What can't you do?" she didn't understand.

"I can't lose you again. Stay with me Mary. Marry me. Be with me always. I love you. Say you'll be with me." He wiped his eyes.

"Oh Darian. I love you too, but, that was the worst proposal I have ever heard. If you truly want to marry me than you'll give me a proper proposal. If you are only asking because you think I am on my death bed, then, forget it. I am not dying Darian and you are not getting off that easily!"

Darian laughed and kissed her hand. There was his Mary back with a vengeance.

ELEVEN

*M*r. Jamison was quite the business man. Always talking to local business owners. Having meetings with the local authorities to get the latest political information. He even conversed with the post man to find out the latest piece of gossip that might be important or well received by the general public.

Mary often overheard him through closed doors since her work space was outside of his office. She could hear him yelling obscenities at whoever was caught in his office. Forcing his agenda on the writers or business owners. Even the authorities were not beyond his tyrannical ways. He never once yelled at Mary Louise the way he did the others. She assumed it was because she did the work the way he liked it.

In the morning Darian left a sleeping Mary and walked to the bakery and ordered a basket of her favorite breads and treats.

He then walked to see Edward Jamison. He was not at all looking forward to this conversation. He knocked on the door and was escorted into Jamison's office.

"What do you want?" Jamison asked in his usual tone.

"It's about Mary," Darian said.

"Who?"

"You know Mary. The young woman who works for you. Does all the work to get your newspaper together." Darian was getting angry.

"What about her?" He put down the papers he was reading.

"She's ill and won't be in to work for a while."

"Tell her to get herself together and get in here anyway," he commanded looking back at his papers.

Darian walked up to the desk and put his hand on the paper to get Jamison's full attention. "She's had an accident. Lost a lot of blood. She won't be in until she's recovered," he said coldly and firmly.

"How long man? The paper doesn't run by itself. If she's not back in a week I'll have to replace her."

"I'll let you know in a week. It would be a big mistake to replace her. She's the only reason I'm submitting any articles to you." Darian walked to the door. He grabbed the handle and turned back to Jamison. "Just so you know, when she's better I intend to make her my wife. You are the closest thing she has to a parent. I'm not asking your permission, you understand, I am informing you of my intent."

"Suit yourself," Jamison responded waving him away and Darian was happy to be getting out of there.

He walked back to the bakery fuming. "What a piece of human waste. How she can stand working for him is a testimonial to her fortitude," he said to himself.

He entered the warmth of the bakery. A smiling assistant greeted him. "Hello Mr. Miles your basket is ready. Your wife will be very pleased with the selection of tasty treats you have ordered."

"Thank you," he smiled. His wife. Yes he liked the sound of that!

She entered her room and looked around. Although it looked the same it felt totally different. He was there with her all of the time. Always there to love, to reassure, with a joke or a piece of trivia. They had a match made in heaven. Two minds, well versed in literature in sync with each other.

His bad habits tamed while hers relaxed. He no longer sought solace in drink and she put down her books. Together they sought happiness in each other's arms. Teasing and flirting became their aphrodisiac. They made love nightly and talked of their dreams in day light.

"You know what I would really like?" she asked him at the breakfast table.

"What, my love?" He enquired.

"I would love to start a school for writers."

He thought she was being fanciful so he indulged her with a gentle smile. "And what would you do at this school?"

"I would lecture on the importance of character development and on the structure of content in a story. I would have group discussions about putting a story together." She said chewing on a piece of bread.

"And what would I do at this school?"

"Whatever you like. You could just stand around and look handsome or you could put together your own recipe for success. Every author wants to be published. Talk about how you got your first book published."

"You are serious?"

"Yes of course. I have given it a great deal of thought. It doesn't have to be a large school. Just large enough that people could come and go as they want, taking the courses that would best suit their interests." She stopped to take a sip of tea.

"And where would you have this school?" His own interest now engaged.

"Here, of course. This is a grand town for inspiration. Plenty of tranquil places to sit and contemplate."

"I think we should do it. We could ask the other authors who submit article for the paper to come up with classes to lecture. I bet they would love a chance to voice their opinions on getting work published."

"You may be right. Why should I do all of the work? Where do we get students?" she asked thoughtfully.

"Perhaps you could run ads in other newspapers around the area."

"This is starting to sound fun!" She was getting her mental juices flowing.

"When you are finished fantasizing we could go for a walk and decide where you want your new school to reside." He stood up as if ready to go.

"Oh you jest. But, I might just call your bluff. I am ready to go when you are." She stood and took their plates to the wash basin.

Darian got his coat and helped her put her coat on. They strolled through town voicing their opinions yeah or nay on every building they passed.

Too large or too small they agreed until they came to a vacant house. It was shabby and in need of much repair. She looked at Darian with eyes glowing.

"You have to be kidding?" He said looking at the mess of a house and then back at her.

"It's the right size and offers us privacy since it stands alone," she was thinking out loud.

They walked around the outside and Darian pointed out all of the things that needed repair.

"Yes, my love, but isn't it beautiful?" she said.

"Obviously she was seeing something he did not. "If you say so," he responded half heartily.

"We could get everyone to help," she added.

"Who is everyone?" he asked. "If you mean the other authors, we don't even know if they can lift a hammer let alone make these kind of repairs." His practical skepticism did not rub off on her.

"You are probably right." She sighed looking longingly at the little house.

"Let's continue on our journey and see if we can find a house ready to move into?" He took her hand to move her along. She just kept looking at the shambles of a home once loved.

They passed several other building but nothing struck Mary Louise's fancy. Darian knew it was a losing battle to try to dissuade her from her heart's desire.

They went back to their regular work routines and did not discuss their new project again. Between writing his articles and working on his latest book, Darian found time to search out the owner of the broken down house and find out as much as he could about the reason for its condition and vacancy. Without telling Mary he bought the house from a family eager to unload it. It had been the home of an elderly Aunt, who had passed away some time before. No one wanted it until Mary came along and they were most eager to see it loved and restored.

When Mary returned home from work she was greeted by a beaming Darian. He scooped her up into his arms. "I have bought you a most wonderful wedding present, but, you must agree to marry me before I give it to you," he boasted.

"Hmmf," she said and walked away.

"Is that all you can say?" He was insulted.

"Is that your best proposal? You wish to bribe me into marrying you? Apparently you don't really know me." She walked over to the coat rack and began unbuttoning her coat and removing her hat.

"What would you have me ask Mary girl?"

"You are a famous and prolific writer. Certainly even you can come up with a few words that would entice me to agree to such a major event in our lives," she said as she went to prepare supper.

Darian was dumbfounded. Mary wanted something from him and he did not know what to say.

They ate in silence and Darian excused himself feigning he needed some inspiration for his latest article. He left her to clean up their dishes on her own and went to the pub.

Ordering an ale he walked up to his friends at the bar. "Gents I have a problem. I want Mary to agree to marry me but she won't budge. Says my proposal isn't proper. I'm over a barrel here. What do I do?"

The men all laughed and teased him. Each one giving him a ridiculous or obscene suggestion.

"Why don't you ask a happily married man instead of those jokesters?" Paddy advised.

"You Paddy?" Darian enquired cautiously.

"Yes, my man. Me and my Kate have been together some eighteen years and it's just like it was in the beginning and do you know why?"

Darian shook his head no.

"Because I give her what she wants," he said grinning.

"I offered Mary a grand present if she'll marry me," he told Paddy "but, she turned me down flat."

"Well you are a lucky man that she doesn't want trinkets, but, what she really wants are words. Do you have any of those?" he laughed.

"What words are you speaking of Paddy?"

"Oh you know sweet talk," he said coming closer. "Like, you're the only one for me. Seeing you makes my day brighter. I can't live another day without you. That sort of stuff. The more you lay it on them more they like it!" Paddy laughed and slapped Darian on the back as he went back to tending bar and conversing with his customers.

So Darian went home and put together his proposal. Only his twist was in the presentation and he knew it would work.

He put it all down on paper and pretended it was his article for the weekly post. He handed it to Mary on Monday morning as she left for work. "Here's my offer for the paper Mary, see that Jamison gets it after you read it."

She nodded, gave him a kiss and proceeded down the street.

When he knew she was out of sight, he put on his coat and hat and followed her stopping at the florist on the way. He purchased a bouquet of every flower in the shop and stopped at the bakery to purchase her favorite treats. If the words didn't work than maybe a scone would help. He hoped it wouldn't come to that.

Darian went to the door and knocked softly. The butler escorted him to the office. Darren held up his finger to his lips so the butler would not announce him.

He waited out in the hall and listened for Mary's response. Finally it came, a noticeable gasp and an "Oh my!"

Darian pushed open the door slowly and found Mary standing with his papers in her hands.

She turned to look at him and Darian walked to her side. "It would make me the happiest man alive if you would agree to be my wife."

Mary started crying and flung herself into his arms. "Yes. Yes I will marry you!"

Darian laid the flowers and scones down on her desk, took the papers out of her shaking hands, and kissed her hard and deep.

Jamison came out of his office. "What's going on out here?" he demanded.

"Darian has just asked me to marry him," she said glowing.

"Well took you long enough," Jamison said walking past them as they were still in each other's embrace.

They both laughed and Mary wiped the tears from her face and eyes.

"What else have you brought me?" She sniffled trying to compose herself.

"Your favorite flowers and pastries," he answered. "I was hoping they would help seal the deal." He said as he opened the paper for Mary to have a scone.

She took one as did Darian and they touched them together as if they were glasses making a toast.

"If you could cook like this I would have married you months ago," she said savoring her scone.

"If you could cook like this I would have asked you months ago myself," he kidded back.

Jamison came back into the room with Edna on his tail.

"I'm so happy for you both," she grinned "When's the happy day?"

Darian responded, "As soon as possible."

Edna and Mary looked at each other and laughed. "We'll see," Edna responded with eyes twinkling. She dragged Mary away talking a mile a minute.

"Apparently there's a lot to this," Darian bemoaned to Jamison.

"Son, you have no idea," Jamison said. "Just let them have what they want I always say."

Darian knew Jamison never let anyone have what they wanted. He was pretty sure Edna was no exception.

By nightfall all of the arrangements had been initiated. They would get married in a small ceremony and have the reception at the Jamison home. Only their fellow authors and a few people from the pub would be invited.

Jamison coerced the joyful couple into agreeing to an article for the paper announcing their happy union. It ended up being a full page with tidbits of information thrown in by the attending authors.

The wedding present from her intended husband of a "house in process of repair," was well received by the bride. She could not stop gushing over its beauty and the glorious repairs that had already been made.

Never was the Jamison home filled with so much joy as on the day that Mary Louise Elmers and Darian Miles became husband and wife.

Their honeymoon get away lasted only a few days as both Mary and Darian had too much work waiting for them upon their return.

They made the most of the few days away with a trip to the shore. They spent most of their time making love and discussing ideas for completion of the repairs on their building and starting the school.

Mary's driving force was the joy of being in love with her new husband. She positively glowed and had boundless energy. If she wasn't working at the newspaper she was giving instruction to construction workers or putting together a format for her upcoming classes. She tinkered with the wording for the advertisement for their first classes.

As you could imagine their home, which was Mary's apartment, over flowed with papers regarding their classes. Darien kept his apartment downstairs as an office and a place to store all of their stories. The school came together slowly and had Mary's nerves on edge. "What is taking them so long to finish?" she would ask Darian nightly.

When they were out together in town and, obviously so much in love, the town's people could not help themselves and would ask mercilessly about babies. Mary would shake her head no. There would be no more babies. She just knew it. She never got her monthlies as most women did. She would smile and shrug it off, but, deep down inside she would have liked a child. Just one would have been enough.

On a bright sunny day in midsummer Darian came to Mary's office at the newspaper to steal her away for a short time. "I need my wife," he told the butler as he escorted Mary to a surprise.

They walked to the school and there it was like a new penny, all shiny and finely finished.

Mary was overjoyed. She jumped around like a school girl glowing over every new item inside. "Oh look at our new doors!" she would exclaim, "and our new hinges!" It was a glorious day in a step toward their future.

Darian and Mary worked on the newspaper ad for new students. They had discussed with their fellow authors about who would teach what course. They were shocked when they did not get a response from their first advertisement.

"Maybe it takes more than one run," Mary suggested.

They agreed to advertise again the next week and to add more advertisements in other newspapers.

Slowly they got responses. As if they had a full student body, they proceeded to conduct their classes.

News that Darian would teach, "How to get a book published," was the most popular of all the courses. Men and women flocked the school for his class.

It was once the students got into the school and were able to take his popular class that the other courses filled up.

Working at the newspaper by day and teaching at the school at night was exhausting, but, her enthusiasm for her work carried Mary Louise through it all.

After many years of running the newspaper, Edward Jamison sold out to one of his competitors. He spent the first few years of his retirement hounding Mary Louise for things to do. He wasn't much of a handyman and his attitude scared the students.

Mary left the newspaper shortly after Mr. Jamison sold it when her position there was eliminated.

The school was functioning and vibrant and offered the serious and not so serious student a chance to try their hand at writing.

Some actually published books and most had articles published in newsprint. The less talented just enjoyed the prospect of something different to do with their time.

There was no name for the school. After the initial students were admitted enrollment was by word of mouth. People came from far and wide to meet Mikail Decature, so much so, that they had to limit access to him.

Our loving couple enjoyed their life together until Mary's untimely demise at the age of 36 when she contracted what was thought to be the deadly Consumption, but, in fact was a terrible influenza virus.

Many women threw themselves at Darian, but, he remained true to his Mary beyond the grave. He continued his novels until her death which silenced his inner ear. Heart sick Darian mourned his beloved wife until his death in 1696.

Mary Louise Elmers

1642 - 1678

married

Darian Milikowski   (shortened to Miles)

who wrote under the pen name Mikail Decature

EPILOGUE

*T*he purpose of this past life regression was quite different from the one for Francesca.

I was opened to this wonderful life in order to relive joyous times, to see myself in a successful light, to see myself as assured and directed toward goals, and know true love. I was loved for who I was and not how I looked.

The obstacle of losing a child did not stop me from achieving other goals. I faced my reality and did not lament over the inability to carry a child.

Michelle Decature was my pen name. No publications were made. I remained the woman behind the man throughout my life.

Abersnethe was a small hamlet north east of Dublin. It was obliterated in the blight of 1806 due to famine. The town was incorporated into greater Dublin when the area went through a period of growth in the late 1800's.

The Shepherd's Daughter

Winifred's story

PROLOGUE

*W*inifred sat like a rock when her Da told her, "your mother has died. She left for you her necklace." He handed it to her roughly. They were both distraught. How could she do this? Leave a child so young and a husband to grieve her.

Winifred took the necklace and held it tight. If she could just hold it she could have a piece of her mother with her. Feel her warm and loving embrace. Her Ma was love and security. Winifred sat rocking herself remembering her mother's comforting embrace.

"Stop that!" her Da scolded her. So she sat still. Not knowing what to do or where she could go. He was not kind to her like her mother was. She could tolerate him because her Ma was always there to protect her. She would stop him when he got too critical.

She remembered her Ma saying, "oh Peter. She doesn't understand your ways. You must be soft and gentle with little girls. She'll toughen up when she grows."

Her Ma stroked her head as she buried it in her shoulder for comfort.

"He won't hurt you child. He spends all day with the sheep making sure they don't wander off. He must be strict so they know who's boss. Do you understand me, Winifred? He does not know about little girls. You will see he is not so bad. We must be patient with him when he treats us sternly because he knows nothing else."

She pulled Winifred from her chest and wiped the tears from her eyes. "When you get a little older you will see he is not so bad. He is actually a nice man when he wants to be. That is the man that I love. And you will grow to love him too." She held the child's face gently in both of her hands. "So dry your eyes and let's go see what we can do to help make his life a little easier."

"What do you want me to do Da?" she asked softly.

Her father just stood there staring off into space with a pained look on his face. "What?" he asked minutes later.

"What do you want me to do?" she asked again louder.

"I don't know. I just don't know." He too was in shock of his wife's untimely passing. It was a terrible thing taking a mother from her child. He knew this from the farm and the sheep. If something happened to the mother ewe the little lambs did not do so well.

"I need to tend to the sheep. Do you want to help?" he asked her.

She nodded her head yes and took his hand as they walked outside of their meager home.

"You stay here and hold the gate open and I will direct the flock into the pen. Do you think you can do that lass?"

Again she shook her head in agreement and dropped his hand. She grabbed the fence and pulled it open all the way.

"That's good," he shouted as he directed the flock into their coral. He made a l sound in his throat as he moved them along. Winifred heard him and tried to mimic what he was vocalizing. She moved her left arm to usher the sheep into the pen as she held the gate open with her right hand.

"That's good. You learn fast," he said taking the gate from her and closing it tight. He latched it shut with a rope noose that he had made years ago. "Let's go find something to eat." Winifred walked back to their home following in his footsteps.

They went into the dark room and her father lit the candle on their small wood dining table.

"Do you know how to cook?" he asked her.

She shook her head no. She was only six years old. Her mother had not shown her how to cook yet.

"We will have to learn together," he said. Looking on the shelf next to the table, he lifted a cloth and found a chunk of cheese. On the next shelf down was another cloth covering a loaf of bread. He took them both to the table and went in search of his wife's carving knife. He found it next to the wash basin and brought it to the table. Slicing a piece of both bread and cheese he handed them to Winifred and said, "Eat."

They sat in silence. Winifred was so sad she could barely choke down the dry cheese and bread. It was something to fill her empty body and soon she felt full. She started to cough and her father got a dipper of water from the bucket on the floor and filled a cup. He handed it to her in silence and she drank it thirstily. She missed her Ma so much. The house felt empty and cold without her there.

"Go lay down girl and get some rest. Tomorrow is a big day," he commanded her. So Winifred got up and went to her small bed. Her Ma had made a straw filled mattress for her. She laid on the mattress but could not sleep. Grief surrounded her and she wept for the mother that was not there to comfort her.

Her father made a fire in the fireplace and listened as his only child wept for the woman he loved and lost. If he were a child he would have wept with her. Instead the man sat in his chair and put his head in his hands and tried to think of how he was going to take care of a child and a flock of sheep by himself.

The next morning Peter went and got a small bucket of milk and brought it to her to have with her breakfast which was more bread and cheese. "Drink this it's good for a growing body." She did as she was told and watched his every move as he prepared their meal. It was the only thing he said to her all morning.

"I have to tend to the sheep. When I get back we will go to the church. Get yourself ready to go," he said as he left her alone in the house.

Winifred did not understand what he wanted her to do, so, she went to her bedroom and sat on her bed. When he came back inside he found her sitting there.

"Are you going to church in your bed clothes?" he asked angrily and she burst into tears. "Aw now don't do that. I told you to get ready for church. Where are your church clothes?"

Sniffling she got up and pulled out the bottom drawer of her two drawer dresser. There neatly folded was the beautiful dress her mother had made for her to wear to church and a pair of pantaloons to wear underneath.

"Here let me do that," he said grabbing the clothes from her.

"I can do it," she sniffled as she took it back from him and turned her back to him.

"I'll be waiting for you by the door. Don't take too long we have to leave for the church right away." He abruptly walked out of her room.

Winifred dressed and made her way to the front door, stopped to put her shoes on and turned to him when she was ready.

Together father and daughter walked to the church in the center of town.

The church had a small group of people inside standing up by the alter. Winifred looked around desperately hoping to see her mother waiting for them there, but, only the neighbors had arrived.

Peter nodded to the Pastor as he held Winifred's hand and made their way up to the front.

"Our deepest condolences to you and your child Peter," the Pastor said.

Winifred clung to her Da since she could not find her Ma anywhere.

"We will have a short service here before we go to the grave site."

Peter ushered her to the pew up front and sat close to her. He rested his arm on the back of the pew and laid his hand on her shoulder.

Winifred looked up to him as saw the pained look on his face. She snuggled closer to him as he held her tightly. This was the first time he had ever done that and it was surprising to her that she felt a sense of security from him. He held her hand as they followed the Pastor to the grave yard. They stood to the left of the Pastor with a big hole in the ground before them. Off to the right of the Pastor stood a large rectangular wood box.

Standing beside her were their neighbors and friends from the church. She heard someone sniffling behind her and as she turned to see who it was her father yanked her back to face forward. The Pastor spoke kindly about her Mama and more women wept softly.

Two workmen from the church jumped into the hole and another two men lifted the box and handed it to them. The Pastor moved and stood before Peter and Winifred with his arms outstretched to shield them. He spoke more words of kindness to her Da while the workmen got out of the hole and moved away from the site.

Peter mumbled a response to the Pastor. Winifred did not know what they were discussing but she knew it could not be good with all of the town's ladies crying behind her.

"Where's Mama? I want my Mama," she cried. Her father scooped her up and burred his face in her shoulder as he too wept for the woman he would see no more.

The neighbors were kind and brought food for them to eat. Meat pies, cakes, breads and treats came on a regular basis for the first month. After that the offerings dwindled and Winifred and her father were left on their own to tend to their needs.

CHAPTER 1

1293

They had been outside with the sheep all day near the cliffs, her favorite spot. She had a rock she loved to sit on and watch the waves below. On her rock her mind would soar. She wanted to be a bird in flight. With her arms outstretched Winifred felt the cool ocean breeze all around her.

If I could fly I would fly to heaven. She felt her soul lift up as high as it could possibly go in the clouds. I would play with all of the angels. She laughed as she envisioned romping on the clouds with the cherubs and winged angels all around her. We would laugh and sing and dance all day.

Today I would be the blue angel and kiss all the sick children in the world and make them feel better. She closed her eyes and turned her face up to the sun. In her own little world she was alive with the joy of being a part of the angelic forces. It would be grand to be a helper for Jesus and Mary. With the sound of the surf hitting the rocks below Winifred felt like an important part of the universe.

"When you are done it is time to take the sheep back home," her father announced.

"Yes Da I am finished." She smiled and got up to help him with the animals. Poor little sheep. They grow and they eat. They grow and they eat and what happens? They get sheered and killed for mutton stew.

Winifred bent down and picked up a fledging lamb. She loved the little lambs. The baby bleated for its mother and the mother bleated back. Winifred rubbed the soft head of the lamb and the head of its mother. She put the lamb down and walked next to them as they headed home.

"Those mother sheep don't like it when you pick up their babies," her father scolded her as he closed the gate.

"I know but I can't help it. I just love to hold the babies so much."

"Someday you will have a baby of your own and you'll see what I mean. Mama's are very protective of their young."

"Really! You think I will have babies of my own? I can't wait. " She smiled and twirled around with her arms out stretched.

"Winifred your head is always in the clouds. Right now we need something for supper."

"Yes Da," she sighed as they trudged back to their home.

Her Da had sent her to the neighbor's house to learn how to cook. His cooking skills were non-existent and hers no better.

Mrs. Beardsley was all too kind in teaching Winifred how to cook. She showed her how to make a stew. Some days Winifred put in too much water and the stew was flavorless and soupy. Some days she did not put enough water in the pan and the meat and vegetables were burnt or scalded. Eventually she figured out how much water to put in and her stew came out perfect.

After church one day she went up to the ladies gathered in a circle. "May I ask you a question?" They all turned to look at her. "Mrs. Beardsley has taught me how to make stew, but, I would like to try something else. Can you teach me how to cook?"

All of the women were excited and started talking at the same time. "Wait. What?" She turned to her Ma's closest friend.

"Yes child. You come to my home after church and I will teach you something else."

"Thank you Miss Ingrid. I"ll tell my Da I am going to learn more cooking," she said as she turned to leave.

"Wait Winifred. Invite your father too. He will probably enjoy a different meal today too."

His eyes lit up. "That was very kind of her. Did you ask her or did she volunteer to teach you?"

"Both. I asked and she volunteered. Come on. I'm tired of the same old stew. I bet she knows how to cook something wonderful!"

So they walked to Miss. Ingrid's home. Inside the little cottage was like being in a flower garden.

The walls had pictures of flowers on them. Her wood furniture had pillows on them with more flowers embroidered on them. Even the tatted table cloths and doilies had flowers worked into the patterns. Winifred gasped in joy and her Da grunted under his breath.

"Da it's beautiful in here!" Winifred exclaimed.

"Why don't you sit here Peter while I show Winifred a few things about cooking." She patted the back of the largest chair in the room. He nodded and sat gingerly on the chair facing the fire. Embroidered on the seat and back were matching flowers. Peter sat trying not to touch them which was near impossible.

Ingrid showed Winifred how to take cooked meat and cheese and slice them thin, place them on thinly sliced bread and spread mustard seed mash with them. "See we pile them all together and spread the mash with it and there you have it. Sunday feast for after church!"

Smiling broadly she and Winifred were enjoying the look of her creation.

Peter helped bring three chairs to the little table and sat uncomfortably with the two women.

Ingrid glowed proudly as she watched Peter and Winifred pick up the dainty sandwiches and take a bite. Winifred smiled broadly and shook her head in appreciation.

Peter stood up and addressed the two women. "Thank you for the meal Mum. I forgot something important I have to do before I go home. Winifred you stay and finish your meal. I will see you at home later." He turned to a surprised Ingrid. "Thank you for your kindness." He left her cottage abruptly.

"I hope he's all right," Ingrid said staring at her closed door.

"Yes he's fine. He is always forgetting something he needs for the farm." Winifred did not know what was going on with her father. She was having a lovely time. She stayed and ate the dainty sandwiches and asked for other ideas of things to cook. Most of what Ingrid suggested were light meals. Not hearty enough food for her Da. She thanked Miss. Ingrid profusely for the lovely meal and went to see what was really going on with her father.

She found him sitting outside their home and sat down next to him. "Are you all right?" she asked.

"Yes I just couldn't take all those little things she called food. A man would starve eating little bitty piles of anything," he shrugged and shook his head.

Winifred laughed. "Maybe Mrs. Wolcott has some other ideas. I just can't eat the same stew again," she sighed.

Later that week, after the sheep were let out to pasture, Winifred excused herself and made her way to the Wolcott home. Mrs. Wolcott was out back hanging linens on the clothes line.

"Pardon me Mrs. Wolcott," she said hoping she did not startle the woman at her chores. Mrs. Wolcott jumped anyway as she turned to see who had called her.

"Oh Winifred it's you. What can I do for you dear?" she said as she clipped a bed sheet to the line.

"At church you said you could help teach me how to cook something besides stew. When might be a good time?"

"Tonight we are having stew, so, that won't be good. Why don't you come over after morning church service this Sunday and we will prepare a roast instead. My boys are big meat eaters, as I suspect you father is too. You can invite him in the evening after you have cooked all day. I am sure he will like it all the more if you prepare it for him." She winked at Winifred.

"I don't know about that, but, Sunday will be grand. Last Sunday we went to Miss. Ingrid's home and he did not like how we made his meal."

"I suspect not. Ingrid eats like a bird."

Winifred laughed. "It was pretty funny watching him pick up tiny piles of food. You should have seen him run out of her house. I have never seen him move so fast."

"You tell him He'll get a manly meal here. Mr. Wolcott and my boys will be here so it will be a meal for a hard working man."

"Thank you Mrs. Wolcott. We won't miss it."

Winifred could hardly wait for her cooking class. She ran to her rock and sat on it in joy. She talked to the birds as they flew over head.

"I get to learn something new!" she called happily. The birds circled over head cawing to each other in flight. "And," she whispered, "Gregor and Dooley will be there too!" Secretly she had a crush on Gregor. He was a handsome boy a few years older than herself. His beautiful dark hair and deep blue eyes were mesmerizing. Everything he did was amazing.

She would see him when she and her Da went to the store for supplies. She would catch a glimpse of him working on his ranch with his Da. She watched him tend to the horses and feed the other animals. "Isn't he amazing?" she sighed.

Sunday morning early she washed her hair and dried it next to the fire. She scurried around getting dressed. She shook out her Sunday dress looking it over for spots of dirt or a place that needed mending.

"What's going on?" her father asked as he watched her tend to her clothing.

"We are going to the Wolcott's after church and I want to look my best," she answered.

"Aren't you getting a cooking lesson?"

"Yes."

"And you want to look good for the food?"

"No Da. I want to look good so Mrs. Wolcott knows I am serious about my lesson." And, so Gregor will notice me.

"Mrs. Wolcott knows you are serious you told her so."

"Yes. And now I want to show her that I am serious." Winifred went looking for her mother's sewing kit   "Please Da, if we make something you don't like, please, please, please just stay until it's time to go! Don't run away like last time."

"I trust the Wolcotts don't have flowers all over everything in their house."

"I don't know, but, promise you won't leave. Please!" she begged.

"All right I promise."

"Thank you Da," she said kissing him on the cheek. "It's really important to me."

"Let's eat before we go to church. It will be a long day before we eat what you cook."

"You eat. I'm not hungry. I have some mending to do before I can go."

"Not hungry. Are you ill? My Winifred never misses a meal."

"I'm fine. I am just too busy to eat. You go get yourself something," she said.

They left for church a little later than usual. As she relaxed Winifred started to feel hungry. She brushed it off telling herself that she would eat something later. She wanted to get to church to show Mrs. Wolcott she was ready for her instruction and to see Gregor.

Even the way he prayed was amazing!

CHAPTER 2

*A*fter the service they met the Wolcott family outside on the church grounds.

"Winifred don't you look lovely today," Mrs. Wolcott exclaimed.

"Thank you Mum." Winifred said happy to know her efforts were appreciated. She looked at Gregor who was standing between his parents. He too was staring at her. She blushed as she caught his eye. He turned away abruptly which disappointed the enamored Winifred.

Mrs. Wolcott took Winifred by the arm. "Let's get our cooking class started. We have some hungry men to feed." Winifred's stomach growled. "I guess we have a hungry girl to feed as well," Mrs. Wolcott laughed. Winifred smiled and her face turned red. She looked around to see where Gregor was going. Emily Wolcott followed her gaze. Well, well, well she thought. Look what we have here. The two females started chatting and the walk to the Wolcott ranch went by quickly.

"Let's have something to eat before we start our class. Cooking can really stimulate the appetite." Emily scrambled up some eggs and added cheese when they were almost done cooking. Winifred had never done that before. Another something new to prepare for her Da.

"Get two plates down from the cupboard please Winifred."
Winifred handed her the plates and Emily dished up the egg dish. She cut two slices of bread and got out a container with preserves in it. "Sit and we will eat before we get started."
Winifred took a big bite. "Mmm this is so good."

"Do you make preserves?" Mrs. Wolcott asked.

"No," Winifred shook her head.

"Try it on the bread. It's just fruit and sweetener. But we love it."

Winifred watched her spread a big spoonful on some bread and take a bite. She followed Emily's lead and did the same. "Oh this is so good. Can you teach me how to make this too?"

"Of course, but, we must wait for the fruit to come to its season."

"My Da will really love this," she said.

"I'll give you some to take home. Save the container for me and I will refill it for you when you are finished."

"Oh Thank You!"

"We have a lot to learn, so, let's finish up."

Winifred ate her meal joyfully and helped Mrs. Wolcott clean the dishes. Emily gave wonderful instructions on how to prepare a roast and took Winifred into the garden to gather some herbs and vegetables.

"You can grow these too. Have your Da prepare a spot and I can help you get started. Didn't your Ma have a garden?"

"I don't remember. It's been a long time since she has been gone. Did you know her?"

"Oh yes. She was a lovely lass. She was a few years younger than me. I remember she had a lovely laugh. Just like your own."

"She did?" Winifred asked.

"Yes and she loved to tease the boys. She would think of a game and when the boys fell into her trap she would just laugh and laugh. Isn't that a lovely memory?" she sighed.

"Do you know why she died?"

"Oh child these things just happen. She got ill and could not get well." Emily rubbed Winifred's arm.

"I miss her so much." Winifred wiped a tear from her eye.

"We all do dear. We all do. Let's check on our roast and prepare the next course," she said changing the subject. She took Winifred into the garden and showed her which vegetables were ready to pick and which herbs they would need. They gathered what seemed like a huge amount to Winifred and washed them with well water. Inside Emily continued her instructions.

"You watch. You will be surprised at how much my Gregor and Dooley can consume. Their Da is not far behind them."

Winifred was happy to do any chore Emily gave her. She even set the table with her instruction.

"Doesn't that look grand? Pretty enough for the queen herself."

Winifred grinned. No one had ever given her such nice complements before.

As dinner time approached the potatoes were set next to the fire and lastly the vegetables were added to the pot. The smell of cooking food filled the house.

The boys burst into the house. "When's dinner we're starved?" Dooley called as he came in. He undid the tie at his neck and went to the fireplace. "Smells good!"

"Where have you been?" his mother asked him.

"We went to the Pastor's home to see about some work he wants done. His wife made us a small meal, but, not enough for this growing lad." He patted his stomach.

"Everything will be ready soon. Where's your Da and Mr. Flanagan?"

"They are out back talking."

"Go get everyone. Supper is about ready."

She hoisted the roast pan and put it on a towel on the dining table. She took a huge fork and knife and lifted the roast onto a platter and left it at the head of the table. She then took the pan back to the fireplace and added some water. She brought a large bowl to the fire to retrieve the vegetables.

The men and boys came into the house talking and laughing. The boys were pushing at each other.

"All right lads, break it up. Your Ma and her student have made us a lovely meal and don't need you two causing trouble." David Wolcott warned them.

"Here take these and go wash your hands. No dirty men permitted at my table." Emily handed them each a cloth.

The boys each grabbed a cloth and handed two to the men as they went out to the well.

She ladled the vegetables into a bowl and handed it to Winifred to take to the table. She did the same with the potatoes and brought them there herself.

All four returned drying their hands and left their rags by the door.

"Come take a place at the table and let's say grace. Winifred you sit by me here and Peter sit next to her. Gregor it's your turn for our prayer," Mrs. Wolcott instructed.

"For what we are about to receive," his voice cracked and Dooley shoved him. "May the lord make us truly grateful. Amen."

Everyone said, "Amen."

Mr. Wolcott stood to carve the meat. "Mum it looks like you out-did yourself this time," he said as he sliced the meat.

"I think it was my helper who made it that way," she responded.

Winifred blushed and Gregor looked at her, which made Winifred blush even more. "I didn't do anything but watch," she admitted.

"Now Winifred, don't be shy," David said.

Dooley grabbed his throat and pretended to choke. Gregor turned to him and punched him in the shoulder hard. Dooley held up his hands in surrender.

"All right boys knock it off," David said.

"Pass the potatoes Winifred," Emily said taking a few as she handed the bowl to Winifred.

Winifred tried to hold the heavy bowl with one hand, but, it was too heavy for her. The bowl started to wobble and Gregor jumped across the table and grabbed it before it slipped out of her hands.

"I'm so sorry," she said her eyes tearing up.

"No, No my fault. I should have known you don't lift heavy things at your ranch," Emily said apologizing.

Peter caught a few potatoes before they fell to the floor and put them on his plate. He grabbed the bowl from Gregor. "Good save son." He exclaimed grinning at Gregor.

Gregor let go of the bowl and sat down.

"Way to go toad!" Dooley added patting his brother on the shoulder.

"Toad?" Peter asked.

"Yeah Toad. You know the way his voice sounds when he talks."

Gregor gave him an elbow to the ribs.

"Hey! Just telling it like it is."

"Boys. If you can't behave at the table you may leave." David gave them a stern warning.

"Yes Sir," they both said in unison.

"Winifred hand me your plate and I'll give you a slice of meat. You want large or small?" David asked.

"Small please," she said meekly.

"Small it is. Peter, my friend, large?"

"Certainly," he responded eagerly.

"Love?"

"Small will be fine," Emily answered.

"Are you sure? Handling all this must have given you a hefty appetite." David teased his wife.

"No. Winifred and I had a bite to eat earlier. Small will be plenty."

"Small it is then," he said passing her plate. "You boys don't want any right?"

"What? Da!"

"OK small it is," he said loading their plates with large slices of meat. Everyone laughed and the meal became a jovial event.

Not only was it delicious, but, the banter between the Wolcott family was very entertaining. Watching Gregor wolf down his meal while no one observed her doing so was just amazing!

Winifred helped Mrs. Wolcott clear the dishes. Not much was left of the meal. The boys must have competed with each other to see who could eat the most. They both devoured as much as they could and then some.

After the table was cleared, the dishes washed and put away Peter thanked their hosts and turned to take Winifred home.

"Thank you Mrs. Wolcott. I really learned a lot today."

"You come back any time Winifred. It was a pleasure. We girls need to stick together and I can't think of a better way than to share my knowledge of cooking."

Winifred ran to Mrs. Wolcott and gave her a hug.

"Now that we are friends. Why don't you call me Emily."

"Thank you Emily." Winifred blushed as she went to join her father.

CHAPTER 3

O n her way home she could not stop talking. "Could you believe those boys. I've never seen anyone eat so much in my life," she exclaimed.

"Yes boys their age do have bottomless pits," her father explained.

"And the food was so good! Don't you think the food was good?"

"Yes it was very tasty."

"Why do boys hit each other so much?"

"That's how boys have fun," he replied.

"They like to hit each other?" she gasped.

"Yes. It's fun."

"I don't see how hitting is fun." She shook her head. "Mrs. Wolcott, I mean Emily, said she would teach me how to make preserves. Do you like preserves?"

"Yes."

"I loved them! We had them on bread. Have you ever had them on bread?"

"Yes. Your mother used to make preserves."

"She did? I don't remember that. I don't remember her very much Da. Is that bad?"

"Hush now Winifred."

"Why Da?"

"You haven't stopped talking since we left the Wolcott's home. Aren't you tired of talking yet?"

"No Da. I guess not. It's just that I had so much fun! Emily made me eggs with cheese on them. And we had bread with preserves and roast. Wasn't the roast wonderful?" She started humming. Her father did not answer her, but, it did not matter to her. She had a glorious time.

They walked into their quiet little home. She never noticed how dark and gloomy it was before.

"Good night Da." She sang as she went to her room.

The next morning she got up early and went to the kitchen to start breakfast. Her father had started a fire in the fireplace before he went out to feed their chickens and cow.

She was going to work today to make their home a brighter place to live. Everything needed scrubbing. No more dark closed windows they needed light inside.

She pushed a chair over to the wash basin and climbed onto it to get the curtains down. It took some time but she managed to get the curtains off of the hooks and threw them onto the floor. She then pushed her chair over to the front windows and proceeded to take them down as well.

"Looks better already," she told herself. She took all of them and put them into the wash basin, added some water and started scrubbing them. Her father walked into the kitchen as she was in the process of cleaning.

"What are you doing and where's breakfast?"

"Oh sorry Da. I forgot about breakfast." She cut some bread and put it on a plate and went back to scrubbing the curtains.

"Is that all?" he asked looking at the meager slice of bread on his plate.

"You want eggs too?" she asked.

"Of course I want eggs! Winifred what's with you this morning?"

"I decided it was too dark in here and I want to lighten it up," she said.

"Can't you do that after breakfast?"

"I suppose," she answered. She cracked some eggs into a bowl and started scrambling them with a fork.

"What are you doing?" he asked.

"Mrs. Wolcott, I mean Emily, showed me a new way to cook eggs. I thought you might like them," she said as she got the pan. She poured the eggs into the pan and took it to the fire. She went to the shelf and got the cheese down and sliced some thin pieces. Grabbing the pan with a rag she rolled it around so the loose egg moved to the sides, threw in the cheese and put the pan back near the fire. She found her Mama's favorite scraper and dished the eggs onto a plate for her confused father.

"Here Da see if you like these. I thought they were grand!" she said as she went back to her washing.

He mumbled something to himself as he sat down with his bread and eggs. A few minutes later he got up and went back outside without saying anything else to her. She looked at his plate and found it completely empty. Winifred smiled to herself as she went back to washing the curtains and took them outside to hang on the line to dry.

She found herself wanting to see Emily for more lessons. Or did she really want to see Gregor and use Emily as her excuse?

The following week she decided she would try her luck and strolled over to the Wolcott home and see when she could have another lesson. As luck would have it, Emily was inside preparing pies.

"Winifred what a surprise. Just in time to help me with some pies."

"Pies? You're making pies? Can I watch?"

"Yes. Come in and you can help. Go wash your hands first."

Winifred ran out to the well. She had forgotten all about Gregor until she ran into him as she was entering the house.

"What are you doing here?" he asked.

"Pies! I'm going to help make pies!"

"Well don't ruin anything," he scowled.

"I won't," she sang as she raced to see Emily.

"What kind of pies are you making?"

"Meat pies."

"Oh boy!" Winifred clapped her hands.

Emily laughed. No one was ever this excited about her making pies before. "I've already made the dough so now I have to roll it out."

Winifred watched with delight. Every step was new and fun.

"I'm going to make lots of pies when I'm grown," Winifred exclaimed.

"I am sure you will," Emily agreed. there was just enough dough left over for a mini pie. Emily formed it into a small shell and filled it with a spoonful of meat filling. Everything was set to bake. "Where is your Da? Is he talking to David?" she asked.

"No he's home with the sheep. I came to ask you when I can have another lesson and here you are making pies."

"Does he know you are here?"

"No," Winifred said softly.

"Winifred you just can't leave without letting him know where you are. What if he needs you? Won't he worry if he can't find you?"

"I don't know. I never left the house before. Usually I go with him."

"Then you better go home. I'll bring your little pie when it's done coking. We don't want him to worry about you."

"Oh all right." She walked home slowly. She didn't want to be alone in that dark house. She loved being with Emily and getting a chance to see Gregor. And she got to make pie!

She walked into her house and to find her Da screaming. "Where have you been? I've been calling and calling for you?"

"Sorry Da. I went to Emily's to see when I can have another lesson and she was making pie. So I watched and got to help." HIs face was red with anger. She was in trouble now.

He grabbed her and shook her. "Don't ever do that again! I was worried sick."

"Sorry Da. I'm so sorry. I didn't think you would mind. I didn't plan on staying there. I just wanted to know more. I'm sorry." Winifred started crying.

"No you are right to want to know more, but, you must tell me before you go. It's not good for a girl to be out by herself. What if something happened to you? I would never know until it was too late. Go to your room."

She ran crying to her room. She was hurt and she had hurt him. All she wanted was a little freedom. Was that so wrong? She wasn't a little girl anymore. She threw herself on her bed and sobbed. She wasn't a little girl anymore. Why didn't he know this? How could she learn anything if she was stuck in the house all the time.

Hours later her Da came to her room. "We have to talk," he said to her.

She sat up her eyes still red from crying.

"I've been thinking that you need to be with girls your own age and not stuck here on the farm. You seem to enjoy cooking with ladies and now it the time you should learn these things," he said.

"What?" she asked.

"I'm saying I think you need to be with women and learn female things," he said awkwardly.

"I can learn that from Emily. She will teach me."

"Emily is not your family. As wonderful as she is, she does not have time to teach you. She has a family of her own to raise."

"What are you saying? You want me to go? Go where?" Winifred could not believe what she was hearing.

"Your mother's sister said she would take you."

"Who is she? I don't even know her."

"Sure you do it's your Aunt Beatrice."

"Beatrice. I don't remember Aunt Beatrice."

"Sure you do. She lives in London."

"Aunt Beatrice lives in London? I have to go to London? I've never been to London!" This conversation was making her dizzy. She wanted to get sick.

"Just for a while. Until I know what else I can do for you."

"How long? How long do I have to live in London? No! No I don't want to go. I belong here with you. You're my Da!" She started sobbing again.

"Now Winifred be reasonable."

"Me be reasonable? You want me to go away! You're my Da and you are giving me away!"

"Just for a little while. So you can learn what girls are supposed to know. I can't teach you that Winifred. I don't know what you are supposed to know. How to cook and clean and dress. I don't know and I don't have time to learn and teach you. Don't you see? Aunt Beatrice knows all these things. She's smart and she's pretty and she wants you to come live with her for a while."

"She wants me to come stay with her?"

"For a while. So you can grow up right. Not stay the chore girl on my ranch."

"I don't want to go Da. I don't want to go!" she cried.

"I know child. But you must become a woman. Don't you see. It's the only way to go." He got up and left her alone in her room.

"The only way to go? Why was this the only way to go?"

CHAPTER 4

*H*er Aunt came to pick her up late the following day. She didn't even have a chance to say goodbye to Emily or see Gregor for the last time.

Beatrice was dressed in a fancy gown the likes of which Winifred had never seen before. The gown was colorful and shiny. Her Aunt was not a tall woman and had blond curly hair. She had some kind of paint on her face. She looked to be a fine lady. Did she want to be a fine lady too? No one cared if she did or did not want it.

Beatrice got out of the carriage and looked at Winifred. "Let me see you child." She made Winifred turn around. "So this is how he raised you. Well I can see I came just in time."

Winifred blushed. What was wrong with how she looked?

"Come child. Say goodbye to your father. We have a big journey ahead of us and a lot to do to get you ready."

Ready for what? Winifred did not care. She wanted her rock and Gregor. She wanted Emily to be her Ma. "He's out with the sheep," Winifred said.

"He leaves you alone on the day you are leaving? Serves him right not to say goodbye."

"Wait! Let me see if he's out by the barn before we go." Winifred went into the house and found her mother's necklace. She put it on as she went to the barn to find her Da. She found him sitting in the barn.

"Da," she said. "Aunt Beatrice is here to take me away. Don't you want to say goodbye?"

"I'm sorry there is no other way," he said as he got up. He hugged her and turned away.

She looked at that pitiful man. What was she clinging to? He didn't even say goodbye in a way that was satisfying. She turned and left him. She headed back to her Aunt and the waiting carriage.

"Is there anything you wish to take with you?" Aunt Beatrice asked her.

"No." Winifred put her hand on the necklace at her throat. "No there's nothing else for me here."

She was helped into a kind of a carriage she had never seen or been in before. They rode in silence. Winifred looked out of the window the whole time. She was being transported to a place that was far away from everything she knew.

"The first thing we shall do is get you some proper clothes," her Aunt said with disgust. "I can't believe he would let you dress like this."

"Yes Mum," she whispered.

"No no not Mum! You are not a servant. You will call me Auntie for that's who I am."

"Yes Mum, I mean Auntie."

"That's better."

Their journey took many hours. They traveled by boat and had a different carriage waiting for them when they landed on the mainland.

The carriage stopped in front of a building that sat close to the street. It had a white stone staircase leading up to the door. There were a few plants growing next to the staircase. Winifred followed her aunt into the house. The home was very large. Everything in the entry was in white and black. White and black flooring, white walls and black banisters leading up a flight of stairs.

"LOUISE!" Aunt Beatrice bellowed. Louise appeared in a servant's outfit.

"Yes Mum."

"Louise, contact my seamstress at once. Tell her I need her immediately. Tell her It is an emergency!"

Louise curtsied and left the room.

"Let us begin by taking you on a tour of your new home. This is the entry, of course. Over here is the parlor where we meet our guests." In the parlor there were two upholstered couches in a pink fabric at right angle to each other and a floor to ceiling dark wood bookshelf running the length of the back wall. The front wall had two floor to ceiling dark wood trimmed windows in it. Through the windows Winifred saw plants growing right up against the house.

"Over here is our dining room." The double doors opened up into a long room with an equally long table in it. There were many chairs on either side of the table, all of matching wood and design. They matched the two chairs at either end. There were two large candelabra on either end of the sideboard that was against the back wall. "Behind here is the kitchen for the servants," Beatrice instructed.

They walked out of the dining room and over to the staircase. They walked up the stairs to the bedrooms. Beatrice opened the first door they came to. "This is the office," she said as they walked into a small room with a single piece of furniture in it. Aunt Beatrice closed the door behind them as they walked out. They continued down the hall. "This will be your room as long as you stay here." Beatrice opened the door to a room that was light and bright. Winifred would have liked it if it were in her own home. This did not feel like her home. There was a soft bed in the center of the room not made of straw. A beautiful quilt lay across it. There was a dark wood carved head board. On the wall that the bed faced was a dressing table and on the wall at the back of the room stood an armoire.

"I hope you enjoy it here Winifred and that we become fast friends."

Winifred knew her aunt wanted her to gloat about what a lovely room it was, but, Winifred could not find the flowery words. "Thank you Auntie, I am sure we will." Winifred had no energy to put into her response. She was in shock. Where am I? Why am I here?

"I will leave you here to refresh. If you want me I will be in my room which is just down the hall. I will come for you when my seamstress arrives. Why don't you rest until then?"

"Yes Auntie," she said.

Her aunt left her and closed the door behind herself. Winifred went to the dressing table and ran her hand across the top. She went to the window and looked out onto manicured gardens. No room for animals here. Close to the house was a table with chairs around it. She walked to the armoire and opened its massive doors. It was empty. She closed the doors and walked to the bed and sat down. It was soft and she sank into it. What was this made of?

There was a knock at the door. Winifred got up and walked over to open it. Her Auntie was there with a very short thin woman. Her salt and pepper hair was pulled back into a tight bun.

"Winifred this my seamstress Madame Lautrec. She will be fitting you with your new wardrobe."

Madame Lautrec marched into the room She wore a tape measure around her neck and had an assistant following he with a note pad.

Auntie Beatrice beamed with pride. Winifred would learn that her aunt was never as happy as when she had a new project. Today Winifred was that project. She was measured and pushed. Commanded to stand tall, turn around, turn back, stand up straight. This went on for what seemed like hours.

"What is it you wish her to have?" Madam Lautrec asked Beatrice. Beatrice mentioned at least six different things Winifred had never heard of. Morning this and evening that.

"How soon can we have them delivered?" Aunt Beatrice asked.

"If I work round the clock it will take at least a month."

"A month! Oh No! She needs something at once. At least one day gown within the next couple of days," Beatrice demanded.

"A couple of days, how absurd! I cannot create genius in a couple of days!"

"Not genius Madame just a simple gown. All she has are the rags she is wearing." Beatrice pointed to Winifred.

"I see. I can try to get something ready by tomorrow evening at the earliest. Two days would be best," the Madame sniffed.

"Whatever you can do will be greatly appreciated Madame." Beatrice gave her most beautiful smile.

Madame Lautrec turned without further discussion and left with her assistant running behind her.

"We are moving along quite nicely. You will have something new to wear to begin your new life." She put her hand on Winifred's arm and squeezed. "Tonight you will meet my betrothed Antonio. A most handsome man. But, you must not tell him so or it will go to his head." Beatrice laughed. "So let's go down and have some refreshments. I am sure you are hungry after our ride." She left the room quickly expecting Winifred to follow her. "Come on," she called and Winifred ran after her aunt down the stairs. She followed her aunt through the hallway and out to the back garden. "It is such a lovely day I thought we would dine outside."

The round table sat on a stone floor surrounded by the walls of the house. The only "outside" was the missing wall that opened to the manicured grounds. Winifred had a glimpse of it from her bedroom window.

"Please sit down Winifred," her Aunt instructed. She walked to the corner and picked up a bell which she chimed and then seated herself.

Momentarily another young woman dressed in servants clothing came out with a silver tray in hand.

"You may place it on the table for us Sylvie. Thank you." Sylvie was dismissed with a wave of Auntie's hand.

Aunt Beatrice moved forward and began serving. She handed Winifred a plate with finger sandwiches. She poured a cup of tea for each of them and handed one to Winifred.

Winifred thanked her aunt and had a vague recall of having tea with her own mother. "My mother liked to serve tea," she said.

"I am sure she did," Beatrice acknowledged. "Tell me Winifred what do you like to do?"

"I like to cook," she said innocently.

"Excuse me?" Beatrice was aghast.

"I started taking lessons from our neighbor..." Winifred let it go. It was too painful to admit she missed Emily and her loving instructions.

"And what else do you like to do? Knit? Sew?" Beatrice sat cradling her cup of tea and studied Winifred's face. "You do look like your mother you know?"

"I do?" Winifred was shocked. Her mother was so dainty and petite.

"Yes, but, you have a lot of your father as well," Beatrice added.

And there it was. A reminder of something she wanted to forget.

"Oh don't pout child. We can fix it."

"How? How can you fix that my Da doesn't want me anymore?" Winifred started sobbing.

"Oh there, there dry your eyes. He didn't give you away. He wanted family, a woman in the family to help you grow to be a proper lady and not some cow hand."

"I'm not...*sob*...a...*sob*...cow...*sob*...hand."

"No of course you're not. But, he is just a shepherd and you don't have a mother to teach you how to be a woman. So, I am here. Her sister. What better woman to teach you than your own flesh and blood? So dry your eyes. You have a roof over your head and food for your belly and someone to teach you all you need to learn. And, if you wish to cook than you shall have a proper teacher to instruct you. How does that sound?"

"Fine." She took her napkin and wiped her eyes and nose.

"Well it is better than fine, but, we will have to wait and see if the student learns her lessons."

There was a knock at the door. "Mr. Antonio is here to see you Mum."

"Bring him here," she ordered. "Antonio is that you?" she bellowed.

"Yes my dear it is I." He came out and bent to kiss her on the neck.

"Come and meet my niece. Winifred this is my betrothed Antonio Renaldi."

A beautifully dressed man bowed to her. Winifred's eyes opened wide He was a very handsome man with glistening eyes that smiled on their own when he spoke. Beatrice was right, he was very beautiful.

"My dear how pleasant it is to meet you at last." He took her hand and kissed her beat up knuckles.

Winifred gasped. No one had ever kissed her hand before. Then she giggled.

"Am I amusing to you?" he asked.

"No. Yes." Then she just blushed.

"Oh I see a woman dressed in a young girls body." He turned to Aunt Beatrice. "My love, we have dinner plans this evening with the Count and his mistress. Do I need to cancel?" He asked looking at Winifred and then back to Beatrice.

"No of course not. Winifred will be here for quite some time and she is exhausted from her journey. She will have a quiet evening, relax, and tomorrow we begin our training. Isn't that so, Winifred?"

She just nodded her head in agreement. The less she saw of any of these people the better she would like it.

"Then I will return for you later for an evening of dinner and dancing." He bent and kissed her hand, bowed to Winifred and left.

"So now you have met my Antonio what do you think?"

"I think he is very beautiful," she said.

"I think you are right. I will have Sylvie draw you a bath. You may lounge and sleep as you wish. Tomorrow we start. For now I must get myself ready for my Antonio and the Count. Come Winifred, we will go up and get ourselves ready for our evening."

Winifred followed her aunt up the stairs.

"Sylvie!" Beatrice bellowed.

Sylvie appeared. "Please draw a bath for my niece in her room. If she needs anything at all this evening you are to get it for her immediately."

"Yes Mum," Sylvie replied dutifully.

Winifred did not know how anyone stood being ordered around as Beatrice did. They all seemed to follow her commands without complaint.

"I will stop in and see you before I go," Beatrice told her as she scurried on her way.

Winifred did not know what she was supposed to do with herself. There was a knock at her door and Sylvie stood with a bucket of hot water in her hand and two men carrying a large basin coming up behind her.

"We are here with you bath Miss." Sylvie said. Winifred backed up into her room and Sylvie walked in and pointed to a spot on the floor. The two men put the basin down where she had directed. She nodded to them and they left. She proceeded to pour the hot water into the tub and turned to address Winifred. "Just ring the bell when you wish for us to come get the basin." She went out into the hall and Winifred followed her to see where the bell was kept.

"Thank you Sylvie. I can do this myself."

"Yes Miss." Sylvie handed her the soap, brush, and towel and left her to her first bath in her Auntie's fancy home.

Winifred took off her clothes and gently stuck her foot into the tub. The water was way too hot. She poured some cool water into the tub and felt it again, much better. She lowered herself into the water and was pleased. This was something she knew how to do. She took the soap and scrubbed herself clean. She rested in the tub until the water got too cool to tolerate. She got out and dried herself with the cloth that was left for her. She put on the night gown and went to the hall to ring the bell. Sylvie appeared quickly

"I am through with my bath. Thank you Sylvie."

Sylvie nodded and scooped up all of the bathing tools and Winifred's clothes as well. Before Winifred could stop her, Sylvie was gone and down the stairs. The two men came back to remove the tub full of water.

"Now what do I do?" Winifred sat on the bed. Oh it felt so nice and soft. She decided to crawl under the covers and see how it felt to lay down. She got comfortable immediately and before she knew it she fell asleep.

CHAPTER 5

Winifred woke with the sun coming through her window. She must have slept all night. She looked around the room and found her clothes near the door, folded neatly and noticeably cleaner. Someone else washing her clothes. This was definitely a different life. She slipped them on and went downstairs. She found a bell in a different alcove and decided to ring it to see what would happen.

A gentleman dressed in servant's clothes appeared.

"Yes Miss?" he asked.

"Is my Aunt up yet?"

"No Miss," he answered.

"Oh," she sighed.

"Would you care for something Miss?

"Is breakfast ready?" she asked.

"Whatever you like Miss," he replied.

"I would like eggs and toast and preserve," she said.

"Yes Miss. And where would you be dining?"

"Dining? Out in the garden."

"Yes Miss. Right away Miss."

She walked to the garden table. The weather was a little cool to be outside but Winifred enjoyed the chance to almost be outdoors. "It's not my special place but it will have to do." Her breakfast was brought to her on a tray with a single rose in a vase as well as her plate of food.

"Anything else Miss?"

"Tea please."

"Yes Miss."

She was eating and thinking about her lovely time with Emily. She wondered about Gregor and how funny it was that Dooley called him

Toad. She missed them so much. Wished they were her family instead of the strange ones she did have. She ate until she was full and sat sipping her tea when her aunt made her appearance.

"You had a good night's rest I hear?"

"Yes Auntie."

"Good. You are an early riser."

The man appeared at the door to take Winifred's tray and acknowledged her Auntie.

"Just tea for me."

"Yes Mum. Anything else for you miss?"

"No. Thank you."

"I see you have learned how to order breakfast?"

"Yes. It's easy when you are hungry." She smiled at her Aunt.

"Enjoy your tea. I will be back in a few minutes."

"Yes Auntie," she said to no one there.

Her aunt came back fully dressed in a day gown.

"We will wait to take you out into town once your gowns come. For now we will start your lessons with manors and etiquette."

CHAPTER 6

Once immersed in her Auntie's schedule, Winifred became an appendage for Beatrice. She would command Winifred to perform some duties not low enough to be deemed servitude but not worthy of her own attention. "Winifred fetch the bell and have Sylvie bring my tea to the sitting room," or, "Winifred clear the table so Sylvie may set it for cocktails."

Winifred felt caught between the two worlds. It was only when Antonio was around did Auntie relinquish her hold and focused her attention on him. "Antonio the beautiful," Winifred called him to herself. It was a wonder he was as enchanted by Beatrice as he was, but, his attentiveness to her requests was unfettered.

"Antonio," Beatrice called.

Antonio's voice rang out across the house. He was mesmerizing with his deep tones and chanting in his native Spanish language. Half Spanish and half Italian his light olive complexion, large dark expressive eyes and thick black hair made him irresistible to many women. There was no woman he would not charm with his focused attention and mischievous twinkle in his eyes. "Yes my love," he answered.

"We must see the construction at Versailles when we are there. I hear the building has gone through many changes worthy of the excursion."

"As you wish my love."

It never ceased to amaze Winifred. Auntie would order him around and he did not seem to mind it. In fact her seemed to relish it. What was it that she did that kept this man so enchanted with her? Winifred shook her head in disgust. Maybe someday there would be a boy who found her so enchanting that she could order him around and he would like it too. Not likely! She would rather sit on her rock than spend time telling people what to do for her. She sat quietly and watched as Beatrice asked Antonio so sweetly for a pillow or to refresh her tea and he most attentively would accommodate her requests.

"Winifred what will you do with your time while we are away," Beatrice asked.

"I am not going with you?" She was surprised. Her Auntie liked to drag her everywhere.

"Not this time. Perhaps on the next trip. We have duties we must attend to." Beatrice responded pushing some hair off of Winifred's shoulder.

"Then I will spend time in the garden here. There is a church a few blocks away I should like to visit as well. It always calls to me when we pass by."

"A church?" Auntie asked in astonishment.

"Our girl has a bit of an ethereal quality about her don't you think my love?" Antonio interjected smiling at Winifred.

"I suppose," she said quietly.

"An angel should visit her flock from time to time," he added winking at Winifred.

Winifred blushed as she stood up. "If you will excuse me I will get ready for my journey into town."

"Certainly Don't stay too long. You never know who might enter those places." Beatrice warned her not having a clue who went to church or why they went there.

"Yes Auntie." Winifred replied dutifully and left the parlor quickly for the sanctuary of her own room.

"You must be patient with her." Antonio added after Winifred had left. "She has gone through much trauma in her short life. Perhaps a respite at the church will restore her joie de vivre. She is a quiet one at heart. Not so full of life as you are my dear one."

"She is an odd one that is for certain. But I will train that out of her. Your watch and see. She will become a fine lady of leisure. Lord knows what THAT man taught her in all those years since my sister's passing. A terrible shame that a girl should grow up without a mother. Why he never married again is beyond me," Beatrice said.

"We could only guess his motives. At least her had the foresight to send her to you for care. She will grow into a lovely young woman despite her upbringing." Antonio rose and walked to the door. "Have your man bring your bags down when they are ready. I will return shortly and we can discuss further your plans to keep me busy and out of trouble." He bent to kiss her on the head before he left the house.

Beatrice sighed. "Finally a lovely man who appreciates my efforts."

Winifred could not wait for them to leave. She heard her Auntie ordering the servants around and the closing of the front door as they went on their latest journey. The house was finally peaceful. Winifred stepped out of her room and rang the bell. She was attended to by the man servant.

"Yes Miss?"

"I would like my meal in the garden please."

"Yes Miss," he said and returned to work.

Winifred changed her clothes into the simplest gown she had. It would have to do for her trip to the church. She ate quietly in the garden and relaxed into her own tranquility. Not the frantic go, go, go her Auntie liked to maintain. After her meal she went in search for something simple to place on her head. A head covering was not something her Auntie would approve of. The latest hat? Yes. A fashion statement? Always. A simple garment to show respect to God did not exist.

Winifred found a cape with a hood and place it over her shoulders. She walked slowly to the church and found it open. The pews were plentiful and the alter was lit with many candles. She felt at home right away. Relaxed she sat in the back and felt the massiveness of the room embrace her. Not like the little church at home, but, welcoming none the less. Many women were kneeling in front of her. Saying their prayers while holding strands of beads. Some women were lighting candles.

A priest made his way down the center aisle. "Are you in need of council my child?"

"No Father. I just wanted to come here."

"You are always welcome in the house of our lord."

"Thank you Father." She crossed herself and went to her knees to prey just like the women in front of her. No birds to take her prayers to God. She spoke softly. "I just want to go home Father. I want to go home." She crossed herself again and got up to leave. She would come back, she told herself, whenever Auntie drove her to madness with activities.

Her days of solitude were filled with quiet activities. She took long walks in daylight around the nearby streets and as much time as possible in her Auntie's garden.

Auntie and Antonio returned from their trip. Boisterous as always and full of her own self worth, Beatrice talked nonstop about their visit to Versailles and the glorious parties and balls thrown in their honor. Antonio, of course, was the life of the party with his flamboyant dance moves and attention to the women at court.

"You should not be so attentive to those other women, Antonio, when you are betrothed to me," Beatrice scolded him.

"You know I have eyes only for you my love," he assured her.

"That's not what the other women think," she answered him.

"Well they do not know my heart. Only what they wish to see." He dismissed her persistence. "Winifred did you get a chance to visit your church? Were the other angels happy to see one of their own?"

"Oh Antonio, don't tease her," Beatrice scolded him.

"I did go to church. Thank you for asking Antonio," she replied blushing.

"And the other angels?" he asked jokingly.

"No angels there. Just lots of people saying their prayers. It is a beautiful church. Much larger than the church back home."

"You will do well to go there. I think it suits you."

"Thank you Antonio. It feels good to me to be there," Winifred said.

"There you go encouraging her solitude when it is her social life that needs attention," Beatrice interjected. "We will begin again on your social etiquette and events just as soon as possible. Tonight we rest from our travels. Tomorrow we begin again." Beatrice got up and was ready to tend to her refreshment.

"I will repose to my own quarters. Ladies it was a pleasure to have your company. My dear, I will see you on the morrow good night." He bowed slightly and left the house.

Beatrice went to the window and watched him as he left. She said nothing and went upstairs to her own room.

Days went by before she had a chance to escape her duties. Winifred stepped out quietly and walked back to the church. She spent days and nights on her knees asking for guidance. Only the priest at the Alter saw the child in prayer. The outward appearance was of a growing girl in prayer. Well adorned in the latest gowns and always gracious in his presence. She would genuflect and be on her way out the back of the church.

One day he met her in the aisle on her way to a pew. "Lass. We have so much to do in this fair city, why are you here so often?"

"Oh Father. I feel at home here unlike at my Auntie's home."

"Certainly you have someone who misses you when you are here. I never see anyone with you."

"No one misses me Father. They know where I am. I return home in plenty of time to go where I have to go and do what I have to do."

"If there is ever a time that it changes you will let me know. Promise me this?"

"All right. Although I cannot see things changing. Even when I ask God. He does not send a message to me here like he did when I was younger and at my home."

"You want God to make changes in your life?" She looked well cared for.

"I miss my home and my friends Father. I am here at my Auntie's home to learn to be a woman, but, I don't like the woman she wants me to be."

"I see," he said not truly understanding her blight. "And what type of woman is that?"

"One who goes to parties all of the time. One who sits and orders the servants around. One who does nothing but talk all day. Talking is exhausting Father."

"When you do this talking do you not tell your Auntie it is not for you?"

"Oh she does not care what I want. She just wants me to be a likeness of herself."

So wise a young girl for her age he thought. "Let me know if there is anything I can do."

"Yes Father. Thank you."

Antonio strolled into the house in search of Beatrice. "Where is the child?" He asked looking around for her.

"She has gone to that God awful church again," she said in disgust.

"The church? Why is she at the church?" he asked.

"She must be asking God for something," Beatrice answered.

"What does she want?" His curiosity turned to concern.

"I don't know Antonio. What does any young girl want?"

"My dear, you must find out what she wants. You cannot have her talking all over town about something she is lacking. What do you feel she is in want of?" he pursued.

"Honestly Antonio I do not know."

"Well if you won't find out then I will. A young girl should not need to go to church so often. Has something happened to her?"

"Why don't you ask her yourself since you are so interested in her whereabouts?"

He got up and went to the door as Winifred entered. She took off the cape and hung it on the coat rack. "May I speak with you Winifred?" he asked with an air of authority.

"Of course," she said. She was curious why Antonio the beautiful would want to speak to her.

"You are gone to the church frequently, do you require some assistance?"

"What do you mean?" she asked.

"Do you need help with something? Do you have something big you need?"

She blushed. "No," she said meekly.

"Then why are you at the church so often?"

"I feel at home there. It makes me feel a part of my life back where I came from." She squirmed as she spoke.

"And you do not feel that way in this home?" he pursued.

"No I don't. Auntie's house is very different from my home."

"I see. Did you spend a lot of time at the church at your home?" he asked.

"Some. I spent time with the people in the church besides being at the church."

"Ah. You miss the people from your town do you?"

"Yes Antonio I do."

"You must make new friends," her Auntie interjected.

"Yes Auntie," she said dutifully and turned to go upstairs to her room.

Antonio waited for her to leave before speaking to Beatrice. "You cannot command her to have friends my love. She needs time to find her own. If she seeks the solace of God in his church we must respect that. She is far from all she holds near and dear. Have compassion for the child. She lost her mother and her father gave her away. She is far from all she finds comfort with. Surely you can understand that?" he enquired.

"Oh I suppose. She is a lost little girl in need of much education and I intend to give her that. You are a kind man Antonio. That is part of why I love you."

He took her hand and kissed it. But, the blinders were coming off. His beautiful and vivacious Beatrice had a heart of stone when it came to her only niece. Despite his plea for a kinder approach the request fell on deaf ears.

Winifred stayed in her room. She did not want to socialize with her Auntie. What did Antonio see in her? She just could not understand the attraction. She crawled back into bed and sought her refuge in sleep.

CHAPTER 7

The next day Antonio came to her room and knocked on her door. "I have a solution for your problem," he told her as Winifred answered her door.

"What problem?" she enquired.

"The problem at hand. The one where you miss your family and friends. You must go for a visit. See if you still want to be there. A trip would do you good and would answer questions about your departure. You could ask your father if he still wants you to stay away. "

Winifred grabbed Antonio's arm. "Do you think I could go? Would Auntie let me? She does not like my Da you know?"

"I do know this, however, she is becoming quite fond of you and would want you to be happy and assured of the reason for being here."

"I would love to go home. I miss my friend Emily and her family. I could go? Really? I could go?"

"I am certain of it. Let's go discuss it with your Auntie and start making arrangements." He offered her his arm and Winifred beamed her most vibrant smile. She was going home!

"GO WHERE?" she bellowed. Beatrice was aghast at the plan.

"To my home. To see everyone I miss." Winifred said joyfully.

"Antonio why would you put such a horrid notion in her head? She cannot go back. Her father commanded her to be gone. He does not want her there. For whatever his reason might be we must respect that." Beatrice glared at Antonio.

"Certainly, my love, a short visit would not interrupt his life and would permit the child to see what she misses. She is, after all, only a child," he reiterated.

"Of course she is a child. No one is denying that. She must obey her elders that is all. We are trying to make a home here for her are we not? Why would you put such a fanciful thought into her head? She must learn she cannot have all she wants in this world," Beatrice said.

At that last statement Winifred ran from the room with tears running down her face. Not only did her Da not want her, her Auntie would not let her go. She was stuck in this nightmare with no way out!

"See what you have done? You have upset her," Beatrice accused him.

"I have upset her? It is your cold hearted approach to her that has upset her. Even her father would probably like to see her. Do not be so forceful on this topic, my love. A cold heart does not suit you."

"Antonio you know I want only the best for her. Why do you torment her with visits to places she cannot go? Let her be. She will find our way is best for her. You wait and see." Beatrice was trying her best to be the softer woman he wanted her to be.

Antonio looked at the closed door at the top of the stairs. His heart told him to go comfort the girl. His thoughts told him to leave her alone. Perhaps Beatrice knew what she was doing. Only time would tell.

Winifred cried herself to sleep that night and every night for a week until she was out of tears. Never once did Beatrice come to comfort her. Another family member who did not care about what she wanted. Antonio's presence was scarce. When she wanted someone to comfort her she was left without anyone.

Beatrice carried on her tutelage as if nothing had happened. Ordering Winifred to stand straight and sit tall. Poise and etiquette were the only things that mattered and it was up to Winifred to fall into line.

When he did show up, Antonio was aloof. His friendship and caring ways were turned off as if they did not exist. Winifred was confused and even more lonely than when she had first arrived.

On her way downstairs for breakfast one Sunday morning she overheard Beatrice and Antonio in a loud discussion. She stopped walking when she realized she was the topic of their arguing.

"But you must include her in our life," Antonio insisted.

"You always want her around," Beatrice pouted.

"She is your niece not a piece of furniture. Surely you understand her need to be treated as family and not as a servant?"

"She is not treated like a servant," Beatrice scoffed.

"Prove it. Show me how her loving Auntie treats her. Never once have I seen you embrace her. She is your flesh and blood. Your sister's only child."

"She knows I care for her."

"How? How does she know this?"

"Antonio why are you doing this?"

"Because I have come to see you as a different woman than the one I fell in love with. Show me you have a heart."

"You know I'd do anything for you."

"Not me Beatrice. Show me you can care for your sister's child. She is not a project for you to conquer. She is a person with needs. Show me you care," he demanded.

"This is ridiculous," she responded.

"Show me," he demanded.

"What would you have me do?" Beatrice asked.

"You have to ask how to show affection to your niece?" he was dumbfounded.

"Why are you doing this?"

"Because I am concerned for all of our welfare."

"Why now? You don't seem to mind how I show you my affection."

"Your affection for me is not the issue. Your ability to mother is," he answered.

"What if I said I don't want to be a mother?" she responded.

"You have taken on the responsibility for something you do not wish to do?" he was shocked.

"I am not her mother."

"I know this. But, who will mother her if you don't? You took her in. Why? Why did you take her if you do not want to mother her?"

"She had a mother, my sister. I felt responsible to my sister. To provide for her daughter. No one said I had to mother her."

"Ah I see. You cannot do what you have no heart for," he said in disgust. "And you wonder why she seeks solace in the church. You have much to learn about life my dear."

"Antonio must we talk about this? There are so many other topics worth discussing besides my niece." Beatrice moved close up to him trying to change the direction of his inquiry with the softness of her body.

He turned and saw Winifred standing at the top of the stairs shaking with her eyes wide open. He looked back at Beatrice and realized he had made a big mistake broaching the subject with Winifred in the house.

Winifred ran up the stairs to her room and closed the door. What was she to do? Where could she go? She dressed herself quickly for an outing and took a deep breath. She ran down the stairs and out of the house all the way to the church. Barreling in the front doors she headed straight for the priest

"There there child. What is the matter?" he asked.

She flung herself into his arms and started sobbing.

"What is it child?"

Antonio and Beatrice walked into the church together and moved directly toward them. The priest looked at them and back to Winifred. Holding her tightly he asked "What is the issue here?"

"They don't love me. They don't want me here," Winifred cried.

"Oh child that is not true," Beatrice said stroking Winifred's back. It was the first time she had laid a hand on Winifred since she had arrived in London.

"This is a family matter Padre," Antonio answered. "The child was sent to her Aunt for care. She is having a hard time adjusting to her ways."

"I see. I see," he said continuing to hold the sobbing girl. "Give us a few minutes to talk alone and I will send her out to you." The Priest said ushering Winifred into a private space. He pointed to the pews for Antonio and Beatrice to have a seat. Finding a handkerchief for Winifred he directed her to a chair. "Sit here my child," he said softly.

Waiting for her to calm down, he sat across from her. "Is it true? Are those people your family?"

"Yes Father," she said barely above a whisper.

"And do you not wish to remain with them?"

"No Father. I want to go back to my home. But, my Da does not want me there. He sent me to my Aunt for care. She does not like me. She just orders me around and makes me wear funny clothes."

"Funny clothes?" he asked for clarity.

She held her arms out for him to see what she was wearing.

"Yes this is the fashion of ladies of leisure. You do not like it? Most women do like it I believe."

"No. It is not what I would chose to wear."

"So you must take the time to adjust to your new life. It is not always easy making changes, but, life goes on anyway. Put some effort into trying to adjust child. It will do your heart good to make the effort. You are always welcome here. Should things get bad you come to me at once and we will see what else can be done. But, for now your care is in the hands of this woman."

"Thank you Father." She was stuck. Her fate was sealed in this horrible situation. There was nothing more she could do to escape.

The priest waited for Winifred to dry her eyes before escorting her back to her Aunt and Antonio. "May I speak with you for a moment," he said to Beatrice.

She looked to Winifred and Antonio before agreeing.

He escorted her back to the same space he had brought Winifred and offered her the same seat. "She is in distress. A child ripped from the only home she has known and sent to another with nothing familiar to her. You must be kind and gentle with her. She will adjust give her time. Children are resilient. It is all in your approach. She has been instructed to come back if things get too bad. So you will take care of her properly or she will return."

Beatrice gave a disgruntled agreement and left his counsel.

"I hope I have done the right thing," the Priest said to himself.

"Come let us go home," Beatrice said to Winifred and Antonio.

Outside of the church she walked up to Winifred and put her hand in the crook of the girls elbow. "What would you like to do today?"

"I would like to go to the park and see the ducks," Winifred answered.

"All right. Let's go to the park. Our studies can wait," Beatrice said with a forced smile.

Winifred had a assortment of tasks to accomplish on a daily basis that kept her focused. Days on end she was taught how to walk and how to speak to people of different stations in life and to foreign dignitaries.

Antonio's presence in their home dwindled and eventually he was gone from their lives. Winifred was not told of the break up and her Auntie did not speak of him ever again.

Her training was constant for four years. She learned what to wear to a variety of occasions. She transformed from an awkward twelve year old to a blossoming woman of sixteen. She had continual social engagements and a vast array of suitors to occupy her time. She ate at the finest homes. Conversed with girls her own age at appropriate times. She had everything that money could buy and a lifestyle that only the elite in society would understand. She hated it. Hated the endless days of proper etiquette, servants tending to her every need and the necessity to wear frilly garments. She still missed the joy of her friendship with Emily. She missed learning how to prepare a meal that was appreciated and substantial. She missed the life of her childhood. The life with sheep grazing and being outdoors for hours at a time without a care in the world. She missed talking to the birds as they flew overhead and going to her little church on Sundays.

While waiting for her weekend invitations, Winifred received a post addressed to her in a hand writing she did not recognize. It was a notice she had not expected.

"It is with deepest regret that the man known as Peter Flanagan has met his maker on Thursday the Eighth of October. Burial will be made on Eleventh of October." It was signed Pastor O'Brian.

"What is it Winifred?" her Auntie asked.

"I must go home," she responded.

"You are home dear."

"No you don't understand. My Da has passed. I must go home."

"Oh dear. I must escort you. I just don't know when I will be able to get away."

"No Auntie. I must do this myself. May I take a carriage?"

"Of course you may."

CHAPTER 8

$\mathcal{W}$inifred went through her armoire looking for something appropriate to wear to her father's funeral. Everything was too ornate or too formal. She decided on a black dress she had worn for a day party. It was form fitting but it would have to do.

She called for a carriage. She would take it as far as the dock. Time was of the essence. She needed to get back in time for the funeral.

God was with her in her travels. There was a boat ready to go to Dublin when she arrived at the dock and a carriage available once she landed at the shore. The carriage driver knew where to find Wallingford and took her directly to the church.

Winifred saw a group of people standing in the graveyard when she arrived. The mourners were all huddled together as she quietly made her way up behind them. She heard the Pastor say.

"We ask thee, or Lord, in the name of the Father, the Son and the Holy Ghost to take this man your shepherd, Peter Flanagan, into your home and keep him."

At the sound of her father's name Winifred gasped. People turned to look at her and some of them began mumbling. The couple in front of her separated and let her step forward. Many were whispering her name and she glanced at them in recognition. Most of them had grown older with silver strands in their hair. She looked around and did not see the Wolcott family but Mama's friend Mrs. Beardsley was there. Many of the young men were strangers to her. How could that be? In all the years she had lived there she had known everyone. Had people moved there after she was made to leave?

The Pastor nodded to her as he continued with his prayers. Two men jumped into the open ground and took their places at opposite ends. The Pastor moved to stand before her as he had done those many years ago.

"Winifred you have grown to be such a lovely young woman," he said quietly holding her arms.

She could not help but look past him as two young men lifted the casket and lowered it to the men in the ground. She started to feel faint and began swaying on her feet.

"Winifred!" the Pastor called to her. But he sounded like he was in a tunnel going farther and farther away.

She woke to find herself in the pastor's office with him and some other people around him.

"Winifred?"

"Yes Pastor," she whispered.

"You with us child? You gave us quite a fright. I thought I was going to have to perform a double ceremony," he chuckled.

"No I am here. What happened?" she asked trying to sit up.

"Just rest a minute. Do you know where you are?"

"I am in your office."

"And why are you here?" he asked.

"My Da has passed and I'm home to bury him."

"Let her up." He said to the others who were hunched over her. He gave her his hand and helped her to her feet. He whispered, "Pretty fancy clothes for going to a funeral."

"Yes. My Aunt believes in overdoing everything if she has half a chance," she replied.

"So where are you off to now?" he asked.

"What do you mean?"

"Are you going back tonight or do you need a room?"

"A room? I am going to stay at my home. It is still my home? Da didn't sell it or give it away?"

"No he lived there alone until he passed, God bless his soul. Tending to his flock that very day."

"Why don't you think I would want to stay there? It's my home. The only place I ever wanted to live. I would have been there for him if he hadn't sent me away!" She was getting emotional and her Auntie would be very angry if she knew.

"Sorry we were under the impression you wanted to leave." He looked around and the others mumbled to each other and nodded their heads in agreement.

"He told you I wanted to leave? Why would he do that? I never wanted to go! We had a terrible fight and he sent me away to live with my Aunt in London. He forced me to go!" she began crying.

"All right lass we believe you. It makes more sense than the story he told us. In any case, you are back now and we're happy to have you."

"Thank you Father."

"So let's take a look at you. The last time we saw you, you were a little bit of a lass." She gave them her best turn. The one her Auntie drummed into her. She put a smile on her face and wiped the tears away.

The men standing behind the Pastor stood with their mouths open. One elbowed the other. "Look Toad the shrimp is back."

"Toad?" She said looking from one to the other. Oh my! "Gregor is that you?" she asked eyes wide.

"The one and only," he answered.

"I didn't recognize you. You're all grown up."

"And so are you," he said smiling at her.

"Yes I guess I am," she smiled back at him.

"OK folks the show is over. Our Winifred has returned and all is right with the world, except of course, the loss of our dear friend Peter Flanagan, may he rest in peace," the Pastor added.

The town folk said, "AMEN," and began dispersing.

"When did you get back?" Gregor asked still looking at her.

"Just now when you were all at the graveside. I got the notice of his passing yesterday morning and rode in as fast as I could to get here."

"You've been riding for two days? No wonder you passed out. Come have something to eat. Ma will be so happy to see you."

"How is your mother? I missed her so much. I used to wish that she was my mother. I loved the time we spent together cooking," Winifred recalled fondly.

"Then you need to come tell her that. She was very sad when you left without saying goodbye. She will be so pleased to hear the truth after all these years." Gregor started walking her toward his family home.

Winifred stopped short. "Oh wait. I have a carriage waiting for me. Let me send him back since I won't be needing him any longer."

Gregor grinned as he escorted her to the carriage.

"Thank you sir. I won't be needing your service any longer."

"Yes Mum," he responded and taped the horse lightly with the reins.

"Yes Mum," Gregor whispered into her ear.

She laughed and elbowed him like Dooley had done all those years ago.

"Oh," he said pretending she hurt his ribs. And they laughed together.

"Ma!" Gregor yelled as they got close to his home. "Ma we've got company. And you'll never guess who it is!"

"Hush Gregor. Dooley has already told me and spoiled your surprise."

Winifred began to run. She missed this woman so much. The woman who should have been her mother. Tears rolled down her face as she opened her arms wide to embrace her.

Emily Wolcott dropped the towel she had in her hands as the grown up Winifred came running to her. She too opened her arms to embrace the daughter she missed.

"I didn't want to go," Winifred said crying in Emily's arms. "He made me leave without saying goodbye to anyone. I missed you most of all. I missed you most of all." She sobbed and the tears flowed as she hugged her mother.

"Me too child. Me too," Emily said. "Let me look at you." She pulled Winifred away from herself to look at the young woman. "Dooley was right," she said wiping her eyes. "You have grown to be quite a beauty."

"I did not say that Ma!" Dooley said.

"Well something close to that," she acknowledged. "And look at the fancy clothes. My, my. Not many places you can wear that dress around here. "

"They're not me. My Aunt has many excuses and places to wear them. But, they're just not me. I love it here. I belong here."

"Ma, Winifred hasn't eaten all day. She needs something. She fainted at her Da's funeral."

"Then you can join us now for a meal and every one after that as long as you like. How long are you going to stay?"

"I'm not going back. This is my home. I hate it there. This is where I belong, on my family land."

The Wolcott men looked at each other. "Winifred things have changed since you left," David Wolcott chimed in. "Your Da was not a healthy man and gave away pieces of the property."

"He did? Why? He had no right. It's my land too!"

"He changed a lot once you were gone. Said you broke his heart leaving as you did."

"Leave HIM! He sent me away! He sent me away to become a woman with my Mother's sister. Who, by the way, was so different from my mother I cannot believe they were related!" She was angry now. "I left him! He had his nerve!"

The Wolcott family looked at each other while she fumed.

"Is the house still mine or did he give that away too?" she asked.

"No the house you can have, but, most of the land has been divided up."

"Who has it? Who had my land?"

"It's not your land any more. Get that through your head. It was given away long ago. The people he sold it to let him graze his small flock on it. But, really it has not been his for a long time," David answered.

"It does not matter Winifred. It does not matter. You are here now and we want you to stay. You belong here. Let's eat and you can answer questions about London. I'm dying to know about London," Emily said dishing up a plate of stew for everyone as they took their place at the table. "Dooley you eating with us?" Emily asked.

Winifred looked from face to face. "Where else would he eat?" she asked.

"At his own home with his wife and baby," Emily answered.

"Dooley is married? To whom?" Winifred asked surprised.

"You remember Sarah the Lumberman's daughter?"

"Yes. He ran the lumber yard outside of town?"

"That's the one. She caught old Dooley and reeled him in like a big ole fish," Gregor said pantomiming a fisherman catching a fish.

"You should be so lucky ole Toad," he said smiling.

"You're not married?" she asked Gregor hoping her old crush did not show.

"Nah. Ole Toad here likes to love em and leave em," Dooley said slapping his brother on the back.

"I see you two still poke at each other." She smiled taking a bite of the hearty stew Emily had made.

"Some things never change," Emily sighed.

"This stew is wonderful Emily. Thank you for inviting me to dinner. I don't know what I will find at Da's house."

"Why don't you stay here tonight. You can have Dooley's old room since he does live elsewhere." Emily grinned at her oldest son.

"Thank you that would be lovely. I just don't think I can face that house yet."

"Good then it's settled. I'll find some linens for that bed and you can put up your things. Do you have a bag of clothes with you?" Emily looked around the floor for her parcel.

"No I left so fast I didn't bring anything with me. Just like when I left here. I didn't take a thing except my mother's necklace." She touched it at her throat. She still wore it always.

"Enjoy your meal and after supper we will get you settled in," Emily commanded her.

They talked about London and her Auntie's home and busy social life. What it was like having servants to tend to her all of the time. How she never did learn to cook, but, could order a meal in several languages. They all laughed at her stories of trying to fit into a world she did not belong.

"Here let's begin with linens for the bed, a candle and candle stick." Emily took her upstairs and opened a cupboard near the bedrooms stocked with supplies.

"You have so much more stuff that my Da ever had in our home."

"You and your father led a meager life, but, you never went without food or clothes. And, you always had a roof over your head," Emily reminded her.

"We did. I never realized how much more you had than we did until just now," Winifred added.

"He had his pride Winifred. No one would deprive him of that."

"Did you always have so much? Oh, of course you did!"

"Not always. We built it as we went along. Your Da lost your Ma and his will to go on. It was only to provide for you that kept him going. He was a broken man in more ways than one," she said.

"But he sent me away."

"For your sake not his."

"Maybe if I had stayed we could have built..." She didn't know what she was saying. "So he just gave me away and finished living? That was four years ago."

"Your Aunt wrote him regularly and told him of your progress into society. She told him you would soon be accepting a marriage proposal and that is when he finally gave up," Emily said.

"But that's a lie! No one is interested in me like that!" Winifred was furious. "Why would she lie like that? My Da gave up because of a great big lie!"

"She probably thought it was for the best. Who knows?" Emily turned and went into Dooley's old room. "Here we are." She opened the door to a small but compact room. Bed in the far corner next to a book shelf. Dresser and desk with a chair at the foot of the bed.

"Oh look at Dooley's old stuff." Winifred ran her hand gently over trinkets on a shelf and keep sakes only a boy would want.

Emily bent to make up the bed.

"Let me help you." Winifred moved next to her.

"It won't be but a minute to finish making it up." Emily tucked in a blanket. "There you are young lady. I hope you have a good night's sleep."

"Thank you so much Emily. It means so much to me to be in your home again."

Emily gave Winifred a big motherly embrace. "You are always welcome here."

She left Winifred to get ready for bed. There was a knock at the door a few minutes later.

"Gregor said you can borrow this to sleep in since you don't have any other clothes with you." Emily handed Winifred an old worn shirt. Clean but too worn to be used as a work shirt.

"Thank you," she said and took it from Emily. She smelled it and smiled. What she would have give to have this shirt four years ago.

As she changed and put it on she felt Gregor all around her like an embrace. It was comforting as she fell easily into a deep sleep.

She was dreaming of her rock out on the cliff and the freedom of being with the birds when she was shaken awake.

"Hey sleepy head. Ma's calling for breakfast. If you want to eat anything you better get up or it will be gone before you get downstairs."

She looked at Gregor and could not figure out how he got to Auntie's house. "OK," she answered him once she realized she was back home. Gregor had grown taller and had gotten way too good looking for his own good. His Toad voice was now deep and rich. She sat up and realized she was wearing only an old work shirt. Not something that was presentable for anyone's breakfast table. Winifred slipped back into her black dress and walked back downstairs barefoot.

"Yeah she looks great. Shhh she's coming."

She heard Gregor talking. He thinks I look great. It made her smile as she walked into the dining room. "Good morning."

"Good morning Love, did you have a good sleep?" Emily asked her.

"Wonderful thank you. Dooley's bed is so comfortable."

"Yeah. Don't tell him that or he'll be back every day to sleep," Gregor answered her.

"And thank you for the use of your shirt." Winifred smiled at Gregor.

"Keep it. It's too old to wear anymore," he said as he grabbed for a roll and some sausage.

"Thank you. I might just do that," she said dreamily.

"Grab a plate Winifred and dig in before the men eat it all up," Emily suggested.

She did as she was told but tentatively looked everything over before she chose what she wanted.

"Here," Gregor grabbed a roll and some sausage and threw it on her plate. "You want eggs you better do it yourself."

"Thanks," she said sitting down next to him.

"Tea?" Emily asked holding up a tea pot.

"Yes please," Winifred said.

Emily got out a cup and saucer and filled it for her. Winifred gingerly moved it in front of herself and took a sip while the men continued to grab and eat at a furious pace. Emily sat at her seat and watched the serene Winifred sitting amongst the high energy men without a care in the world.

"Thanks Ma gotta go," Gregor said as he grabbed another roll. He kissed his Ma on the cheek and then Winifred on the cheek. "Glad you're back," he said as he ran out the door.

"Later Love," David said kissing Emily on the other cheek. "Will you be here when we get back?" he asked Winifred.

A surprised Winifred sat motionless. "I don't know," she answered.

"Hope you decide to stay," he said walking out of the door after Gregor.

"What was that?" Winifred asked staring at the door.

"That, my girl, was breakfast at Wolcott manor," she laughed.

"Is it like this every day?" she asked turning to Emily.

"If there is something that needs tending to. Otherwise, it's half that fast and they eat twice the amount. I don't know which I prefer." Emily sighed sipping her tea.

"You know what I missed most when I left?" Winifred asked.

"What's that?"

"I missed your cooking lessons. When I told Auntie that I wanted to learn to cook she nearly died. Cooking in London is done by the servants not by the elite."

"Oh is that so?"

"Yes. If the servants weren't there all day every day Auntie would not know how to take care of herself. She only knows how to order people around. Do anything herself? Never!"

"Well here on the farm we do it all every day, don't we lass?"

"Yes we do." The two smiled at each other.

"But, first I have to find something to wear besides this dress. Anything I left at Da's house would be way too small for me now."

"I have a few things you could borrow. You do need something more practical to wear," Emily agreed.

CHAPTER 9

"*L*et's walk into town and see if there is anything we can use to make you a dress. I need a few supplies any way."

"That would be lovely. I miss it here. I can't wait to see everyone." Winifred got up to help with the dishes.

"No sit down. You are still a guest. I don't want you to get your fancy dress all dirty."

"Please Emily let me help. I feel like family coming home. You were always more a Ma to me than the one I had and lost."

"Thank you. That's so nice of you to say. You do feel like the daughter I never had."

"See we belong together." Winifred gave her a quick hug.

They walked into town and chatted like they had never been apart. Emily reintroduced her to all of the shop keepers as they went about their business of finding materials for Winifred's new wardrobe. Winifred helped her carry the supplies she needed. They were giggling over something when they got back to the Wolcott home.

"Where have you been Ma? We're starved," Gregor asked looking around for something to eat.

"You are always hungry and what do I tell you?"

"Wait it's on the way," he said mocking her.

"And do you always get fed?" She raised an eyebrow to him.

"Yes," he sighed.

"So?"

"I waited for you and I'm still starved."

"Boys!" She shook her head as she put her parcels down. Opening a package she handed a loaf of bread to Winifred. " Take the knife over there and slice it all up please."

Winifred happily did as she was asked.

Gregor came up behind her and whispered in her ear, "Make mine extra thick." She scrunched her neck. His words sent shivers down her spine and made her heart go all aflutter.

"Gregor leave that girl alone and go wash your hands," Emily commanded as she took the stew pot from the fire and forked the meat onto a platter.

"It's OK Ma she likes me." He turned to Winifred and winked at her.

Winifred laughed and blushed as she watched him leave the room.

Emily sliced the meat and scooped potatoes from the pot and put them around the meat.

"All right boys come and get it," she called. "Better stand back Winifred if you know what's good for you." Emily warned her as the men came barreling into the house. They each grabbed a plate and headed toward the food. David, Gregor and three farm hands attacked what was laid out. Winifred tried to get out of the way while the men went after the food but got caught between the meat platter and the pile of bread. When Gregor came to get his portion he went one way around her to get his bread and back to get at the meat. Somehow they ended up face to face when Gregor came at her for a quick kiss on the lips. "Mmm tastes great," he said and moved away to the table to sit and eat his meal.

Winifred was shocked. Her first kiss from the boy she had wanted as a young girl and it happened so fast she did not have time to respond. She looked around but no one else seemed to have noticed what had happened.

"Winifred. Grab a plate love and eat something before these hounds eat everything," Emily called to her.

"Yes mum," she said softly. Looking around the only place to sit was next to Gregor. She sat tentatively.

"Who you calling a hound?" David asked.

"You. You old dog," she answered.

He barked and they played. He barking at her and her hitting him away. This distracted all of the farmhands while they were devouring their meal.

"You all right?" Gregor asked softly.

"Yes," she said quietly as she blushed.

"Do you mind that I did that? He asked quietly looking at her.

"In front of everyone I do," She whispered back.

He looked around. "No one saw it," he said.

"I mind if others saw it," She whispered again.

"So it's OK if no one saw it?" he pursued.

"Yes," she said quietly.

"Da." He yelled practically in her ear. "When we're done today I'm gonna walk Winifred over to her place to check it out. You OK with that?"

"Sure son. Be careful to watch for snakes. That place has been empty for a while," David called back.

"OK we will," he yelled. He was smiling at Winifred the whole time.

Winifred was never so nervous to walk home as she was today. Gregor rolled up his sleeves as he escorted her home.

"You're awfully quiet," Gregor said as they walked.

"I don't know what to expect when we get there," she said. "I haven't been there in four years."

"I expect that it will be the same as when you left. He didn't do much after you'd gone."

"I still can't believe he lied about me going away. I never wanted to leave. You do believe me don't you?"

He shrugged. "Sure. Doesn't matter though. You're back now."

They approached the house which was more like a shack. "I don't remember it being so small," she said.

"Yeah. Places get smaller as we get older."

She stood in the middle of the dark room and looked. Gregor walked up next to her and put his hand on her shoulder.

"It looks the same but feels so small." She walked into the space that was her room. A little cubby big enough for her small bed, a two drawer night stand she had used as a dresser, and a child size chair. Sitting on the chair was a doll her mother had made for her. The bed was lumpy with straw poking out of it. A worn out quilt was thrown on top. Looking at it made her want to cry. She walked back to the front room and looked at the fireplace they used for their stove and the tiny kitchen area next to it. Even the dining table looked smaller. The stairs between her cubby and the kitchen led up to the loft where her Da stayed.

She climbed the stairs and looked around. It was cold and musty and had no life to it. She felt tears well up in her eyes She walked back down the stairs and out the door to the front of the house. Wiping her face she turned away from him. "I don't know what I am going to do. I can't live here. It's awful. Reminds me of him and death."

She walked around the back side of the house to see the small pen they used for the sheep broken down and empty. "Where are the sheep?" she turned to him.

"They got sold off to pay his debts. Winifred wait!" He called to her and started running after her. "Don't! Winifred Don't!" he screamed.

She stood at the cliff's edge and looked down at her rock. The place she felt closest to God. Today it was a sad little boulder overlooking the rocks and the water below. She burst into tears and covered her face with her hands.

"Aw Winifred. Don't cry." Gregor came up and put his arms around her and walked her back away from the edge.

"I don't know where to go. I don't know what I am to do," she sobbed. "I don't know where I belong. I hate London. Don't make me go back there."

"No one is making you go back there. We'll talk to Ma. Maybe she knows what you can do."

"I love your family. Why couldn't I have been born to your family?" she sobbed.

"We love you too."

"Really? You do?" She looked up at him.

"You've always been a part of our family. Even when your Ma was alive you felt like family," he agreed as he walked her to his family home.

"You're just saying that to make me stop crying," she sniffled.

"Yes. But, it's true."

She laughed and stopped to look at him. "You're a nice man Gregor Wolcott." She grabbed his shirt and pulled him closer to give him a quick kiss on the lips.

Gregor seized the moment to let his passion loose. He grabbed her hard and kissed her feverishly on the lips. He slid his hands up her back to hold her head in both of his hands. They devoured each other. She gasped for air as the kissing went on and on.

Coming up for air Gregor looked at her. "Geez-us Winifred you can kiss."

She elbowed him in the ribs.

"Who taught you how to kiss like that?" he asked rubbing his side.

"What? No one taught me. It must be you."

"Well you had to learn somehow."

"I was in London for four years remember?"

"Yeah I remember. It was quiet around her when you were gone."

"Really? Did you miss me?"

"Kind of."

"Kind of? Gee thanks."

"I didn't know I would miss you until you were gone. You were hear all the time. Talking to Ma. Cooking with Ma. You were like a pesky little sister. Then you were gone and it was really quiet. Ma was sad and lonely. And, then you came back. "And, whooee. You look like this." He mimicked female curves with his hands. And your all grown up and you kiss like there's no tomorrow." He shook his head.

"Is that bad?" she was confused.

"Bad? Oh hell no. I mean, gosh no. Well you know what I mean. But Winifred." He grabbed her shoulders and looked her square in the eyes. "You should not kiss guys like that unless you mean it."

"Mean what?" she asked.

He rubbed his face with his hands. "Unless you mean to have more kissing and other stuff."

"I'd like more kissing." She smiled at him. "What other stuff?"

"Just other stuff."

"Like what?"

"You kiss like that and you don't know about the other stuff?"

"No. Tell me. What other stuff?"

He looked around to see if anyone was around.

"Like rubbing and grabbing," he said softly.

She gasped and stepped backwards. "Rubbing and grabbing what?"

He laughed. "Rubbing and grabbing each other. I thought they taught you this stuff in London?"

"They most certainly did not!"

"So who taught you about kissing like that and not about the rest?"

"NO ONE! I did not like the boys in London. They just tried grabbing me for a kiss and I would hit them hard in the arm."

He laughed, "No really. Who taught you?"

"You want to know who taught me?"

"Yeah"

"Really?" she asked coyly.

"Yeah!"

"You did you big idiot! You kissed me and I kissed you back. Geez Gregor. I told you I hated the boys in London. You're the only one I've ever wanted to kiss. Ever since we were kids. Geez." She walked away from him talking to herself. "Who taught you to kiss Winifred? Who? Who? Who?"

"Wait! What did you say?"

"You heard me."

"You wanted me to kiss you when we were kids?"

"Ugh!" she sighed.

"Why didn't you say so?" he pursued.

"You didn't even know I was alive. You just said you thought I was a pesky little sister. If I had told you that I wanted you to kiss me you would have run away or pushed me down." She walked away shaking her head "Boys!"

"So wait! No one taught you how to kiss like that?"

"Isn't that what I just said?"

"And you saved it for me?" he smiled.

"Yes Gregor. I saved it for you," she sighed.

"Well isn't that something?" he said putting his arm around her shoulder. "Isn't that something?" he said again proud of himself.

Winifred started running to get away from him and ran inside his parents home. "Emily can I help you get dinner started?"

"Thanks love, but, it's almost done. You can set the table."

"Good. I have a big problem and I need your help," she said getting the plates and the silverware.

"Is he ten hands high and goes by the name of Gregor?" she asked.

"What? No! I went to my house, my Da's house and it's awful. I can't live there. What am I going to do? I can't go back to London. I just can't!"

"Oh Winifred I am so sorry. This is too big a problem for just me to give my advice. Let's talk about it over supper and see if we call can't come up with something for you."

"I'm not going back to London," she said emphatically.

Dinner was a challenge. She couldn't look at Gregor. She stared at her plate pushing the food around. What do I do? Where do I go? She sat and waited for someone else to broach the subject.

"Well I say you just stay here until we come up with a better plan," Emily volunteered as the three others ate in silence.
The tension between Gregor and Winifred was like having a fifth person in the room.

"What's going on here?" David asked looking from Gregor to Winifred and then his wife.

Emily just shook her head no and that stopped David's questions for the moment.

"I just can't go back to London," Winifred said her voice cracking with emotion.

"No one is sending you back dear," Emily said softly.

"That house is not livable Da. Winifred said there are too many bad feeling in it," Gregor volunteered. Winifred nodded her head in agreement and wiped a tear from her cheek.

"All right so she stays here. We have room," David said looking from face to face. It was done! He settled it. Why wasn't everyone happy? "Someone tell me what's going on?"

"I appreciate the offer Mr. Wolcott, but, I can't intrude on your family like that."

"Mr. Wolcott is it? What is going on here? Someone better answer me!"

"Not now David. This is more important. If Winifred doesn't want to stay with us she doesn't have to. Where can she go? Who can she stay with?"

'I'm not going back to London!"

"We know!" The three Wolcotts said in unison and then started laughing.

Winifred's tears flowed down her face, but, she smiled just the same.

"I'll stay at Dooley's," Gregor offered.

"You can't stay there they have a new baby. You'll just get in the way," Emily answered.

"Winifred can stay at Dooley's," Gregor suggested.

Emily turned to Winifred. "Have you ever cared for a baby?" Winifred shook her head no.

"Well that's out. You really need to have experience with a baby to work with one."

No one could come up with a good solution. "Why don't we sleep on it and see if we **can** come up with a solution in the morning," Emily said as she got up to clear the dishes. Winifred got up to help her.

"Isn't that what I said?" David asked and no one answered him. They all went their separate ways.

CHAPTER 10

*W*inifred did not sleep well. She tossed and turned all night. Where can I go? Kept circling around and around in her head. By morning's first light she got up and put on her dress and walked to the property she grew up on. Out to her rock she went to sit and contemplate. She sat uncomfortably on the little rock and watched the sun rise in the sky. She listened to the birds cry and the water crashing against the rocks below. "Take my prayer to our Father little birds. Ask him what I should do? Where I should go?" The tears flowed down her face as she sat.

"Come with me," she heard a voice say. She closed her eyes and waited for the rest of her message. Surely her Father would tell her more.

"Winifred come with me." She turned around and saw Gregor standing behind her.

Wiping her face she laughed. "I thought God was telling me to go with him. Was that you?"

"Come on." He held out his hand to her. She took it and got up. He put his arm around her neck and pulled her in to kiss her brow. "I did not sleep at all last night thinking about you leaving. I thought how empty the house would be again without you there. You belong with us and you know it don't you?"

She agreed.

"Then don't fight it. Stay."

"I can't live there with you like a sister, Gregor. I'm not your sister."

"I know. I realized last night, for the first time, that you are supposed to be my wife, and, I gotta tell you Winifred that scared me. It scared the hell out of me."

"What are you saying Gregor?"

"That we should be together and not separate. Marry me Winifred. Be with me always."

"I would love to marry you Gregor. I have always wanted to be with you."

"We have to talk to Ma and Da.   Da is going to explode. Ma will calm him down, she always does."

They walked the rest of the way home with arms around each other. It felt normal and natural that they should be together like this. In some ways it felt like they were an old married couple. Together they walked into the house that was bustling with activity and stood in silence until everyone stopped and looked in their direction.

Gregor let go of Winifred and walked to the kitchen to talk to the hired hands. "Boys, I need to speak to my parents privately. Do you mind taking your meal outside today?"

"Not at all." They looked from him to Winifred and grabbed their plates and walked outside. No one said a word.

He motioned for Winifred to sit down and this time he sat next to her. David stood at the counter drinking his tea and stared at Gregor.

"David," Emily said softly. "Let's hear what he has to say." She dragged her chair next to his and made him sit down. She placed her hand on his hand and waited for Gregor to begin.

"I tossed and turned all night trying to figure out a place for Winifred to stay. Where could she go? Who could she help? Who would need her the most? When I thought of her gone from here I felt empty. Like it felt when she left the last time. I remembered how Ma said she felt alone and that's how I felt when I thought of her gone from here. I thought of every old man or old woman who could use someone to care for them and when I saw her helping them I felt alone and empty. "Why can't she just stay here?" I asked. I saw how happy Ma was and full of life this house was. And I said, "I want that. She belongs here." I felt a voice say, "She's not your sister, son." And that's when I knew. I knew she is supposed to be my wife. But, I'm scared Da. I never wanted a wife before. I don't know how to treat a wife. It's just Winifred and I want her to be with me always."

"And what about you Winifred? David asked. "What do you want?"

"I have loved Gregor as long as I can remember. When I was in London other boys wanted to kiss me and I was repulsed. They weren't

Gregor. I feel I belong here. I am home here and I want to stay here with Gregor."

"Is THIS what has been going on in my home?" David was furious.

"No Da. Nothing has been going on."

"No Sir."

"David! Don't jump to conclusions," Emily warned him.

"You knew this was happening?" he demanded from Emily.

"No I knew they were seeing each other as adults for the first time, but, I have not seen or heard anything that you have not seen or heard. Have you seen or heard anything?" she asked him.

"No, but..." He hesitated.

"No buts. They are young and falling in love. You remember the joy of first discovery. For heaven's sake David, when could they possibly have done anything? She just got back to town and Gregor works with you all day. This is fate stepping in and making things right. Your son is coming to you as a man and asking his father for advise and direction. Aren't you Gregor?"

"Yes Ma."

"And Winifred. Our sweet Winifred is back to make our lives whole again. Should we not embrace her as a daughter-in-law as much as we embrace her as our daughter?"

"OK Emily I get your point."

"I hope so David. Look at them. They both look scared as jack rabbits. Really children this should be a happy day. Have no fears and no worries just joy!"

They both let out a breath they did not realize they were holding.

Winifred smiled as she looked at Gregor. He smiled as he turned to her and kissed her on the lips.

"All Right!" David said trying to break them apart with his words. "You want to get married. What's next?"

"This whole thing, this revelation is new to me Da. It hasn't sunk in yet. Can't we wait a while before we make the next step," he asked staring at Winifred the whole time.

She moved her hand into his and gave it a squeeze. It startled him like a little shock. He felt her say, "We belong together." His look turned to surprise while Winifred just continued to smile.

They settled into a new routine. "My love," Gregor said to her when he came into the room after a long day at work. "I have missed you terribly all day."

"I know," She would say softly to him as he held her tight.

"How do you know?" he nuzzled her neck.

"When you think of me I feel it here," she said and put her hand on her stomach.

"How do you know it's me thinking of you," he looked at her smiling face.

"Because no one makes me happy and warm inside but you," she whispered and kissed him on the neck.

"Geez Emily. Were we that sappy when we first got together?" David asked rolling his eyes.

"Hush David. I think it's sweet. I've never seen either of them look so happy," Emily sighed.

"Well if it goes on much longer I'm going to be sick," he scowled.

"No you are not. Suck it up. You know it doesn't last forever. Let them enjoy it while it's fresh."

"What's for dinner?" David asked loudly.

"We've got meat and potato mash so go wash up while Winifred and I get it to the table."

"Come on son. Let's go wash up before they eat it all without us."

Gregor did not hear him. He was talking softly to Winifred.

"SON! LET'S GET CLEANED UP."

Gregor lifted his head and looked around "Da?"

"LET'S GO!" He motioned to the door.

"Something wrong?" Gregor asked as he followed his father out to the well.

"No we have to clean up for dinner. Do you think you two could..."

"What Da?'

"Not be so romantic all of the time? It gives your mother ideas."

"What kind of ideas Da?" he asked innocently baiting his father.

"Gregor. A man doesn't always want to talk so romantically to his wife all the time."

"Why not?"

"You'll learn. It's not the same after a while. Gets old. Could you save it until you and Winifred are married. Or, just not in from of your Ma and me."

"Sure Da. But I like talking to her. She's got lots of interesting ideas. Did you know she can tell when I'm thinking about her? Isn't that the damndest thing?"

"Yeah. She's special son. Let's go get something to eat." David shook his head as he followed his son back into the house. Gregor had it bad.

They all laughed through dinner. When the subject of the wedding came up Gregor and Winifred sat looking at each other silently.

"What are you thinking Winifred?" Emily asked.

"We decided on a month or two. However long it takes to get the church and festivities ready." She said turning away from Gregor and looked at Emily.

"When did you decide that?" Emily was surprised.

"Just now," Winifred said looking back to Gregor.

"I guess I missed it. I didn't hear you discussing it."

"Really? We discussed it at length. How long do you think it will take to get ready?"

"If I can get all of the church ladies going a couple of months would be fine. What are you boys doing about a house for these two?" She asked turning to David.

"We have our eye on a piece of property by the river, but, I know Winifred wants to stay near the cliffs, don't you Winifred?"

"Whatever Gregor wants is all right with me It doesn't matter to me as long as we are together."

"Better take her up on it boy while she is in a good mood. Let's talk to old man Shively in the morning. Maybe young love will inspire him to let go of a few acres. That way our properties will butt up against each other and we can add more cattle to the ranch. Never hurts to have more livestock. Who knows when we will have more mouths to feed." David patted Gregor on the back as he got up from the table.

"Ma. I'm going to take Winifred for a walk before we turn in."

"You go. I'll finish up here and find out what's eating at your father."

"Good. He's been acting weird lately." Gregor took Winifred by the arm and led her out of the house.

Emily found David looking out past the barn at the property owned by old man Shively. "What's going on David?"

"Did you hear them discuss the wedding at all?"

"No. Why?"

"Gregor made a comment that she knew what he was thinking. Do you think that's possible?"

"What I think is that these two were practically raised together and they know their way around this world that we raised them in."

"That must be it."

Gregor and Winifred walked hand in hand until they were out of sight of his family home.

"I used to sit on my rock and ask the birds to take my prayers to God. I guess it worked because he brought you to me."

"I like that. I like that a lot." He nuzzled her ear. Kissed her neck, her throat and returned to her lips for deep kisses.

"All right you two. Time to come in. Let's talk," David yelled into the night.

CHAPTER 11

*G*regor took Winifred's hand and pulled her close as they walked into the house together.

"First thing we need to discuss is sleeping arrangements." David started as they took their seats.

"It's not proper for you two to be under the same roof while you are engaged to be married. You, Gregor, will go and stay at Dooley's for a while."

"I thought you said I'd get under foot there?"

"You will but it's the best solution," David said.

"I could stay there. I don't have any experience with babies. but, I could learn. I like babies," Winifred offered.

"We thought about that. To start Gregor will be there. If it gets too tense you two will switch places. For now, you get your clothes and head on over there. Dooley and Sarah will understand when you tell them what is happening. If either of them gets upset with you being there, come back and we'll escort Winifred over there. You can see each other in the day light as long as someone is with you. You got that?"

"Yes Da."

"Yes sir," Winifred answered.

"We plan on speeding up this engagement, but, you still need a place to live. Even if old man Shively agrees to selling us some land it would be months before we could build a decent house. You sure your Da's place is unlivable?" David asked Winifred.

"It's terrible. Gregor can testify to it."

Gregor nodded his head in agreement.

"OK then. Let's get going. I want to talk to Dooley. See if he or Sarah know of a place that's vacant. Let's go!" David got up quickly and ushered his son upstairs.

Winifred sat in shock at the quickness of this decision and action.

"You will thank us later Winifred for now your safety is our concern. Once you are wed you will have more freedom. But for now, you are under my constant watch. Consider me your shadow. We have a Wedding dress to make and arrangements to prepare. Do you want to contact your Aunt for advise or participation in any of these plans?"

"She should be off to Europe. I don't know when she will be back. I am sure this little wedding would be too tame for her liking. I'm just a little country girl to her. But, thank you for suggesting it."

"Emily we are on our way. I'll be home late. There are a few things we need to discuss with Dooley. Don't wait up, although I know you will." He bent to kiss his wife. "Winifred get your sleep. these wedding plans take a lot of energy."

Gregor came down stairs with his clothes rolled all together.

"One kiss son and then we're out of here," David said.

The two accompanied by his parents had a chaste kiss and Gregor turned away. He turned back to her and said, "Me too," and then left.

"What was that?" his mother asked after he closed the door.

"Pardon me?" Winifred asked.

"He said, "Me too," and I didn't hear what it was in response to."

"I told him I loved him," she said as she moved to go up the stairs.

CHAPTER 12

A vacant cottage sat on the church property behind the cemetery. It had belonged to Sara's, mother's, sister's, nephew and had been donated to the church after he was lost at sea. It was perfect for their needs. A small two bedroom with a loft that overlooked the gardens surrounding the cemetery. The Wolcott men set out after work in the evening to refresh and repair the cottage.

The two married men took the opportunity to give Gregor advice on how to treat his wife. He found the information unnecessary and ridiculous. This was Winifred he'd know her forever.

Emily and Sarah at the same time helped her sew her dress and gave her advice on what husbands expect. All of it Winifred found embarrassing and horrifying. This was Gregor after all. She'd know him forever.

On the day of the wedding the bride was nervous and the groom impatient. It was most unusual that the groom's father escorted the bride down the aisle while his mother stood in as matron of honor. Dooley stood beside Gregor as best man.

The ceremony was short and heartfelt. The Pastor's words fell gently on the two people who only had eyes for each other. The glow on each of their faces radiated their love. When it was time for the groom to kiss his bride, Gregor was tender as he held her face in both of his hands.

The whole town turned out for the reception which was jovial and raucous. The music played loudly as Winifred sat serenely enjoying the festivities. The men hoisted Gregor into a ceremonial dance.

One drunken stable hand came up to the newlyweds and said, "For the bride's pleasure we anoint the groom with honey and oil so he may taste as sweet as she is." And then he poured some liquid onto Gregor's head.

David went charging after the hand and was helped in escorting him out of the church hall.

Winifred laughed as she tried to wipe the concoction off of Gregor's head and face.

"What do you say. Do I taste as sweet as Bill says you are?" He bent in for a kiss. Winifred obliged her new husband with a taste of their future. "Yes, my husband. You taste like perfection."

"I think it's time for us to leave," he said dragging Winifred out of her chair.

"We can't go before we have some cake. It wouldn't be proper," she scolded him.

They cut their cake and everyone cheered. The elder ladies took over cutting pieces for everyone there. Gregor and Winifred danced while feeding each other their cake. When the music stopped and the cake was eaten he whispered in her ear, "Can we go now?" and she agreed. They ran hand in hand out the back of the church and around the cemetery to their new home.

Gregor turned to Winifred and said, "Close your eyes." When she did he opened the door. He pulled her inside to see the finished house for the first time. "You can open them now."

She looked around at the freshly scrubbed walls and polished floor. "Oh Gregor it's beautiful!" she marveled. "Just what I wanted!"

"I know," he smirked. "I felt everything you wanted."

She smiled as she walked from room to room. Every little detail was perfect. She walked into the second bedroom and found a sheet of cloth covering a piece of furniture. "What is this?" She looked at him puzzled.

"Lift it off and find out," he said.

She removed the cover and found a glistening cradle underneath it. "What is this for?"

"It's for the baby you said we would have within a year," he answered trying to contain a smile.

"I never said that Gregor! I never said that!"

"OK," he laughed. "My Ma said we probably would have one that soon."

"You!" she laughed pushing him as she ran out of the bedroom. Gregor chased after her laughing as well and their honeymoon began.

Days and nights they spent in each other's arms. Making love was only interrupted by the occasional need to eat or sleep. They lost themselves in each other. With one exception. Winifred tested Gregor's sensitivities daily. She would slip out of his embrace at sunrise and go out to greet the day in prayer. When she wanted his company she would send a message telepathically. "Come find me."

Gregor woke with a start. Surprised his glowing bride was not in his arms. He got up and left the house knowing she would be outside facing the sunrise with two cups of tea in hand.

"How did I know you would be out here?" He greeted her with a kiss. Winifred just smiled. He was getting better and responding more rapidly that she had anticipated.

One morning he came outside to find her talking. "Not yet," Winifred said to no one there. "I'm not ready."

"Who are you talking to?" He asked taking his beverage from her hand.

"Your son tells me his ready and waiting."

"My son?" Are you with child already?" He turned her around to look at her face.

"No Gregor. He is waiting for us to create his opening. I told him I'm not ready yet. He will wait until the right time whether he wants to or not."

"So My Ma was right about giving us the cradle?" he said smugly.

"No your Ma was hoping to have another grand baby to spoil. She has no say in when we have children." She kissed his cheek and went inside to start their meal.

"Are you sure? She can be very persuasive."

"I am sure. This is between you and me. God knows when the right time will be. He will not be consulting your mother for advise on this issue."

"Does our son have a name?"

"Of course. What name do you like?"

"I think Gregor is a fine name."

"Sure you do. Really? Any other thoughts. I cannot call Gregor and have you both answer.

"How about Samuel?" she asked.

"No. How about Aillil?" he asked.

"Now you are being ridiculous. Think about what names you really like. How about Benedict?"

"You just liked Benjamin the neighbor boy," he teased.

"I did not. I only liked you. Come on now," she said softly. "Just think and feel. What name do you prefer?"

"I'll let you know. Let's eat first. Before I have to wear out my brain."

"How about Thomas?" she asked as she prepared their meal.

"Thomas is a nice name. Thomas Wolcott. Has a nice ring to it."

"More tea?"

"Yes. What about Adam? Adam Wolcott. Good strong name Adam."

"Hmmm. Adam is a good one," she agreed. She dished up their food and handed him a bowl. "Richard or Robert? No, doesn't feel right."

"My grandfather was Edward Wolcott."

"Very regal," she said. "Edward is a good one."

By the end of breakfast they had a half dozen names under consideration.

Gregor insisted they practice baby making just in case they forgot how it was done when the actual time arose.

Winifred agreed knowing she was playing with fire. Any opportunity would be taken by the anxious and ready soul. Her desire to please Gregor outweighed her unwillingness to be a mother so soon.

As it turned out the baby's urgency to be born overruled her desire to wait and she conceived him in their first month together.

CHAPTER 13

*H*er pregnancy was rough. The first stage made her violently ill. Winifred was worn out with the nausea and Gregor was beside himself with his inability to stop it.

"Ma I don't know what to do. She's just so sick all of the time."

"It will pass son. Let me see if I can find some herbs to calm her stomach. "

Emily came to the rescue bringing peppermint leaves to the cottage. Winifred looked awful. She was pale and her lips were dry.

"Oh my lass. Look at you. Let Mama Emily fix you up." Emily prepared some peppermint tea which Winifred glared at before taking a sip.

"That tastes good. I hope the baby likes it. I just can't lose any more of my meals." She rocked herself in the rocking chair Gregor got for her.

"Let me make some soup and toast for you."

"No smells please Emily. I can't stand the smell of meat right now."

"Not to worry. I'll make it at home and bring some right over. You continue to sip that tea."

"I will. Thank you Emily," she said resting her head on the back of the chair.

Emily left her and pulled Gregor aside. "She looks terrible son. Watch her and make sure she finishes all of her tea. Winifred says that smells are making her ill so I'll prepare it at home and be back shortly with some soup. You look like you could use a good meal yourself. "

"I'm OK Ma. I'm just worried about Winifred."

"You can't take care of her If you're weak. Give me a few hours and I'll be back."

"Thanks Ma." He smiled as he went to tend to his wife.

Winifred was dozing in the rocker which Gregor took as a good sign. True to her word Emily came back with some soup, a loaf of bread, and a pie.

"Let her eat what she wants in small amounts. Several small meals may be easier to handle than a large one."

"Thanks Ma. Everything looks delicious."

"I'll be back to check on you. Eat son you need you strength. Anything you would like for me to make?"

"Whatever you bring will be appreciated," he said.

Winifred woke as Emily was leaving.

"Ma brought some soup. Want to try a bit? She said small meals would be best."

"Yes. I'm starved," she said.

He gave her a small cup of soup and Winifred stared at it. Slowly she took a sip. "Mmm good," she sighed.

"Please go slow. I don't want to see it again."

"Me neither," she said taking her time. Winifred was exhausted after she ate. She handed Gregor her bowl. "I need to lay down," she told him as she started to get up.

"Sit with me a while Love. I don't get enough time with you these days."

Despite how she felt she stayed in the chair and looked at her husband. "What's wrong?"

"Just worried about you. I've never seen anything like this. Ma says it will pass."

"She's the one with experience. I'm counting on her to know what to do. Wish my Ma was here to tell me how she did it."

Emily came back later with more food. "This is for Gregor to keep his strength up. Someone has to take care of you son and I can't be here all of the time." Winifred looked over the home baked goods hungrily.

"How's our little mother doing?" Although Winifred stood a few inches taller than Emily. Her petite frame and recent weight loss made her look very fragile.

"So far so good. I ate some soup and it hasn't come back to visit."

"Good. Just go slow. Even though you may be hungry give it a bit before you have something else to eat."

"Emily did my Ma have a hard time when she was pregnant with me?" Winifred asked.

"Let me think. We didn't see much of each other except at church on Sundays. I do remember your Da coming to church alone on a few occasions saying she was ill. Could have been when she was carrying you. We didn't talk about things like that. Most girls had their Ma to help them over the rough parts. Every woman knew what was happening we never discussed it in public."

"Oh." Winifred felt let down. Any bit of information would sooth her longing for a connection to her own mother. "What about you? Did Gregor make you ill when you were carrying him?"

Coming out of the kitchen when he heard his name, Gregor joined the conversation carrying a big piece of pie on a plate.

"I didn't make you sick did I Ma?" He bent over to give his Ma a kiss on the cheek.

"Oh yes you did." Emily said patting him gently on the face. "Both you and Dooley gave me quite a time of it in the beginning, but, then it passed. With you it seemed to go quicker, but, that may be because I was tending to a very active little boy and did not have time to think of myself."

Gregor shoveled his pie into his mouth as Emily talked.

Winifred looked at the pie. "Oh that looks good. May I have a piece?"

Gregor looked to Emily.

"Give her a small piece son. She won't know if she can handle it unless she tries some."

Gregor came back with a tiny sliver. Winifred laughed looking at the pathetically small amount but took it eagerly. She took a deep breath before placing a small bit in her mouth chewed and waited. She shook her head. Not such a good idea after all. She lurched from her chair to find her basin and ran into the bedroom.

Gregor sighed in exasperation and shook his head. He came back to the front room with the pie and handed it back to Emily. "I'll have some at your house if Da doesn't finish it first." He turned and went to find Winifred. She was sitting on the bed with the basin in her lap. Gregor went to the pitcher on the side table and poured some water into a cup. He handed it to her and watched as she rinsed her mouth.

"I'll never eat pie again," she moaned.

He took the basin and walked it outside to dispose of its contents and rinse out the basin. When he returned Winifred was lying down her eyes closed. He ran his hand over her head. "Looks like it's soup and tea for you." When she didn't answer he went back to see his mother as she was getting ready to leave.

"At least she kept the soup down," he told her.

"When she wakes give her more peppermint tea. If she holds that down try a bit more soup. I'll talk to the ladies at church and see if they remember what soothed their stomach. I know it doesn't seem so now, but, It's a blessing having a child." She rubbed Gregor's arm. "She'll get over this I promise."

"Thanks Ma," he said as he escorted her out.

True to what most of the women said, Winifred's sickness left as quickly as it had begun.

She and Gregor played joyfully as they fought over who could eat the most. "Are you carrying a horse in there? I have never seen any woman eat so much."

"Oh. And how many women have you watched eat?" she asked.

"Just Ma and Sarah on a regular basis. Special occasions at church events. Most ladies just pick, pick, pick at their food. Not devour it like a barnyard animal."

"Who are you calling a barnyard animal?" She was shocked at his insensitivity.

"I'm not calling you an animal Winifred, I've just never seen you eat so much and so often."

"Hmm." She harrumphed as she made her way to the bed to lay down.

Gregor followed her and lay beside her. She turned her back to him.

"Aw Winifred. You know I love how you look. I was just kidding." He put his arm around her.

"Except when I'm eating." Her voiced cracked and tears fell from her eyes.

"Are you crying?" He was surprised.

"I've never been pregnant before Gregor. I can't help that I am hungry all of the time. I just can't get full. The least you could do is be more sensitive to my situation," she sniffed.

"I love your situation." He turned her toward him and stroked her back. Winifred's tears just kept on flowing. No matter how he tried to soothe her she took it the wrong way. Gregor stopped talking and just kept rubbing her back.

The next day at their midday meal Gregor finally broke down and spoke to his Da and brother.

"I don't get it. Whatever I say comes out wrong and she cries. She eats like a horse and when I mentioned it that made her cry even more."

Dooley and David looked at each other and laughed. "Whatever you do, don't tell her she eats like a horse," his Da warned.

"Sarah once ate a whole chicken in one seating. It's like their possessed. But say anything and you're sent out of the house. Take it from me little brother, the less you say the better off you will be."

"She's creating a life." Emily joined the conversation. "When you hold that child for the first time you'll forget what happened along the way to get you there. Counting ten little fingers and ten little toes all perfectly formed is the best medicine to what ails you now." She cut into a freshly made pie and served each of her men a piece. His Da and brother nodded in agreement as they took their pie and began eating.

"But Winifred..." he started.

"Winifred is responding to what's going on in her body. She cannot control it. It controls her. The sooner you accept it the happier you will be." Emily scolded him.

"And the sooner you get what you want." David chimed in rolling his eyes and looking at Emily.

Emily shook her head "That's all you boys ever think about."

"Well it is when it stops," Dooley added.

"Be kind to her Gregor and you'll get your Winifred back." Emily added as she left the table to start cleaning the dishes.

"Listen to your mother son. She's a wise woman," David said loudly hoping Emily heard him.

"Yeah and if you're lucky," Dooley added quietly. "You'll get the part when they're insatiable. It's the best part of the pregnancy."

David elbowed his son to be quiet and pointed to his wife.

Gregor got up quickly. "I think I need to go check on my wife." He said as he left the house.

"Yeah. You do that," Dooley said to no one as the door closed.

Winifred's pregnancy progressed normally and as night fell shortly before their first anniversary her labor began.

After dinner Gregor ran into his parents home. "Winifred is in labor. What do we do?"

"You'd think you haven't seen a birth before," His Da answered.

"Oh David. This is Winifred not his cow. Go home to her son and I'll get the midwife. Do what you can to make her comfortable and we'll be there soon."

"Thanks Ma." He kissed her cheek and ran out of the house as fast as he came in.

In the wee hours of the following morning while the men stood in the kitchen discussing what needed to be done on the farm that day and who would take over Gregor's work, Gregor stopped talking and held out his arm. "Wait!" He said stopping his Da and brother from talking. "He's here!" And a baby's cry was heard throughout the house.

Emily came out of the bedroom. "It's a boy!" she said wiping her face.

Dooley and David turned to Gregor. "How did you know?" Dooley asked. Gregor just shrugged as the two men patted him heartily on the back. He turned to his Ma, "Winifred is fine," she said. He gave her a great big hug and headed toward the bedroom to his wife's side.

"He's a beautiful lad," the midwife said as she cleaned the baby.

"Devon has finally joined us," Winifred said softly to her husband who had hold of her hand and was kissing her face over and over again.

"Devon McGuire Wolcott," he said looking at his son for the first time. "A nice strong name for a strong boy." Gregor uncovered the blanket to see for himself. Yes. Two tiny arms with ten little fingers waved spastically. The same for his legs with ten perfect little toes. And the little package that made all men proud of their creation right where it should be. Devon let out a hearty cry. "OK son," Gregor acknowledged as tried to reposition the blanket.

"Here let me show you how they like it," the midwife said giving Gregor his first lesson as a father. She tucked and rolled the blanket around him making the tiny tot look like a sausage. "Nice and tight just how they like it." Devon stopped crying immediately.

"That was amazing," Gregor acknowledged. He picked up the baby awkwardly.

"Hold him like this," the midwife said. "They need their head supported until they can hold it up for themselves."

Gregor thanked her and carried the baby out to the family for the men to see him for themselves. "Meet Devon McGuire Wolcott," he said proudly as the men turned to see the newest addition to their family.

"He looks just like you did when you were born," David said as he took his grandson in hand.

"That's not saying much," Dooley chimed in and Gregor gave his brother a shove. "Nice job," Dooley added as he looked over his father's shoulder at the new born.

CHAPTER 14

*T*heir second year together began with a whole new set of rules all determined by the new baby. Gregor started going home for his mid day meal to check on his little family. He didn't want to miss a thing when it came to Devon's accomplishments and, of course, he missed his wife.

On rare occasion he came back to work smiling and Dooley shook his head. "You always had the luck of the Irish."

"I am a lucky man indeed," he admitted.

"You ready for a second one so soon?" Dooley kidded him. "Winifred said there won't be any more so we're going to give Devon extra love."

"I guess it's up to me then to add to the family," Dooley boasted.

"You trying to tell us something?" Gregor asked.

"Yes. We didn't want to say anything yet, since you all are so over the moon about Devon, but, Sarah is expecting."

The men all cheered and patted Dooley on the back.

"You could have said something earlier," David said. "A new baby is always good news."

"When is she due?" Emily asked joining her men.

"She's still at that awful sick part, so, maybe in summer."

"That's wonderful. Another baby." Emily grinned.

Devon grew like he was reading a manual. Joy filled their home as he was applauded for each new accomplishment as if he were the master of the universe.

He was walking by his first birthday and his proud parents walked him all over town.

On bright sunny days Winifred took him to her favorite rock and sat him in her spot holding him tightly around the middle.

"Dat," he said pointing at the birds as they flew.

"That's a bird," she told him. "See the water. It splashes against the rocks." She pointed down the cliff to the water below.

"Dat," he said pointing to the water below them.

"Doesn't it sound nice and relaxing?" she asked him.

"Dat," he said.

"Shh. Listen to the water. Hear how nice it sounds hitting the rocks."

He leaned forward and then back to smile up to her.

"Yes the sound is so nice and tranquil. Here is where we ask the bird to take our prayer up to God. What should we ask for? How about a nice big cake for your birthday?"

"Dat," he said.

"Let's go home and wait to see if God answers our prayer."

Devon eagerly started walking and stopped mid way home. "Uppy Uppy!" he demanded.

"Someday soon you will walk all the way home on your own."

Birthday one was followed by birthday two and birthday three. Before birthday four Winifred took Devon to their special rock and sat with him as they listened to the water below. Coming toward them was a flock of birds in flight.

"What should we ask for this year?" She was hoping he would ask for little tools to help his father at work.

"I want to draw. Stuff to draw."

"You want paper and charcoal sticks?"

"Yes. I like to draw."

"You don't want tools to help Da at work?"

"No. I like to draw," Devin insisted.

"OK son. We shall see if God can bring you what you want."

Later that evening, after he went to bed, Winifred told Gragor what Devin had requested.

"I say we give him both. We already have some tools his size. He can learn to help me and have something for fun as well." Gregor kissed her neck and started rubbing her back.

"What if they don't have charcoal for drawing at the mercantile?"

"Then we'll make some for him. He's only four Winifred he doesn't need much He'll probably grow tired of it soon anyway. Boys his age go through lots of toys."

"I suppose you are right," she said. She had a nagging feeling inside of her that with Devon that was not the case at all.

Devon's birthday dinner with the family was a wonderful party. With Emily's help she prepared enough food to feed their growing clan and then some.

Dooley and Sara came with Amelia now age five and a half and Aaron age three. Sarah excused herself just as they arrived at the cottage and ran outside. Everyone looked to Dooley for an explanation. "Sarah's pregnant again, " he said with a sigh. "Just when it was starting to get good again we're right back with the awful part."

"Oh Dooley," Emily said as she went after Sarah to help her.

"Congratulations," Gregor and Winifred said in unison. They looked at each other and laughed.

"Care to join us?" Dooley taunted.

"Not on your life," Gregor said under his breath.

"We can't have any more," Winifred added softly.

"You could if you tried a little harder," Dooley kidded.

"Oh he tries plenty," Winifred kidded back.

"You get what you get," David said. "Emily would have liked to have had a daughter, but, it just didn't happen. Winifred's mother only had one child. Maybe it runs in the family."

"You can have one of ours, old man." Dooley patted his brother on the arm.

"Thanks," he mumbled.

Emily and Sarah rejoined the group and the festivities resumed.

Devon appreciated his gifts, but, rejoiced at the pencils and paper the most. He spent many an evening drawing contently. Winifred make it a point to hang his pictures on a special wall just for his art work.

Gregor took Devon with him to work regularly and taught him how to use his tools. "He's really very good with them. He listens tentatively and applies the right effort. He's just always more interested in drawing."

"Maybe he'll be a famous artist?"

"Maybe. Not much money or need for it in these parts."

"He's still young. Like you said before, little boys change as they grow." She tried appeasing Gregor but, they both knew that Devon was developing in ways beyond their control.

Birthday after birthday Devon grew more interested in different types of art. He wanted colors and ground seeds with oil to paint pictures. Despite his interest in art he went dutifully with his Da to work. If a barn needed repair, Devon was there for the fine details needed to square corners or make doors hang straight.

Dooley's family kept growing. Every other year another child was added. When baby number five was in the works the Wolcott men decided to build them a new house.

Despite his tender years, Devon's artistic talent was developed enough to help Sarah's request merge with the men's abilities.

He worked side by side with his father doing all of the finishing work as they moved room to room.

"You did this?" Winifred asked as she lovingly stroked the frame to the baby's room.

"Yes Ma. And all the other bedrooms as well," He said proudly.

"You have accomplished quite a lot Devon."

"Nah. It's really very easy."

Sarah waddled into the house as they were all touring it "I'm so glad to see you Devon. There's something I would like added in the kitchen."

He followed her into the large kitchen with lots of open cabinets. I hear the latest thing is to have doors on all of these. I suspect it is to hide what's inside. Could you make me little doors for these here on the bottom so the babies won't get into my supplies."

"Sure Aunt Sarah. Let me get my paper and we can figure out what you want."

Winifred and Gregor looked at each other with pride and then to their son who acted so grown up and had no fear of venturing into something new.

"How do you know how to do this?" Winifred asked Devon later as he sat over his paper with his pencil.

"It's the same thing I'm already doing only smaller." He had it all figured out. Made it simple.

The new baby was born in the midst of the chaos of construction at the new house. Devon worked diligently and slowly through his calculations and construction. His tenth birthday came while working on her kitchen project and Devon asked for some tools to be used in wood working that were not used or needed on the farm.

His mother happily went in search for them. Treated them delicately when she had them in her hands. She had no idea what they were for but Devon wanted them and needed them. How could she refuse?

Move in day came while Devon was still working on his project. Emily and Winifred offered to watch the children while the men did the work and Devon could get some work done in peace.

The older children stayed with Emily and David for a while giving Dooley and Sarah a chance to get the new house set up and the baby onto a regular schedule.

Devon continued to work at his project and, although Sarah was anxious to have it finished, she was warned not to pressure Devon. He was slow and methodical. One by one the cabinet doors got finished and Sarah marveled at his workmanship.

She came to collect her children on a day that Winfred was there helping. "Wait until you see my modern kitchen," she boasted. "It will be the envy of every woman in town."

Winifred and Emily could not wait to see it. They helped gather all of the children and their assorted possessions and walked them to the new house. The home was built on the land that had originally been allocated to Gregor and Winifred. The house stood in all its glory. A beautiful two story structure. With six small bedrooms and a larger one for the parents.

"How many children do you think they will have?" Winifred whispered to Emily.

"There's no guessing with the way they are going," Emily whispered back.

Winifred let go of the children's hand that she was holding when they entered the kitchen. She gasped at the workmanship her son had executed. There in a line up were perfectly sized little doors on little hinges all around the room.

Sarah beamed, "Isn't it glorious?" She opened and closed each door to give them a try.

Winifred joined her with equal enthusiasm. "My Devon did all this?" she asked as she too opened and closed each door.

"Yes our Devon did this and now everyone will want these in their homes."

Emily joined them and could not stop raving about what her grandson had done. "He is a genius I tell you. Wait until Maggie O'Brien sees this! Devon will have a profession for the rest of his life. Aren't we glad now that we got him all of those drawing tools?"

Winifred smiled to herself. Everyone was taking credit for what she had provided for her son It didn't matter. His workmanship stood for itself.

That evening at home as she and Gregor crawled into bed they talked about their son.

"You should have been there. Emily and Sarah raved about Devon's expert craftsmanship taking credit for helping him along."

"He did do a fine job," Gregor agreed.

"Fine job? It was perfection All those little doors on little hinges moving as they should."

"You are a proud Mama." He held her in his arms.

"Of course! What's the matter Gregor? You don't sound as proud as I thought you would be."

"I am proud, he applied himself and did a fine job, but, he is just a boy. Others will want him to do the same for them and what happens when he gets bored with their project? Besides, I like having him work with me. If he does other kitchen projects I will not see him."

"You are such a good man and a good father. He will always seek your counsel. He loves you. Even if he doesn't say it. He is growing into a fine man because of how you treat him. Someday he will be a good husband because of how you treat me."

Winifred and Gregor sought comfort in each other's embrace. Their son was growing up faster than either of them liked.

Over the next couple of years Devon did work on a few kitchens for neighboring families. The job were never as pleasant as the one he did for his Aunt Sarah and Uncle Dooley. The home owners were demanding and wanted the work done quickly. Devon in his youth did not have the patience, temperament, or experience to deal with the ungrateful customers.

"I cannot do what they want at the speed they demand." He cried in exasperation.

"Let me talk to them son. We can straighten this out," Gregor offered.

"No Da. This is my project. I should handle it."

"Tell them what you told us Devon. If they will not let you finish at your own speed then you must be done, Now!" Winifred was angry at how these ungrateful people were treating her son.

"But, I am half finished."

"Devon. Your Da gave you his suggestion and I gave you mine. Go out to our rock and take it to God and wait for the response. Either that or finish what you have started and take no more projects. I will not have you upset our home with their inconsiderate stupidity." She went outside to release the tension he brought into their home.

"You heard us Devon. Decide what you want to do and do it. You know you always have work with me."

"Thanks Da. I need a break. I'm going for a walk."

"Don't stay out too long. You know your mother worries."

"Yes I know," he said as he left their home.

"Where is he going?" Winifred asked when she came back inside.

"He's going for a walk. He knows not to be gone too long."

Devon walked to the church and sat in the pews. It was a comforting place that gave him the space to think. Unfortunately the people he had done work for also went to this church. He worried that those people would seek solace at the church when he was there.

He left the church and continued walking. There was another place that always intrigued him. He walked several towns away to the Monastery Tallaght and stood just looking at the building. He looked at it like a builder. How did they construct it? Big grey stone blocks. A huge building with no windows! He stood across the street and just looked at it. Behind the wrought iron fenced yard were young boys playing. Just the sight of this building relaxed him. He did not know what he was going to do with his problem, but, he liked standing there and just looking at the Monastery.

He turned and found his way home. His mother was sitting by the fire when he got home. Mending clothes she looked up when he entered. "How are you? Did you decide what you are going to do?" she asked.

I'll go to the Abernathy's house in the morning and explain. Either they let me work at my own pace or I am done. I cannot work with the pressure they impose. If they want me to finish then I will. If they cannot wait then I'll be done now. Either way no more kitchens for me."

"That's good son. Sounds like you came to the right decision."

"Thanks Ma. And thank God for me."

She smiled "You know me too well."

Devin finished the project and was grateful not to have to work in private homes again. He went back to work with his father, but, his heart was not into it. During their evening private conversation Gregor shared with Winifred, "Devon spends a lot of time staring off into space. I don't know what he is thinking. He doesn't confide in me."

"Oh Gregor, I pray for his safety and direction and I am told he is fine and protected. I guess we need to have faith that he is where he needs to be."

Devon began to spend more and more time walking to the Monastery. He could not explain it. He was just drawn there. One day he got up enough courage to go inside.

"Yes son, what can we do for you?" A man not much older than himself approached him.

"I've come by here many times and I just wondered what you did in here all day."

"We pray and we teach. A simple life but a rewarding one. Do you need some prayers? Are you in need?"

"No. No. My Ma taught me to pray when I was little. And I'm fine if you mean am I hungry. No, I'm just drawn here. Do you mind if I just sit here a while?"

"You are most welcome to stay as long as you like. We will begin our next prayer path soon. You may join us if you like. I am Brother Michael, and you are?"

"Devon. Devon Wolcott."

"Brother Devon you come back as often as you like." Brother Michael left him alone.

Devon felt he had been welcomed by the grace of God. Being called Brother Devon opened up a feeling that went deep to his core. He was at peace. He felt he had found a door that he had been looking for. He sat through the prayers and did not know what to think. It was strange and comforting at the same time. He left in a daze. He went home and said nothing to either of his parents.

At work the next day he begged off early saying he felt ill and went to the Monastery instead. Several times a week he felt ill and sought refuge at the Monastery.

Most of the men there told him similar stories to his own. They had families but did not belong in their world. They tried their hand at menial labor or worked at home but only felt alive in the house of God. He went to his Mother's rock and sent his prayer up with birds only to have his feeling verified. He belongs in the house of God.

It took Devon months before he could broach the subject with his parents. Christmas was coming and he just could not go on working with his Da. He loved his family deeply so the conversation he was about to have with them was painful.

"Ma, Da it's been coming for some time." No not like that.

"Da, Ma you may be wondering where I've been." Yes, that was better.

Winifred came into his room. "Why don't you tell us what is the matter son, so we can help you figure it out." She opened the door he was afraid to walk through.

"Where's Da?"

"He's cleaning up at the well He'll be in soon come out and talk to us. You know we are on your side no matter what the issue is."

"I'll be out in a moment," he told her.

Winifred stood pensively by the fire. Her son was in trouble and she was ready to help. "God help me to help him," she prayed.

Gregor came in and saw her by the fire. "What's going on?" He asked her as Devon made his way out of his room. They both turned to watch him.

"Sit down Ma, Da."

"I can't Devon just tell us and we will help as best we can."

"There's nothing wrong, but, I've come to a decision."

They stared at him waiting.

"Devon?" she asked.

"I love you both, you know that. I just can't go on working with Da, I just can't."

"Is that it?" Gregor asked.

"Is it a girl? We were concerned it might be a girl," Winifred asked.

"A girl! What girl? No, God, it's not a girl. For a long time now I have had a pull to something different and I just did not know what it was. When I worked on those kitchens for those awful people I just couldn't take their criticism. So I went to find peace in the house of God."

"You went to church?" she asked.

"Not exactly, well yes. I went to the Monastery at Tallaght. First it was odd and then I got to like it. It's like everything you ever taught me Ma and more. So much more. I talked to the brothers and they welcomed me in. I feel like I belong there. Ma, Da I want to be a monk." He let out a big sigh.

A monk. A MONK! He wanted to be a monk.

"Say something," he urged.

"A monk is quite a big step Devon." She did not know what to say. Gregor left the house without saying anything. Devon moved to go after him and Winifred stuck out her arm to stop him.

"Leave him alone for a while. He is as shocked as I am. This is not something we foresaw for you. Are you sure? A monk son?" she asked.

"Ma. I hate working with animals. I am an artist. I told them they needed to add windows to their building and they were excited by my ideas. Imagine that. I get to live in the house of God and I get to do what I love best. Create and construct. They even suggested colored glass windows. Imagine me creating something that important? It's everything I ever wanted."

She knew right then she had lost him He found his passion and his comfort. All the things she had with Gregor their only child had found at age thirteen in the house of God. She had led him there as a baby and God was taking over. He was so young to be making such a big decision, but, make it he did.

"Go to bed son and rest. Your Da has to deal with your news in his own way. He will come around as I will. Everything will work out as it was planned."

"Thanks Ma. I knew you would understand." He kissed her quickly on the cheek and went back to his room and closed the door.

CHAPTER 15

*W*inifred sat up in the front room waiting for Gregor to come home. Her head was spinning all she could do was pray. "Please bring me peace and tranquility. This news is quite a shock. Please bring me peace and tranquility. I need harmony and balance in my home and my life. " She said it over and over again trying not to let the upset into her heart.

The thought came to her. "He has found his peace. Who am I to judge where he finds it?" She let that sink in and then she was fine. "He HAS found his peace. Who am I to judge where he finds it?"

Relaxed she got up and went to bed alone. In the morning she got dressed to go to her in laws house She was certain Gregor had gone there.

She knocked on Devon's bedroom door.

"Yes," he called.

"I am going to Gram's house. I'll be back soon. Get something to eat if I am late."

"Da?" he asked.

"I'm going to find him. I'll be back."

She walked to her in laws home remembering how she felt about Gregor as a young girl. Here she was again looking for her love. She knocked softly on the door and Emily met her.

"He was here and then he left. He is shocked and completely crushed. He does not know what he did to Devon, but, he feels guilty. I tried to talk to him. He is just in a state of shock. He said there was someplace he had to go and he left this morning. Can't you do that thing you two do to call to each other?" Emily asked.

Winifred laughed. "You know about that?"

"You used to do it all the time before you got married. David and I were always surprised by it. No two people were ever able to do what you two did. Now your beautiful boy needs that connection to be his strength as he makes a major change."

"You are right and I came to that same conclusion last night. As closely connected as Gregor and I are, I cannot make his decisions for him. I do have an idea of where he might be."

She closed the door behind herself and stood out in the open. From her heart she asked, "Where are you my love?" and sent it out into the either. Without direction she started walking. She found herself going to her spot on the rock. Sitting like a little lost boy was Gregor. His arms on his knees looking out at the sea.

"I never understood why you liked this spot so much," he said without turning around. "Even Devon would come here on his own. So I came to see what draws you here and maybe somehow it would help me to understand how our boy got so mixed up that he wants to run to a monastery."

She went to her knees behind him and put her arms around his middle like she did for Devon when he was little. "I watch the water hitting the rocks and I listen. I let the sound of the ocean calm me down. Just relax to the sound. Relax. All is well. Our son is content."

Gregor took a deep unsteady breath. She relaxed her grip and put her hands on his shoulders and gently massaged his neck.

"Relax and let go of the pain. All is well. Our son is at peace. He is not dead. He is not gone. He has found his true calling. Like you, I worried all night and then I asked myself, Who am I to judge where he belongs? Who are we Gregor to be so selfish as to want him in a life that makes him so unhappy? He loves us and it is that love that has brought him to a higher love. Not the love that I would choose for him, but, one he has chosen for himself. We have each other. He has our love to take with him into his future. Certainly we want our son to have all that he yearns for. Don't we?"

He took her hand from his shoulder and kissed it. "You always know."

"I don't. But I know where to go for the answer. Come let us go love our son the way we do best. I am certain he had a fitful night waiting for you to tell him you still love him."

They walked hand in hand. Taking a deep breath before they went inside. Devon was standing next to a pile of his possessions outside of his bedroom door.

Winifred gasped. Gregor moved forward to engage his son. "Sit down Devon and we will discuss this."

"You can't stop me," Devon started.

"We're not going to stop you. Your mother and I were very surprised by your announcement. It has taken each of us some time to deal with what you said. We have some questions for you first before we take the next step. Grant us that much."

"All right." He went to sit down and grabbed a pillow to put in front of his stomach.

"I'm going to start breakfast." She filled the kettle with water. This simple ordinary activity would help her stay focused and balanced as they went into the unknown.

"First. Is there something I did to drive you to this decision?" Gregor started with his biggest fear.

"No Da. Working with you is great. Helping at Aunt Sarah and Uncle Dooley's home made me feel like I was starting to really matter. You weren't keeping me with you to get me out of Ma's way. When Aunt Sarah asked me to fix her cabinets I felt I was doing something important. As soon as I started doing the same work for those other people, I don't know, I felt like I was going in the wrong direction. I started walking after work to get rid of those bad feelings and I found myself at the Monastery. At first I just stood outside and looked at that building. It was amazing! It took me a long time before I went inside and that was unbelievable. It felt right being there. The brothers said I could stay and pray or I could go. They were so nice. We started talking about what I do, you know, draw and construction. They said they needed work done there. They didn't ask me to come and live there, but, it just feels right. I feel like I belong there. They're the friends I always wanted."

"You can't work there and live here?" Gregor asked.

"No Da."

"Your father and I love you," Winifred started. "You know that will never change no matter where you go or what you do. Of course, we want you to stay with us. We are a family. But we understand that you feel that this is where you belong. If you get there and sometime later you change your mind you are always welcome to come back. You understand?"

He shook his head in agreement.

"You are always welcome here. It is your home too. " She poured some tea for each of them. "We want you to go with our love and we want you to go with peace in your heart that you are making the right decision."

"Thanks Ma."

With tears in her eyes Winifred kissed his head. "That offer is forever son."

"OK Ma. Can we go now?"

"Now? Are they expecting you to move in now? Today? Right this moment? Can't we share our meal together first? It might be the last for..." She did not know when or if she would see him again.

"Son. You sprung this on us last night. Surely you understand we have more questions about your welfare that to just let you go there. We want to meet, whoever is in charge. Find out how and where you will stay. God entrusted you to us. This is a monumental move with changes that affect all three of us for all time. Let's eat first and you can tell us about where you will live and what you will do there," Gregor insisted.

"But they are expecting me!" Devon insisted.

"Well they can expect you and your parents to show up together. After we have the breakfast your mother has prepared for us." Gregor ushered Devon to the dining table where Winifred had served up his favorite breakfast meal.

"Leave your belongings here and we will bring them to you if you are truly able to stay. Don't be surprised if they send you home today and make you wait." Gregor instructed him.

"Why do you say that Da? I'm ready to go."

"I know you think you have given it a great deal of thought, but, the church has their own ideas and ways of taking in their brethren. "

They waited while Winifred washed and dried the dishes. Walking in silence Winifred's mind wandered to the day he was born. The day he took his first step and the times he sat on her rock pointing to the birds. A tear trickled down her face. He wasn't fully grown and he wanted to take this great leap into his future.

Gregor saw her wipe away the tear and put his arm around her shoulder. He kissed her head and whispered in her ear. "I feel the same." Acknowledging the close union they share.

The size of the Monastery was daunting. A large grey stone building with its iron fence surrounding young boys who were kicking a ball around on the grounds. The boys were calling to each other as they played.

Devon opened the gate and waited for his parents to enter before closing it behind himself. "It may be prayer time. If it is, we must be quiet and sit in the back of the chapel until it is done."

Winifred was overwhelmed by the size of the chapel. Long wood pews filled the massive room. Looking around she was amazed at how dark it was. Candles lit the room but no windows were anywhere. Monks in prayer was a beautiful sight. Their voices rang in deep rich tones harmonizing during their chants. It was unusual and soothing. As they exited the chapel many of the monks nodded to Devon as they passed him. He nodded back to them and seemed more at ease than Winifred and Gregor wanted.

After all of the monks had left the chapel they were met by a very large robust man in his dark brown robe. He dressed just like all the other younger men. Father Hesper he called himself and offered to talk to them in his office.

"Your son has shown quite an interest in our order. I must admit his knowledge of construction and his creative talents would be most appreciated. We have talked extensively about opening walls to let some light in. This building was built at a time that religion was considered unacceptable. There were many attacks and the building was constructed as a fortress as well as a house of worship. Your son's brilliant ideas would bring this old war horse into the fourteenth century in a style that would encourage worship and release the old focus on fear."

"We are concerned, sir, that he is making a rash decision that will affect his future adversely. Is there an age when men are admitted? Or, a trial period when they can live here and be released if it doesn't work out?" Gregor wanted his son home.

"Men take their vows at any age. We prefer that they are older, however, Devon seems convinced that he belongs here. It is a hard sell to convince a young man to chose something else when he has his head set in one direction."

Gregor understood this but he still wanted his boy back home. "Where would he stay if he lived here?"

"Each man has a private space. The common grounds are where we dine and work together. We have a school here for orphaned boys. Gardens out back that grow what we eat. We are self contained as far as taking care of our own needs. Devon has made friends quickly with some of our brethren. They take their vows once they have progressed in their studies and proven to be committed to the faith. Each man must decide this for himself."

"What if he wants to come home or if his family needs him?"

"He is not being kept here against his will. If his presence is needed at home for any reason he is not forced to stay here. We find most men, once they decide to join us, prefer to stay here. We ask that during the first months that the family refrain from visiting. This gives the young man space and time to adjust to his new life style. Our prayer path is rigorous and takes some getting used to," he laughed jovially. "Let me get Brother Michael to show you around. He and Devon became fast friends. I realize this is a big decision that you must make as a family. Devon is most welcome to join us whenever you see fit to let him go. I trust I will be seeing you again soon." Father Hesper walked to the door and spoke to the man outside. "Please get Brother Michael. Devon and his parents would like a tour of our building and grounds." He turned back to the Wolcott family. "Do not hesitate to find me if you would like more information. Ah, here is Brother Michael now."

"Brother Devon you came back so quickly. I'm glad to see you. Are these your parents?" Michael's smile was warm and friendly.

"Yes my parents. Winifred and Gregor Wolcott. This is my friend Brother Michael."

Michael gave them a small bow as a greeting and directed them toward the hallway. He walked them slowly through the building showing them an empty living quarter. A very small room barely large enough for the bed and night table next to it. They walked to the very large dining hall and outside into the garden. The vegetable garden was massive and there were cows grazing in the field beyond the garden. He directed them into the back entrance to the pulpit. They walked through the area where the elders prepared for their service and into the chapel. He stood in the middle of the room and faced the wall behind the crucifix. "Did Devon tell you about his plans for adding glass to our Abbey?"

Gregor and Winifred looked at each other and said, "No," in unison.

"It's a beautiful drawing of the colored glass he plans to use to build it. It will make our humble Abbey look like a Cathedral. It is very impressive. You should show them Devon. I am sure they would like to see you work."

"Thank you Brother Michael for your time," Winifred said.

"We would like to speak to Father Hesper again," Gregor added.

"Certainly. Right this way." He directed them behind the chapel to the hallway of offices. His door is second on the left."

Gregor knocked on the door and waited for a response.

"You may enter," the voice boomed.

"Father Hesper. We are ready to leave. Should we decide to let Devon join you, when is a good time for us to return?"

Devon held his breath. Was his father really ready to let him go?

"During the week would be best. Sunday is God's day and we are in prayer all day. Good to see you again Devon. Thank you for bringing your parents to meet me. Enjoy your day." He dismissed them and returned to his paperwork.

Devon walked with his parents and felt their stress. When would his parents realize this is where he belongs? He walked slowly off the Monastery grounds and looked longingly at the building. Gregor waited to get home before he talked to his son.

"So you think this is where you want to live?" Gregor's questions began.

"Yes Da."

"And what will you do when you miss your mother's cooking?"

Devon laughed.

"I am serious son. What if you don't like what they make to eat?"

"Da. It's just food." He laughed and shook his head.

"You are still a growing lad. I have seen you eat your weight in your Ma's potato mash and kidney pie. I've seen you devour one of your grandmothers fruit tarts in one sitting. You think they cook like your family?"

"I don't know Da."

"Did you see how small their rooms are?" Gregor persisted.

Devon signed.

"Did you? You'll go stark raving mad living in a room that small!"

"I'm not staying in my room all the time Da. There's lots of work and prayers to be done."

"And what about prayer? A whole day in prayer every week. Do you think God wants to hear that much from you?"

"Oh Da."

"Oh Da. Is that all you can say? What is it about that place that draws you away from us Devon? Why there and not here in our home?"

Winifred felt his pain. His father's torment was her torment as well. His desperate questions brought tears to her eyes. They were losing their son and there was nothing they could do to stop it. "That's enough Gregor," she said and walked out of the front room and went to her bedroom. She sat on her bed and felt like crying. Why did this have to happen so soon?

"Someday you'll understand Da." Devon said as he left the house and slammed the door behind him.

"What is wrong with this family?" Gregor yelled. " One day we are fine and the next day everything is upside down!"

"Didn't you hear him?" Winifred got up and went to the bedroom door. "He told you how much he hated working with the town folk and how much he felt he belonged with the men at the Monastery. It's not about you Gregor. It's about him! His desires. It's his life. It hurts me too. God knows it hurts me too, but, who are we to decide his future? Do you really want him miserable and by your side? Or, do you want him happy doing what he feel he has to do? Did you see him at that place? He was relaxed. They like him there. They admire his work. He wants to be there Gregor. He loves us, but, we are only his parents we are not his future. His future is calling to him and we are the weights holding him back."

"Winifred." He hung his head. "I just don't want to lose him like this."

"I know Gregor. I know. But, he is not dead. He is alive and, God willing, will thrive in their presence. Did you see what he envisioned for that church? Big glass windows of different colors. Can you imagine sunlight coming through colored glass into that chapel? It sounds amazing. And our son, your son, wants to create that. How can we deprive God of all that talent?"

"Why aren't you more angry?"

"What good would being angry get me? He's made up his mind. My anger isn't going to change that. Come let's go talk to our boy while we can. My heart breaks for our loss and is overjoyed for his decision for his future. This is a big step for him. One that will influence the rest of his life. Let us celebrate his life like we do every year. Let us be the parents he needs us to be."

Gregor got up and put his arms around her shoulder. They walked in silence out to find their son.

Devon was sitting in the yard waiting for them. "Ma. Da." he said as they came to him.

"Come inside son, we need to talk," Gregor said.

Devon entered the house and sat down. He jiggled his foot nervously waiting for his father to continue.

"Your mother and I have discussed this in detail and we want you to know the truth. Our hearts are broken. But, we want you to have the future you want and think you deserve. We ask that you give us this day to hold you and love you before we turn you over to the Monastery."

Devon jumped up and hooted. "You are really going to let me go?"

"We are son," Winifred answered.

CHAPTER 16

"*T*hanks Ma." He grabbed her and hugged her.

"Thanks Da." He gave his father a big hug too.

"What should we do with our last day together?" Gregor asked.

"I think we should start by seeing your parents and then Dooley and Sarah before we have a family outing." Winifred suggested and the two men agreed.

They shared a quick meal and made their way to the family. It was a bitter sweet goodbye. Lots of hugs and promises by Devon that he would keep in touch. Everyone knew it would not happen. Once he was gone he would be gone from them forever. Dooley took the news better than the rest of them. Rough housing with Devon and telling him he was happy that he wouldn't have to see him around his wife anymore. Devon blushed with embarrassment at the comment. Sarah was sweet thanking him again for the fine job he did on her kitchen. Devon blushed again but stood a little prouder for the complement.

Winifred packed a picnic and the three of them went to her rock and relaxed together. Gregor asked Devon about the window he was going to install at the church. They discussed the construction in fine detail. Winifred stood back and watched with tears in her eyes as father and son came together for the last time.

"Let me know if you need some help installing the window son. It may be quite a project for the Brothers."

"Thanks Da."

It was the offer of support she knew her wonderful husband would give at any time to their only child. She made his favorite dinner that night and Devon said grace.

"Thank you Father for blessing me on my path. Thank you for the two wonderful parents who have brought me to you. Bless this home with prosperity and joy. And for all that we are about to receive we are most humbly grateful."

Winifred stared at her boy, and for the first time saw the man he was to become.

Gregor said, "Amen."

The next morning they got up, they ate, and walked their son to his new beginning. At the door to the Monastery Winifred broke down and wept. "I love you so much. No matter what happens I will always be your Mama."

Devon held her in a strong embrace until her weeping subsided.

"My boy," was all that Gregor could say. Devon threw his arms around his father's neck and held on.

He stood back and smiled broadly. "Here I go," he said.

Father Hesper came out to greet them. "You have a fine son here. You should be very proud of his work and his dedication to God."

"Thank you," Winifred said wiping her eyes. Gregor shook his hand and the two left their son to the unknown. They held each other as they walked home and did not let go for the rest of the day. That night they slept wrapped in each other's embrace.

The house was brutally quiet. Winifred left Devon's room as it was and closed the door. It was the only way she could feel his energy. Slowly they grew to accept his absence. The quiet that was so harsh at the beginning became the norm. Gregor went back to work at the family ranch and took on most of the responsibility. David was slowing down and Dooley became a father for the sixth time. Days became weeks. Weeks became months. Months became years.

The hardest times were on Devon's birthday. Winifred still had the family over and they gave a toast to his life and his health in his absence.

"Today he is seventeen. I wonder what he looks like?" she said feeling melancholy.

"I am sure he is a strapping lad," Emily offered.

"Looks like his Da, but, trimmer like his Ma," Sarah added.

"Do you think he eats them out of house and home?" Winifred asked laughing.

"I am sure of it." Emily laughed with her.

"Thank God I have mostly girls," Sarah said crossing herself.

The next day Winifred was cleaning up from the party. Gregor was getting ready to go to work. Distracted by the need for repairs on the barn roof.

"Da should put a new roof on it instead of continually making us repair this old one," he said as he finished dressing.

Winifred felt awful. Something wasn't right. "Why don't you stay home today? I feel a chill coming on." She wanted him home to take care of her.

"You all right?" he asked kissing her forehead.

"No I don't feel right. Please stay home with me."

"I'll come home early. That old roof won't go anywhere with all of the work we've done on it."

She hugged him hard. "Hurry home. I miss you when you are gone."

"I won't be long." He kissed her cheek and went to work.

Winifred continued to clean the house and still felt awful. She felt the urge to sit down and when she did she felt a cold, harsh snap in her gut and she knew.

"G R E G O R !" she screamed.

She sat staring into space. Bursting into her house without knocking was Dooley.

"Come quick there's been an accident! " He grabbed her by the arms and pulled her to her feet.

"Dooley. He's gone," she said.

"We don't know that for sure. Come on Winifred." He dragged her as he ran. But, she knew. She felt the warmth leave her body. Like a big knife stabbing her and leaving her drained. She had heard the sound of a big book slamming shut and a voice saying, "It is done!"

They ran to the barn where a group had gathered and laying on the ground motionless was her beautiful Gregor.

Emily was beside herself crying as David dragged her away from her lifeless son. She saw the ranch hands wiping the sweat from their faces while the Pastor stood over Gregor saying a prayer.

"Father let Winifred in," Dooley called. She move to his side and dropped to her knees. There was nothing to say. He was gone. All of her men had left her. She looked up to Dooley. "Get Devon!" Dooley looked at her. "You must get Devon!" she insisted.

"OK Winifred we'll get him. We'll get Devon."

Somehow the arrangements were made for the funeral. Winifred was in such a state of shock all she could do was stare into space. People talking sounded like they were far away. And then he was there. The vision of a young Gregor approaching her wearing a brown robe.

"Mother," he said in a deep voice and embraced her.

"Oh Devon. Oh Devon he's gone. How could he leave me? How could he leave me so soon?" She wept in her son's strong arms.

"It's OK Ma. Everything is going to be OK."

"How son? How could this be? We had a wonderful life. A beautiful son. We had it all. How could he leave?"

Devon held his frail mother in his arms. He looked around for Dooley. "What happened?"

We were working on the roof and he fell. Hit his head. Gone in a flash," Dooley said wiping his eyes.

Devon spoke at his father's funeral. Winifred did not hear a word. He held her and walked her home. He thanked everyone for their well wishes. Wrapping her in a big blanket, Devon started a fire and made some tea. He forced her to drink it and eat some pie.

"I'm not hungry," Winifred said.

"I know, but, no one makes pie like Gram," he said lovingly.

After her meal he walked her to bed. "Sleep Ma I'll be right out here."

She slipped into a restless sleep. When she woke she called, "Gregor."

"No Ma it's me Devon."

"Son. You're here?" And then she remembered the terrible event that brought him home. "I am sorry I took you away from your place. "

"Don't be sorry. I need to be here. You ready to eat? The neighbors brought food."

"You eat. I'll have something later."

"Can you sleep or do you want to sit by the fire?"

"A fire sounds nice." Devon helped her to the front room.

"Father Hesper will be here soon. I need to speak with him."

"Sure son whatever you need."

When Father Hesper arrived Winifred stood to greet him. "You'll excuse me I need to rest."

"Certainly Mrs. Wolcott. Devon and I will be right here when you get up."

The sounds of the two men speaking lulled her to sleep. When she woke it was dark. She got up to see if Devon was still there. She found him on the chair by the fire alone.

"Your friend is gone? "

"Father Hesper had to return to the Monastery. He will return when he can."

"And you. When will you return?"

"I am here for you Ma. I'm not going back yet."

"Thank you Devon. This means a lot to me. When you left before it was I consoling your father. Who knew you would be back to console me?"

"Ma. Who owns this house. Did Da ever buy it?"

"I don't know. It may still belong to the church. Why son?"

"Just asking," he said.

He made her a plate of food for her and took some for himself. They were chatting when Father Hesper returned.

"Father, I need to go out for a while. Could you stay with my mother. I won't be long."

"Are you all right with that Mum?" Father Hesper asked her.

Winifred agreed and Devon slipped out. "Would you care for something to eat? Our neighbors have outdone themselves. There is no way I will be able to eat all of this food before it goes bad."

Father Hesper got himself a plate full of food.

"We have not heard from Devon since he left four years ago. How is he doing at your church?"

"Your son has adjusted very nicely. He has learned his prayers and has taken his vows. The window he promised is under construction. He works slowly but diligently. His father consulted with him at the abbey on a few occasions. Did you know this?"

Winifred was surprised. "No! He never said anything to me. I would have liked to have known that."

"Perhaps he did not want you to go through the grieving process again."

"You are probably right."

Devon returned and sat the them. "Ma I asked Father Hesper to join us here because I have something big to discuss with you that involves us all."

She looked at both men. "All right son. Are you OK?"

"Yes Ma. I am fine It is you I am concerned about. I just talked to the Pastor about this house. Just as I feared Da never bought this cottage. It is a part of the church property. The Pastor said you are welcome to stay, but, he is not certain that another couple won't need a house in the future."

"But this is my home!" she cried.

"Ma listen to me. It is part of the church property. It does not belong to you. Without Da there is no one to take care of it. How will you live? You have no one to take care of you."

"Devon. My God, I'm going to lose my home too?" She was slipping back into shock.

"No Ma. Listen to me. Are you listening?"

"Yes son. I hear you."

"Good. I talked with Father Hesper at length and told him about you. How you taught me about God and how to pray. He said it is because of you that I am such a devoted Monk. "

She smiled warmly at her son.

"It is because you are of strong morals and filled with spirituality that he has agreed to make you an offer."

She looked at Father Hesper.

"We want you to come with us Ma and stay at the Monastery. There are no women there so this is a very special offer."

"Son?" Winifred was confused.

"Mum. I have discussed it with the other Brothers and the church hierarchy. Because you are Brother Devon's mother and under the present circumstances, we have room for you to stay at the Monastery. Everyone works there Mum, and you would be no exception. We have need for housekeeping help, and if you decide to join us, that would be your duties. Your quarters would be secluded away from the men in a private wing off of the sanctuary. We will provide all of your meals and you would be the only mother permitted to see her son regularly on Monastery grounds. There are many young boys in the orphanage who could benefit by a woman's influence especially one who is so morally grounded. This would be a great help in their development," Father Hesper concluded.

"What do you say Ma? It is the best solution to all of our problems."

"Devon I am overwhelmed and I am honored. I need some time to think about it. Can you wait until morning for my response?"

"Sure Ma."

Father Hesper got up. "I must return to the Monastery. Please be assured that we want you to join us. It could be the answer to all of our prayers." He bowed slightly. "Brother Devon I will send someone to retrieve the response in the morning." He turned to Winifred. "I hope I will see you soon."

She got up as he left. "I must rest son. I think this has become one of the biggest days of my life."

She tried to sleep but the pending change in her life kept her awake. "What am I to do? Gregor, what should I do ?" The silence was deafening . Leaving her home would break her heart. Seeing her son daily would definitely restore some of her spirits. If she stayed in the house she would think of Gregor all of the time. Miss him all of the time. People would pity her all of the time. She did not want that. I can't stay here. The house belongs to the church. What if some young couple needs it? Where would I go? This question brought the only answer. She would have to go the Monastery. Father Hesper and Devon had made all of the arrangements. She hadn't seen her son in four years and here he was acting like a grown man. Taking responsibility for his widowed mother. The Monastery did that for him. Turned him into a concerned, thoughtful and caring man. She would have to thank Father Hesper for many things.

Winifred woke early and looked around her home quietly. What could she take and what would she have to leave? She prepared some tea and started breakfast. Devon got up to say his morning prayers and found his mother sitting by the fire looking out the window at the sunrise.

"You are up early," Devon bent to kiss her on the cheek.

"I am getting ready for my new beginning," she said.

"You are?"

"Yes. I decided to join you at the Monastery."

Devon gave a big sigh of relief. "I am glad. We will do well having you there and you will have a roof over your head. I can watch you better with you there," he grinned.

"And I can watch you," she grinned back. "I'm not sure what I can bring and what I should leave." She looked around at all of her possessions.

"We will figure it out. Brother Ezekiel will be here soon and we can discuss how to move your possessions into your room. I'm a bit envious. I had to leave everything behind."

"As you can see, I kept everything for you."

"I can hardly take these things now," he laughed.

"What about your art supplies. I could keep them in my room for you when you want them?" she offered.

"Always the caring Ma. You know Father Hesper wants us to call you Sister Winifred?"

"Of course you will have to call me Ma. I am not your sister!"

Devon laughed. "It will be nice to have you there. I missed you and Da."

"We missed you too. More than you could ever know."

Arrangements were made for her possessions which were mostly family keepsakes. Some of her fondest items went to Dooley and Sarah's children for their own new beginnings. The rest were left in the cottage for the next tenants.

Winifred adjusted to her new surroundings with far greater ease than she would have ever thought. Her serene temperament blended well with the tranquil environment in the Abbey.

She performed her cleaning duties thoroughly and quietly, She kidded with the Brothers about their slovenly ways . Most of them stopped calling her Sister Winifred and resorted to calling her mother. Her gentleness was appreciated since the majority of the Brothers had very traumatic early lives. These difficult family circumstances is what brought them to seek out the solace of the monastery.

Winifred spent a great deal of time with the young orphaned boys. She loved them and enjoyed listening to their stories. They sought her out for a hug, when they scrapped a knee, or to show off their latest find (a shiny rock or a dead bug.)

Unlike the boys and men he mentored, Father Hesper came from a privileged background. He chose service to the church over a life of wealthy extravagance. Charmed by her level of interest despite her lack of education, Father Hesper tutored Winifred daily in spiritual philosophy.

Winifred lived the rest of her days at Monastery Tallaght. She only left the grounds when she received notice of Emily and then David's passing. She made her final venture to Dooley and Sarah's home when she learned of the birth of their seventh child.

Devon's creation which they called lighted glass, now known as stained glass, took him seven years from the first inspiration to its completed installation. He produced every aspect of the process. From life size paper patterns of each piece to blending the colors for every piece of glass. By introducing elements that captured color when heated over open flames. His creation which he called "Opening in Prayer" was a flower with many petals. The center showed the petals tightly together and the outer ones opened wide. The center of the flower was in darker shades and lightened as they opened. The Building of a scaffolding took more time and effort than expected. Hoisting the glass structure into place was a nightmare. The beauty of the piece was far superior than anyone had imagined. People came from far and wide to admire the workmanship for many years.

The Monastery became her home and Winifred felt blessed to see her son's dedication and growth into manhood.

Winifred passed quietly one morning when her beloved Gregor came to take her home.

Winifred Flanagan
1232 - 1308
married Gregor Wolcott
1248
gave birth to one child
Devon McGuire Wolcott
1249

EPILOGUE

*B*rother Devon Wolcott's accomplishments at the Monastery Tallaght were numerous. Besides the monumental task of adding a stained glass masterpiece to a weight bearing wall.

He aided many youth in their desire to learn how to construct.

He taught boys how to draw using perspective.

He created a fund for wayward boys with the meager inheritance from his grandparents will.

He created refuge for his mother, who was destitute, upon her husband's untimely demise.

He treated his mother with respect by offering her shelter and a sustainable job.

He fed the poor weekly as one of his chosen penance.

Despite his aversion to barnyard animals, he created whimsical pens for the chickens.

He created escape doors for the animal enclosures should the structures catch fire.

He created a play yard for the indigent boys.

Considerate of many. He preferred solitude to socializing.

He continued to visit "The Rock of Winifred", as he called it, past her demise.

Aunt Beatrice was a broken woman for quite a while after the breakup of her pending marriage to Antonio Renaldi and abandonment by her niece Winifred. Once she regained her sense of self worth she became an enterprising woman and started a school of etiquette for young girls providing for others what she had done for Winifred. She taught poise, manners, linguistics, dance and dress among other necessities for ladies of leisure. Her style of schooling caught on and brought her great wealth. Later in life she met and married a Duke. They spent the rest of their lives together socializing and catering grand affairs.

Antonio Renaldi went on to love many women in his life. He eventually settled on a woman whose nationality closely resembled his own.

The purpose of exploring the life of Winifred Flanagan is to open the past knowledge of higher prayer. Her realm was small, but, her impact great. Winifred maintained her faith in the face of unexpected changes and insurmountable grief. This was shown to us first in the early loss of her mother, when ripped away from Emily, during Devon's departure at a such a young age, and finally with Gregor's passing.

Winifred was rewarded for the way she dealt with her losses with an overabundance of joy and spirituality. The love that she shared with all of the little boys helped to sustain her through the grieving process for her beloved husband and well into her old age.

She was the maternal light to many who sought her.

Where Francesca fell down without this level of spirituality opened to her Winifred flew with the birds. Her assent into heaven was joyous for herself and all who greeted her, especially, her true love.

The tiny town of Wallingford perished due to disease when great plagues swept Ireland.

The Monastery at Tallaght was destroyed completely by the Dutch. No remains of the early structure are in existence. A new Monastery has been built on its sight.

Winifred's rock still remains.

coming soon . . .
by Susan Latner
The Teller
**The first book in the Atlantis Trilogy
another book in the Know My Light series**

Johanna Jasmine, a wild and willful young girl, is taken to the church to be raised. Through constant discipline she becomes a focused and dutiful woman. See her trials and tribulations as she discovers who she really is. Wife, mother and seer of truth.

See how she handles her psychic powers and the ramification it has on her family. The beautiful Johanna must wield her power and tame her enthusiasm through her life's tangled web.

The Teller - One who tells the unknown.

CPSIA information can be obtained at www.ICGtesting.com
Printed in the USA
BVOW01s1131220816

459597BV00007B/1/P